Praise for *Bearded Gospel Men*

"They had me at memes, and they kept me hooked with bearded gospel legends as every page turned. I'm fairly certain my beard is thicker and shinier than ever thanks to this book."

Jake Holland,
YouTube/Twitter star

"Bearded or not, we can all use a few heroes and role models to inspire and guide us as we explore what it means to follow Jesus. *Bearded Gospel Men* introduces us to a diverse group of examples with a tone that is both irreverent and deeply meaningful. I'm going to share it with my sons."

–Chris Wignall,
Executive Director of the Catalyst Foundation

"Short chapters: check. Hilarious: check. Challenging: check. Pictures of insanely gorgeous beards: check. I was laughing within thirty seconds. I highly recommend it!"

–James Kelly,
Founder of FaithTech

"*Bearded Gospel Men* is at once inspirational, insightful, and hilarious. The writing, laced with delightful wit, offers an encouraging glimpse into the lives of bearded brothers of the Beloved."

–Bradford Loomis,
Recording artist/singer/songwriter

"This is a work of both whimsy and profundity, at once silly and sublime, filled with hirsute hijinks and hair-raising insights. Jared Brock's and Aaron Alford's playful humor is irresistible—many times I positively chortled, and even a few times guffawed—and their vivid portraits of

31 manly (and maybe bearded) men are riveting and convicting. This is a book to make you both laugh and think. Even more, this is a book to make you want to be more, well . . . manly. And more godly. I'm even thinking of growing a beard."

–Mark Buchanan,
Author and professor

"Uncle Jared has a bigger beard than anyone except God."

Cain Greene,
Age 4

BEARDED GOSPEL MEN

BEARDED GOSPEL MEN

THE EPIC QUEST FOR MANLINESS & GODLINESS

JARED BROCK AND AARON ALFORD

W Publishing Group
An Imprint of Thomas Nelson

HarperCollins Publishers
Since 1817

Published in Nashville, Tennessee, by W Publishing, an imprint of Thomas Nelson.

Thomas Nelson titles may be purchased in bulk for educational, business, fund-raising, or sales promotional use. For information, please e-mail SpecialMarkets@ThomasNelson.com.

Meme designs by Aaron Alford.

ISBN 978-0-7180-9930-5 (SC)
ISBN 978-0-7180-7502-6 (e-book)

Library of Congress Cataloging-in-Publication Data

Library of Congress Control Number: 2017946593

17 18 19 20 21 LSC 10 9 8 7 6 5 4 3 2 1

Dedicated to Robino Kent and Ronaldo Zacharias, two of my favorite somewhat-bearded gospel men.

–J. B.

Dedicated to Dad, Mom, and Andre, the family in whom I learned what it meant to be a man and live the gospel. The bearded part I figured out later.

–A. A.

Contents

Introduction

THE MANIFESTO

BY JARED BROCK

Charles Finney. George Müller. D. L. Moody. Jolly Old Saint Nick. What do all these men have in common?

Beards.

Your humble authors have experienced a vast array of diverse Judeo-Christian traditions and have discovered one powerful thing that unites the Protestant, Catholic, and Orthodox worlds: follicle faithfulness.

Men have been growing facial foliage since the beginning of time. While it's not officially mentioned in Genesis, we're pretty sure that in the *Beardginning*, God created the heavens and the beard.

Did you know that Abraham had a beard? Of course you did. So did his son Isaac. Though not as hairy as his caveman brother, Esau, Jacob is often depicted with a manly mane. King David wore a beard, as did his wise-guy son, Solomon. It goes without saying that Moses' face was well forested, and Aaron's beard is specifically mentioned in Psalm 133.

Technicolor-dream-coated Joseph also had a crumb catcher until Pharaoh turned him into a smooth-cheeked Egyptian. Noah (a.k.a.

Russell Crowe) had a beard, obviously. And let's not even pretend that Methuselah was baby-faced. Job, Elijah, Jeremiah, Ezra, and the apostle Paul—all bearded.

Do you know who else had a twenty-four-hour five o'clock shadow? Jesus "The Man" Christ.

And if we believe what we see on the ceiling of the Sistine Chapel, then the bearded Michelangelo certainly was a prophet painter for knowing even God Himself displays Santa-like plumage.

Is there a connection between hairiness and holiness?

Yes.

One might even say that we are justified by face. Every hair is a prayer, every collar cover an offering of love. Beards teach men contentment—when you have a beard, you have enough.

Throughout history, Christian men have gloried in male-pattern magnificence. Saint Benedict of Nursia wore a superb double-forker. The benevolently bushed Euthymius wouldn't allow clean-shaven monks to enter his Judean Desert monastery. Saint Francis of Assisi had a beard, and now there's a pope named after him. He's clean-shaven, but we're praying for him.

Let's pause for a moment and consider all the people who didn't have a beard. Hitler. Mussolini, Stalin, Mao. The Devil himself (pointy goatees don't count).

The documentation of beardliness is a hallowed tradition. Abbot Burchard of Bellevaux wrote *Apologia de Barbis* in 1160 as "a treatise on the biblical, theological, moral, social, and allegorical implications of beards."[1] In 1531, Pierio Valeriano Bolzani wrote *In Support of Beards for the Clergy* after the (beardless) Pope Clement VII thought about forcing priests to manscape their forested faces.[2] Little did he know that a beard covers a multitude of chins. As nineteenth-century orator Thomas S. Gowing once declared in a speech, "Though there are individual exceptions, the absence of Beard is usually a sign of physical and moral weakness."[3]

Of all the great Christian men who wore beards, none stands so highly as the headless martyr Sir Thomas More. On the day of his beheading, the tufted knight supposedly positioned his beard away from his soon-to-be-severed neck, saying, "This hath not offended the king."[4]

Beards mean leadership. John Knox, Menno Simons, and George Müller founded entire denominations, most likely on the strength of their beards. The well-bearded General William Booth founded an army on the strength of his food saver. Hasidic Jews, Quakers, Greek Orthodox, hipster pastors, and worship leaders—all bearded. A beard confers instant leadership. It's the difference between "Mister" and "Sir."

Speaking of bush-faced worship leaders: David Crowder or those unbearded Newsboys? We rest our case.

Just look at the history of *Beardianity*: Charles Spurgeon, Saint John Chrysostom, Lactantius, James the Greater, Saint Nicholas, Saint Patrick, Dwight Moody, Gregory of Nyssa, Charles Finney . . . beards, beards, beardy beards. Why do godly men choose to grow their own neck scarves?

Because it's the right thing to do.

Yet, despite a clear biblical and historical bias toward beardliness, a number of Christian institutions and Bible colleges have, throughout the years, created policies that expressly forbid the cultivation of facial manliness. Historical anti-beards include Bob Jones University, Moody Bible Institute, Pensacola Christian College, and even the Salvation Army—despite General Booth's titanic topical topiary. In fact, Liberty University's 2009 dress code insisted that "facial hair should be neatly trimmed."[5] So much for liberty.

Hear these words, baby-faced college deans: Dihydrotestosterone, the chemical that promotes beard growth (and sadly, balding) is God's gift to man-folk. For it is by grace we are saved through face, not of ourselves, lest any man can boast. Beards or baldness—perhaps God has chosen whom we will serve.

But don't take our word for it—we barbates stand on the shoulders of elegantly bearded giants.

Growing a beard is a habit most natural,
Scriptural, manly, and beneficial.
—C. H. SPURGEON

The beard must not be plucked. "You will not
deface the figure of your beard."
—SAINT CYPRIAN (EVEN HIS STATUE HAS A BEARD.)

The nature of the beard contributes in an incredible
degree to distinguish the maturity of bodies . . . to
contribute to the beauty of manliness and strength.
—LACTANTIUS

The beard signifies the courageous . . . the earnest, the active, the
vigorous. So that when we describe such, we say, he is a bearded man.
—SAINT AUGUSTINE

[God] adorned man like the lions, with a beard, and endowed
him, as an attribute of manhood . . . a sign of strength.
—CLEMENT OF ALEXANDRIA

You need biblical proof, you say? Then let there be no shaves of gray about it. I will give you three, nay four proclamations, but be forewarned: if we hear the Word of God, yet fail to do what it says . . .

If my head is shaved, then my strength will leave me,
and I shall become weak and be like any other man.
—JUDGES 16:17 ESV

The men were greatly ashamed. And the king [David] said,
"Remain at Jericho until your beards have grown and then return."
—2 SAMUEL 10:5 ESV

You shall not round off the hair on your temples
or mar the edges of your beard.
—LEVITICUS 19:27 ESV

The LORD God said, "It is not good for the man to be
alone. I will make a helper suitable for him."
—GENESIS 2:18

So there you have it. We, like sheep, have gone astray—shave henceforth at your own peril. And so I exhort you, as Paul did the Corinthians, "Be imitators of me, as I am of Christ" (1 Cor. 11:1 ESV).

WELCOME TO THE PUB

BY AARON ALFORD

Of the seven dwarves, only DOPEY had a shaven face. This should tell us something about the custom of shaving.

—TOM ROBBINS

Now that you hold in your hands these hallowed pages (paper or digital), let us begin with a little clarification. What exactly do we mean when we say "Bearded Gospel Men"? What defines a Bearded Gospel Man? Are you a Bearded Gospel Man? The first part and the last part are the easiest to define. The words *bearded* and *man* shouldn't require a lot of explanation. If you have scruffy stuff growing on your face, there is an 89 percent chance you are bearded, and you are a man.

But what does it mean to be a Bearded *Gospel* Man? That's the clincher. The shortest answer is that, along with having a manly mane, you can proclaim that most basic of Christian tenets, the Apostles' Creed. But of course a Bearded Gospel Man is something more than just a well-churched dude with a beard. It's a man who's letting himself be changed by that gospel. A man who is striving to truly embody that gospel.

And if a Bearded Man is striving to be a Bearded Gospel Man, he knows he can't do that on his own. He needs the grace of God, the company of good friends, the kinship of true community, and the wisdom of that great cloud of witnesses. It's in that spirit of friendship, community, and wisdom that we present this book.

But first, a little history: Bearded Gospel Men started as a Tumblr blog and Facebook page by Pastor Joe Thorn. It was a joke, really. Mainly memes about beards and good-natured barbs about the superiority of the unshaven, mostly in the context of Christianity and church life. Bearded Gospel Men gathered momentum and eventually became a community of tens of thousands of people. We began to offer not just joke memes, but content about the Christian life, church history, and masculinity, and we received some great feedback. As BGM grew, we attracted more people from the entire spectrum of the Christian faith, from Franciscan friars in Brazil to good ol' Baptist boys in Alabama. Brothers from around the world were united in their love of the beard! We also gained a lot of followers who would not consider themselves "Christian" by any stretch of the imagination, and for a time we struggled with how to see this Bearded Gospel Men thing. Until we landed on the image of a pub.

Pub is short for "public house," and that's what we wanted to be: a pub that happens to be owned and operated by Christians, where everyone is welcome to hang out. If people wanted to share a few laughs at the bar, they'd be welcome to do that. If they wanted to sit down at a booth for some chitchat, they'd be welcome to do that too. Or if they wanted to take some time to talk about deeper things, there would be some comfy chairs by the fireplace for serious conversation. Since then we have endeavored to be a place where everyone is welcome, everyone is treated respectfully, and everyone leaves feeling a little happier for having come for a visit. We won't ooze Christianese all over the place, but faith is smack-dab in the middle of all this.

It's in the spirit of the pub that we welcome you to these pages. In each chapter, you will meet some of history's greatest Bearded Gospel Men. Introduce yourself. Listen to their stories. Some will make you laugh; a few may get you a little misty-eyed. Ask questions. Let these men challenge you. There are no antismoking bylaws in effect at this pub, so grab your pipe and take a little time for reflection while you thoughtfully stroke that beard (an action that is scientifically proven* to make you wiser!). It is our hope that as you surround yourself with these godly men, you will be spurred on to thought, prayer, and action.

The bar is open. The fireplace is lit. Old friends and new await you.

Welcome to the pub.

* Not actually scientific or proven. But it feels true, doesn't it?

THE JOURNEY

BY JARED BROCK

People loved darkness instead of light because their deeds were evil.

—JOHN 3:19

Men today are not a stellar species. We do most of the murdering. We commit almost all the rapes. We wage the wars, commit the felonies, and precipitate the global economic crashes due to our greed and stupidity. Over 95 percent of Fortune 500 companies are controlled by men. We run the big banks, the conglomerates, and the military industrial complex that has slaughtered tens of millions of our fellow brothers. We created the porn industry, rigged the electoral process, and degraded God's creation on a scale never seen before in history.

What is wrong with us?

Seriously—what is so broken inside the male heart that makes us want to dominate, seek, kill, and destroy?

The answer, in short, is darkness. We live in the dark. We suffer in silence. We allow our sin to fester.

We need help.

For the most part, the Christian resource industry hasn't helped. My friends in the Christian music industry tell me their record labels actually have a target market in mind: Her name is Jenny. Jenny is married. She is twenty-five to thirty-four years old. Jenny is a stay-at-home mom. Jenny has two kids. Write your songs for Jenny.

In the Christian publishing world, women do about 70 percent of the book purchasing. So who do you expect publishers to gear their books toward? I don't blame the publishers—they're just fulfilling demand. The truth is, most devotionals aren't made for men. Publishers don't write a lot of books for men in general, because men couldn't be bothered to sit down and read them. This is our fault. So their books are geared to women. Not that there's anything wrong with birds or flowers, but we wanted to write a devotional we'd want to read ourselves.

So here's the plan: each day for the next thirty-one days, we're going to introduce you to some of our favorite Christian dudes throughout history. These guys lived their faith in real, tactical, practical ways that led millions of people closer to Jesus, in big efforts and small acts of love. Each entry will also include a verse of the day, a quote to contemplate, and a prayer.

But this book isn't meant to be read alone. Each entry also contains three questions to answer with a partner or small group of brothers. Genesis 2:18 makes it pretty clear: "It is not good for the man to be alone." Like going to war, or making an exodus from Egypt, or taking a journey to Mordor, we need one another's help along the way.

There are thirty-one days on this book's journey, but don't beat yourself up if you miss a day. Take your time. If it works better for you, take a full year to go through this book with your friends. It's better to use a good system that works than a perfect system you'll later abandon. Just take it one day at a time.

It's time we help ourselves. It's time we form bands of brothers to help one another through life. It's time to go on a healing journey together.

First John 1:7 offers us a double incentive to do so: "If we walk in the light, as he is in the light, we have fellowship with one another, and the blood of Jesus, his Son, purifies us from all sin."

Together we find our healing. In surrender we find our strength.

CHAPTER 1

Ignatius of Antioch

LION FOOD (AND LOVING IT!)

BY AARON ALFORD

Meditation: Dear friends, let us love one another, for love comes from God. Everyone who loves has been born of God and knows God.

—1 JOHN 4:7

Quote of the Day: I will gladly die for God if only you do not stand in my way.

—IGNATIUS OF ANTIOCH

The Colosseum had a good crowd that day, and the cheers of thousands rang in the ears of the man being led in chains into the arena floor. Moments later he felt himself hurled to the ground, landing in a cloud of dust inches away from the gaping, roaring maw of a hungry lion. The beast reared up, and in an instant the man felt the slash of its claws across his face.

Now that's what I'm talkin' about! he thought.

Ignatius of Antioch didn't set out to be devoured by lions, but he would've been mightily disappointed if his friends had prevented him from getting there. We don't know what his final thoughts were in the moments before he was devoured by bloodthirsty beasts, but we do have an extensive record of his thoughts on his way to the Colosseum.[1]

Born in the first century, Ignatius may have had a most unique experience with the Lord Jesus. Some writers of his day claimed that it was none other than little Ignacio who Jesus took up in His arms when He said, "Truly I tell you, unless you change and become like little children, you will never enter the kingdom of heaven. Therefore, whoever takes the lowly position of this child is the greatest in the kingdom of heaven. And whoever welcomes one such child in my name welcomes me" (Matt. 18:3–5).

If this was the case, the little boy who was borne up in the embrace of Jesus and giggled in His lap grew up to become someone who in return carried Jesus to the world. It may be for this reason that Ignatius was also known by another name: Theophorus, "God bearer." However he came to faith in Christ, Ignatius became one of the most important and influential leaders of the church of his time.

Whether or not it was he who Jesus took in His arms as a boy, Ignatius lived close enough to the time of Jesus' earthly ministry to have been discipled by none other than the apostle John, and one of the main themes both in John's gospel and in his letters is the unity of the church and loving one another. It's in John 17 that we hear Jesus pray "that they may be one as we are one" (v. 11), and in 1 John we read, "Dear friends, let us love one another, for love comes from God. Everyone who loves has been born of God and knows God" (4:7). John instilled in Ignatius a passion for love and unity that would become a hallmark of Ignatius's life.

Ignatius took over leadership of the church in the city of Antioch after Evodius, who himself took over from the apostle Peter. Ignatius's leadership of the church came at a unique time for the early Christians (who first began to be called "Christians" in Antioch), as the land was ruled by the Roman emperor Trajan.

Trajan had an interesting outlook on the burgeoning movement of Christianity. While he couldn't find any real reason to see them as a threat, neither could he tolerate the Christians' rejection of Caesar as god. In a letter to his friend Pliny, who was governor over the region containing Antioch, Trajan's solution to the Jesus-follower problem read more or less like this:

> Dear Pliny,
>
> I like what you're doing with the Christians. Threaten them a bit, and if they renounce their belief about this Jesus-god, set them free. No harm, no foul! I don't think we need to bother seeking them out, but when we do find some Christians (the kind that won't recant), it's probably best if we just go ahead and kill 'em.
>
> Your pal,
>
> Trajan

Trajan may have had a somewhat lax attitude in regard to persecuting Christians, but it was enough to send many to their deaths, and it was under these conditions that Ignatius was arrested and tried under Trajan himself. An early document carries this account of his trial:

> Trajan said, "Do you then carry within you Him that was crucified?" Ignatius replied, "Truly so; for it is written, 'I will dwell in them, and walk in them.'" Then Trajan pronounced sentence as follows: "We command that Ignatius, who affirms that he carries about within him Him that was crucified, be bound by soldiers, and carried to the great Rome, there to be devoured by the beasts, for the gratification of the people."[2]

On the way to Rome, Ignatius wrote seven letters to churches and pastors whom he met en route, or with whom he was otherwise in contact. Throughout these letters, common themes occur, and we can see the issues about which Ignatius was most passionate. As it did in the gospel and letters of his mentor, the apostle John, one theme that appears in each letter is the unity of the church. He felt it was of utmost importance for each of the local churches to live in harmony, obedience, and love with one another and their local leadership: "Wherefore, as children of light and truth, flee from division and wicked doctrines; but where the shepherd is, there do ye as sheep follow."[3]

It's interesting to note that one of the leaders to whom he wrote was none other than the former runaway slave mentioned in the book of Philemon, Onesimus. Ignatius, again encouraging unity, wrote that Onesimus, now the bishop of Ephesus, was "a man of inexpressible love, and your bishop in the flesh, whom I pray you by Jesus Christ to love, and that you would all seek to be like him. And blessed be He who has granted unto you, being worthy, to obtain such an excellent bishop."[4]

Another significant theme that comes out of these letters was Ignatius's absolute commitment to be a witness for Christ as a martyr. In fact, it became his passion. Well-meaning Christians did not, of course, wish to see him dragged off to be used as a lion's dinner, but Ignatius counted it an honor and pleaded with them not to interfere with Trajan's sentence:

> I write to the Churches, and impress on them all, that I shall willingly die for God, unless you hinder me. . . . Allow me to become food for the wild beasts, through whose instrumentality it will be granted me to attain to God. . . . May I enjoy the wild beasts that are prepared for me; and I pray they may be found eager to rush upon me, which also I will entice to devour me speedily, and not deal with

me as with some, whom, out of fear, they have not touched. But if they be unwilling to assail me, I will compel them to do so.[5]

When he at last reached Rome, Ignatius the God bearer got his wish. In the account of his martyrdom, it's recorded that his final prayer before entering the Colosseum was again "that mutual love might continue among the brethren."[6]

In the twenty-first century West, we live in a highly individualistic culture, a culture that often seeps unseen into our faith. When a church split can happen over whether the correct lyrics to "How He Loves Us" should be "sloppy wet" or "unforeseen," it does us well to remember Ignatius and his passion for church unity. Whenever he helped local congregations to live in unity and obedience to their leaders, Ignatius was being a living answer to the prayer of Jesus, the prayer His dear friend John had written down: "that they may be one as we are one" (John 17:22).

It's doubtful many of us will be called to give witness to Christ by becoming food for beasts in the Colosseum, but we are called to give witness by means of our unity and love for one another, just as Ignatius was. Ignatius's poetic exhortation to the Ephesians, reminiscent of the apostle John's, is one we can receive just as if it were written to us:

> Therefore in your concord and harmonious love, Jesus Christ is sung. And man by man, become a choir, that being harmonious in love, and taking up the song of God in unison, you may with one voice sing to the Father through Jesus Christ.[7]

CONTEMPLATION

1. Have you ever been tempted to leave the church you are a part of? Why?

2. How might you encourage unity in your local congregation? Do you need to forgive anyone or ask forgiveness?
3. How might you encourage unity in the church as she is represented in your city?

PRAYER

Holy Spirit, grant us the grace to live in humility and in unity with the entire body of Christ.

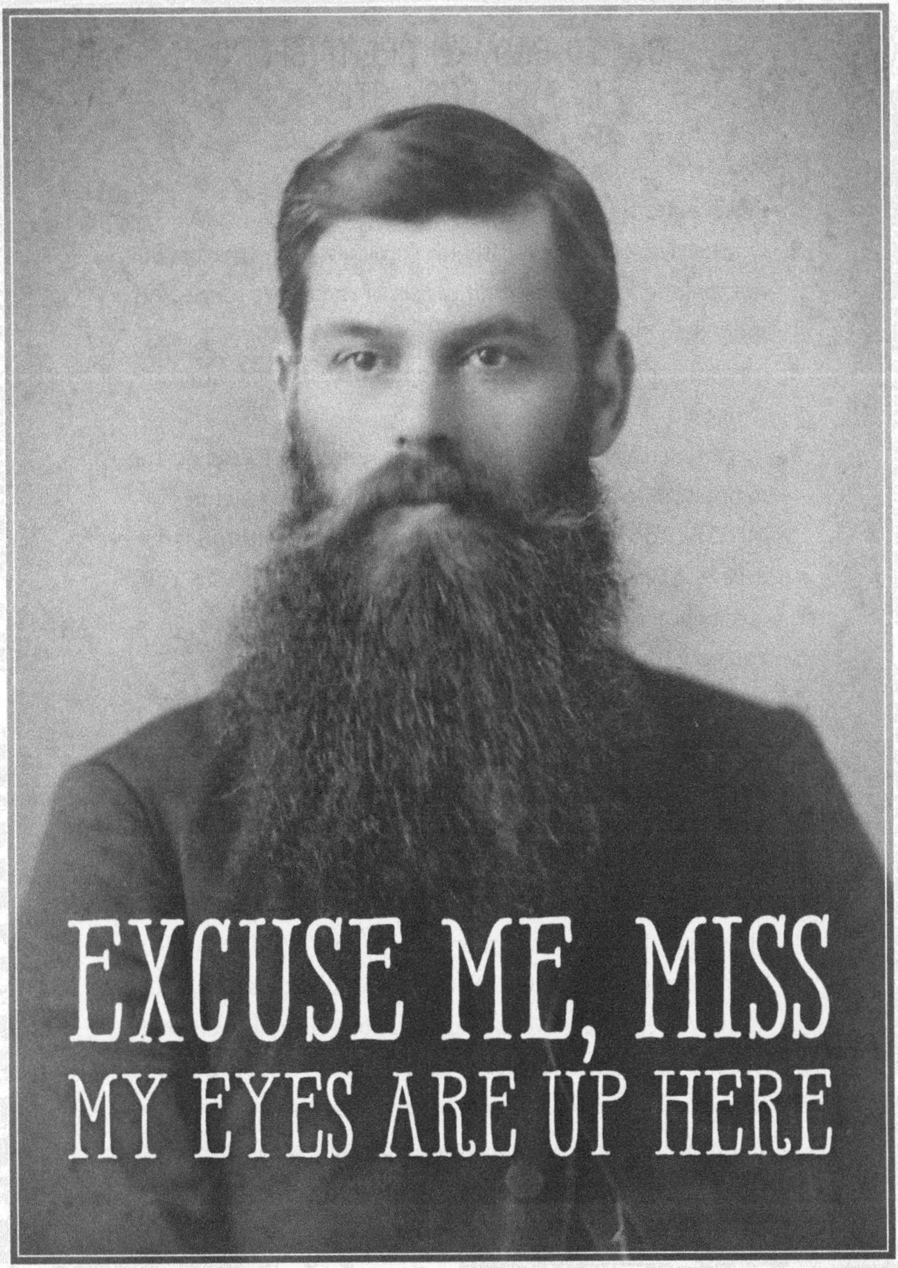
EXCUSE ME, MISS
MY EYES ARE UP HERE

HOW TO GROW A GREAT BEARD IN FIVE EASY STEPS

BY AARON ALFORD

1. Reach puberty.
2. Don't shave. Admire your stubbly studliness in the mirror. (But not for long, lest you commit the sin of vanity. We suggest no more than nine seconds.)
3. It's getting itchy. Don't shave. No good thing comes without struggle.
4. It's getting really itchy. *Don't shave!* To steel yourself against the temptation to pick up a razor, we suggest sticking pictures of Mr. T, ZZ Top, Rick Rubin, and Gandalf on your bathroom mirror. Believe in your dreams! (Also, you may want to look into a high-quality beard oil product.)
5. You now have a beard! Enjoy it. Stay away from beard-endangering things like scissors, small fires, and people who say, "I liked you better without a beard." Take it with you wherever you go. Tell it your secrets. Get used to Duck Dynasty comments. Use it to defend yourself against dark forces. Slay orcs. Chop down trees by looking at them sternly. Start a tree farm in your whiskers (a nice Douglas fir should be ready by Christmas). Use it as inspiration to write that novel you've been meaning to get to. Audit the philosophy class it's already taking. Accept the inevitable advances of a virtuous woman. Flee the inevitable advances of the dissolute. (Or take a vow of celibacy; it's up to you.) Resist the temptation to use its power for evil. Let it help you improve your painting technique as it explores the possibilities found in neo-Expressionism. Endure

countless questions about how hot it gets in the summer. Use it as a haven for small animals awaiting adoption. Be patient and forgiving when your friends fall into the sin of beard envy. Use its dimensional portal (this commonly appears at the six-month mark) to explore strange new worlds and visit alternate timelines. And no matter how much it begs, never, ever feed it after midnight.

CHAPTER 2

Good King Wenceslas

THE MERRY CHRISTMAS BOXER

BY JARED BROCK

Meditation: The King will reply, "Truly I tell you, whatever you did for one of the least of these brothers and sisters of mine, you did for me."

–MATTHEW 25:40

Quote of the Day: Christian men, be sure . . . ye who now will bless the poor shall yourselves find blessing.

–JOHN MASON NEALE

In Canada we have a peculiar winter holiday called Boxing Day. Contrary to popular belief, we don't (generally) go around punching people for buying us ugly Christmas sweaters. Boxing Day is celebrated in Canada, Great Britain, and most of the Commonwealth. It's basically our version of Black Friday, minus the guns and stampedes. But we also celebrate Black Friday, so Boxing Day could more accurately be called Return-the-Stuff-You-Hate-and-Buy-the-Stuff-You-Want Day. If you ever buy a Christmas present for a Canadian or a Brit, be sure to include the receipt and store hours.

But Boxing Day wasn't always such a shallow, commercial celebration. Originally, British employers of a certain caliber gave gifts to their employees, often in the form of a box full of presents for their families. That's one theory, anyway. Boxing Day might also refer to the box that was traditionally placed at the backs of churches on Christmas Day to collect offerings for the poor. Either way, these gifts for the poor and working class were given on the day after Christmas, which also happens to be the feast day of the first Christian martyr: Saint Stephen.

And here's where Good King Wenceslas comes in.

You've probably heard the song. It was written by John Mason Neale and published in 1853, but the music originated in Finland three hundred years earlier. Like every Christmas song he ever covered, Bing Crosby sings a creditable version.

"Good King Wenceslas" is an odd Christmas carol. It mentions no nativity, no bearded wise men, no baby Jesus in a manger.

Good King Wenceslas looked out
On the Feast of Stephen
When the snow lay 'round about,
Deep and crisp and even;
Brightly shone the moon that night,
Though the frost was cruel,
When a poor man came in sight,
Gathering winter fuel.

"Hither, page, and stand by me,
If thou know'st it, telling
Yonder peasant, who is he?
Where and what his dwelling?"
"Sire, he lives a good league hence,
Underneath the mountain,

Right against the forest fence
By Saint Agnes' fountain."

"Bring me flesh, and bring me wine,
Bring me pine-logs hither;
Thou and I shall see him dine
When we bear them thither."
Page and monarch, forth they went,
Forth they went together,
Through the rude wind's wild lament
And the bitter weather.

"Sire, the night is darker now,
And the wind blows stronger;
Fails my heart, I know not how,
I can go no longer."
"Mark my footsteps, my good page,
Tread thou in them boldly;
Thou shall find the winter's rage
Freeze thy blood less coldly."

In his master's step he trod,
Where the snow lay dinted,
Heat was in the very sod
Which the saint had printed.
Therefore, Christian men, be sure,
Wealth or rank possessing,
Ye, who now will bless the poor
Shall yourselves find blessing.

It's inspiring, isn't it?

But here's the funny thing: Good King Wenceslas wasn't even a king.

Good Wenceslas, whose real name was Václav, was the bearded Duke of Bohemia in the year 921. Duke Václav was instrumental in bringing Christianity to the Czech Republic. He instituted the Latin rite and laid the foundation for what is now the magnificent St. Vitus Cathedral, the jewel of Prague's ancient castle complex.

But he didn't last long. A group of wealthy nobles plotted with Václav's younger brother and ran him through with a lance when he was only twenty-eight. He was immediately declared a holy saint and righteous king, whose power wasn't based in a crown but rather his character. He was martyred, sainted, and made the patron saint of the Czech Republic and, one assumes, their delicious *trdelnik* pastries. If you ever visit Prague, you can check out his skull, which now stands, sadly, beardless.

The stories and tales of the good duke's kindness went far beyond just one Christmas gift to a poor country serf and gave rise to the medieval concept of the "righteous king." A local biographer recorded the notion in glowing terms: "Rising every night from his noble bed, with bare feet and only one chamberlain, he went around to God's churches and gave alms generously to widows, orphans, those in prison and afflicted by every difficulty, so much so that he was considered, not a prince, but the father of all the wretched."[1]

Now all of this is likely legend, of course, but that's really not the point, is it? This Christmas carol isn't just about a Czech royal who died 1,081 years ago.

It's about us.

If we have the ability to vote, to use our freedom of speech, and to gather together to worship, then we fall into the category of "rank possessing." If we have a house, a car, clean water, and food, we fall into the category of "wealth possessing." We are rich, and we have the opportunity to act like kings. We can follow in the snowy footsteps of good Duke Václav and celebrate the true meaning of Boxing Day. Perhaps we can find a box of blessing for the poor and, in doing so, find ourselves truly blessed. As we walk in the footprints of faithful greats, who themselves followed in the footsteps of Jesus, we find warmth in the ground on which they trod.

CONTEMPLATION

1. Where do you possess rank and wealth?
2. Are you stewarding your influence and affluence well?
3. How can you "gather winter fuel" for those who face difficulty?

PRAYER

Father of the rich and poor alike, make us saints in helping those who have less than we have.

BE THE FACE
YOU WISH TO SEE
IN THE WORLD!

ON BEING A BIBLE DONKEY

BY AARON ALFORD

Being yourself can be frustrating, especially if you're me. I try my best to live with integrity, purpose, and humility, but much of the time I fail. I'm stubborn and stupid, and sometimes it seems like I'll never get my act together. In short, I feel like a Bible Donkey.

Growing up in churches that mostly used the King James Version of Scripture, my church friends and I took particular delight in the sections of the KJV Bible that referred to donkeys. Giggling gleefully, we would call one another "Bible Donkeys." We were the epitome of Christian maturity. I'm sure you, dear reader, were never so juvenile.

The Bible mentions donkeys on at least eighty-seven occasions. God told Moses, "If thou see the ass of him that hateth thee lying under his burden . . . thou shalt surely help with him" (Ex. 23:5 KJV). Then, of course, there is the most famous Bible Donkey of the Old Testament, Balaam's Bible Donkey. God famously used Balaam's donkey, an ass who could not speak—a dumb ass—to prophesy a warning to Balaam and save his life. (He's been using Bible Donkeys to speak ever since.)

I don't want to remain a Bible Donkey, but I'm coming to terms with the reality that, like Balaam's donkey and every other donkey before and since, I can be stubborn, stupid, and insensitive. Perhaps you can relate. But don't worry; such traits don't exclude us from God's kingdom. Balaam's donkey wasn't the only donkey God used for His glory. There's a story in the gospel of Mark about a colt (the foal of an ass):

> [Jesus said,] "Go to the village ahead of you, and just as you enter it, you will find a colt tied there, which no one has ever ridden.

> Untie it and bring it here. If anyone asks you, 'Why are you doing this?' say, 'The Lord needs it and will send it back here shortly.'"
>
> They went and found a colt outside in the street, tied at a doorway. As they untied it, some people standing there asked, "What are you doing, untying that colt?" They answered as Jesus had told them to, and the people let them go. When they brought the colt to Jesus and threw their cloaks over it, he sat on it. Many people spread their cloaks on the road, while others spread branches they had cut in the fields. Those who went ahead and those who followed shouted,
>
> "Hosanna!"
>
> "Blessed is he who comes in the name of the Lord!" (11:2–9)

Mark is usually the most succinct of the gospel storytellers, charging through his account in just sixteen chapters. But here Mark spent a significant amount of time on a seemingly small incident. He didn't say, "So the disciples obeyed Jesus and fetched a mule." No, Mark took his time with this story. It's almost as if the little jackass is the star of the show.

So let's look at this colt. He was young, and he was tied with a rope. He was not in a stall—he was alone in the open street, possibly neglected and uncared for. In fact, he'd never been sat upon, and donkeys are pretty much good for one of two things: carrying people or carrying stuff. This one had been used for neither. Then a couple of disciples showed up, freed him of his bonds, and brought him to the Lord. It's then that the poor, neglected donkey found his purpose: carrying Jesus.

If there's a lesson to be learned from these Bible Donkeys, it's this: It is a noble thing to be used by God, but it doesn't require nobility on our part. When that colt went riding into the city carrying Jesus, no one was looking at the donkey. The shouts of praise were not for the little beast of burden. But when the disciples threw their cloaks on that burro's back, he must have felt a certain glow of dignity for carrying this Most Excellent Passenger. The little colt had never been useful for anything, and now here he was, carrying the King of kings.

So it is with us. We find our purpose and our dignity when we are what we're meant to be: beasts of burden, carrying Jesus.

So don't worry about being a dumb Bible Donkey. Jesus knows what you are, and He loves you anyway. He knows you're stubborn. He knows what you sound like when you think you're being eloquent ("Eeee-aaawwhh!"). But He's chosen you. He sent His disciples to you to set you free of the ropes that bound you. He brought you to Himself, and He clothed you with dignity.

His burden is light, and it is His great pleasure to use Bible Donkeys like you and me to carry Him into the world.

CHAPTER 3

Saint Boniface

VERSUS THE MIGHTY THOR!

BY AARON ALFORD

Meditation: See, the Lord, the LORD Almighty, will lop off the boughs with great power. The lofty trees will be felled, the tall ones will be brought low.

—ISAIAH 10:33

Quote of the Day: Let us be careful shepherds watching over Christ's flock. Let us preach the whole of God's plan to the powerful and to the humble, to rich and to poor, to men of every rank and age, as far as God gives us the strength, in season and out of season.

—SAINT BONIFACE

The great oak towered above the people gathered at its trunk. They did not love this tree, but they reverenced it all the same for fear of the god it stood for. He was temperamental, violent as a storm cloud, destructive as a hurricane's wind, and the only way he could be satisfied was through sacrifice. But no animal sacrifice would do. It had to be human. If they did not satiate their god in this way, they feared for their very lives what terror he might visit upon them.

It was to this tree Boniface the Christian missionary came, ax in hand, ready to challenge their capricious god. The missionary had been among them for years now, and many of their kin had abandoned the gods they had feared in favor of this God the Christian preached. This God, he had told them, did not demand human sacrifice, for He Himself had become a sacrifice. This God was greater than Thor and Odin and all the Viking gods they worshiped and feared, said he, and he would prove it. The Christian swung back his ax, and it fell upon the tree with a *crack*.

Boniface had not intended to become a missionary when he entered a monastery as a teenage boy, but the call had found him nonetheless, and it would lead him one day to singlehandedly challenge a god.

Born sometime between AD 672 and 680, Boniface, whose name means "Good Fate," was an Englishman at a time when Christianity was still young in England, having only taken root among the Anglo-Saxons around the year 600. He showed himself to be brilliant in his studies and could have lived a comfortable life of secular pursuits. But Boniface set his mind on higher things and gave himself to a religious education. He entered a monastery, and there he studied the Scriptures and became a priest at the age of thirty. He excelled as a preacher, and soon the monk wanted to use his gifts in service as a missionary, particularly to the people of Germania (modern Germany), a place in which the gospel was just beginning to be preached. So, in the year 716, Boniface forsook the security of monastic life and set forth.

Paganism was widespread in Germania and its surrounding territories, in particular the worship of Nordic gods such as Odin and Thor. Where Christianity did exist, it was often entangled with and diluted by local superstitions. There were also rogue Christian missionaries with little training or education in the basic tenets of Christianity, which brought even more disorder. Boniface arrived on the scene in the midst of this time of confusion. There was a desperate need for a man with Boniface's wisdom, intelligence, and passion.

He was made a bishop and set to work organizing the burgeoning church of Germania. Boniface found himself enjoined to the tasks of both preaching the gospel and reforming and correcting existing churches from error. Where Christians had once been scattered and more or less unaccountable in what they taught and practiced, he tried to bring unity, orthodoxy, and right worship. Holy men and women from his native England heard of Boniface's difficult work and came to assist him. With their help, along with support and encouragement from people near and far, Boniface was able to bring unity to a scattered, disjointed church.

But the roots of Viking paganism ran deep, and the Nordic gods were still worshiped and feared in many places. One such place was Hesse, where superstitions and witchcraft fueled such dread as to inspire human sacrifice. Central to their worship was the veneration of trees, in particular a giant oak tree called Thor's Oak, or the Thunder Oak. The few Christians who lived in the area begged Boniface to demonstrate the power of the Christian God over the mighty Thor.

So Boniface came to the oak tree and made a proclamation to the gathered worshipers. "Here is the Thunder Oak," he declared, "and here the cross of Christ shall break the hammer of the false god Thor!"[1]

He took an ax and swung it into the venerated tree, and the *thwack* of the ax resounded through the woods. Just then, a great wind came blowing down from above. The people thought for sure that the fearsome Thor was about to take his hammer and strike Boniface with a bolt of lightning for his insolence. Instead, the mysterious wind blew hard upon the oak itself. The oak tree began to crack and pop where

Boniface had fixed his ax. Then, as if torn apart from the heavens above, the oak tree split into four pieces and fell with a great crash.

The tree known as Thor's Oak now formed the Christian cross on the forest floor. The cross of Christ had broken the hammer of Thor. Many pagans believed. The God of Boniface was mightier than Thor, than Odin, than any false god. What's more, one small tree was left standing next to the ruins of the oak. It was an evergreen, a fir. Pointing to the little green tree that ever pointed heavenward, Boniface explained that this tree, the "young child of the forest," would now symbolize God's gift of himself in Jesus.[2] Like the endless life given by Christ, this tree was ever green and ever humble. The Christmas tree was born. The people forsook the slavery of fear and embraced the Good News of the mighty and gentle Jesus.

Boniface understood the Germanic love of trees not to be an intrinsic evil, but something to be baptized, transformed into a new, Christ-centered life. As if to further exemplify this, Boniface did not merely destroy Thor's Oak, but transformed its remains into something beautiful. He used its timber to build a chapel dedicated to Jesus.

Eventually, Boniface gave his life for love of the German people and the gospel. On June 5, 755, at about the age of eighty, Boniface and several other priests and deacons gathered to baptize and confirm a group of new Christians in their faith. But a gang of men fell upon them with swords, men who still lived in fear of their pagan gods. Several of the neophyte Christians ran, but Boniface and at least thirty-seven others were killed. Boniface entered into the fullness of the endless life he preached about in the Christmas tree and left behind a legacy of the transformational power of Christ, who takes our fears and transforms them into faith.

Eternal God, the refuge and help of all your children,
we praise you for all you have given us,
for all you have done for us,

for all that you are to us.
In our weakness, you are strength,
in our darkness, you are light,
in our sorrow, you are comfort and peace.
We cannot number your blessings,
we cannot declare your love:
For all your blessings we praise you.
May we live as in your presence,
and love the things that you love,
and serve you in our daily lives;
through Jesus Christ our Lord.[3]

—A PRAYER OF SAINT BONIFACE

CONTEMPLATION

1. Boniface left everything that was familiar to follow God's missionary call. Do you think God might be asking something similar of you?
2. It's tempting to see only the negative aspects of the culture around us. What do you see that might be "baptized" and brought to fullness in Christ? What might you do to build something good and not just tear down what's bad?
3. Are you, like the people gathered at Thor's Oak, living in fear of any false god? How might the cross of Christ break that fear?

PRAYER

Jesus, break in us any fear or superstition; let us live confidently in Your love.

FRET NOT,
YOUNG BEARDER.
ITCH TOO
SHALL PASS.

THE BEARDITUDES

Blessed are those who strive for beardedness,
for they shall be satisfied.

Blessed are those who endure suffering for beardedness's
sake, for great is their reward in manliness.

Blessed are those full in beard, for they shall
inspire the beardless toward beardom.

Blessed are the bearded who eat messy foods, for
their flavor shall endure forever and ever.

Blessed is he whose face knows no razor,
for the Devil stays far from him.

Blessed are those who resist the scraping of
their faces, for they shall be comforted.

Blessed are they who hunger and thirst for
beardedness, for their necks shall be covered.

—Taken from the NBT (New Bearded Translation)

CHAPTER 4

Moses the Black

THE MURDERER MARAUDER MARTYR

BY JARED BROCK

Meditation: "Even now," declares the LORD, "return to me with all your heart, with fasting . . ."

—JOEL 2:12

Quote of the Day: Fasting helps to express, to deepen, and to confirm the resolution that we are ready to sacrifice anything, to sacrifice ourselves, to attain what we seek for the kingdom of God. . . . Prayer is the reaching out after God and the unseen; fasting, the letting go of all that is seen and temporal.

—ANDREW MURRAY

Moses the Black, otherwise known as Moses the Strong or Moses the Robber, was a fourth-century desert father—a monk at the edges of society—in Egypt. His real name was Saint Moses Murin the Black, literally meaning "Moses the Black Ethiopian," which really seems redundant if not overtly racist. Today he is seen by many as the patron saint of nonviolence.

Moses was the slave of a government official in Egypt before he escaped (or was banished) for committing a violent crime—a theft or murder, depending on the account you believe. Moses was a huge and incredibly violent man who led a gang of seventy-five bandits that roamed the Nile Valley. They robbed villages and murdered the inhabitants. To give you an idea of how much rage filled our future bearded saint, consider this story:

During one attempted village raid, a dog wouldn't stop barking and woke up the villagers. Moses swore revenge on the village. Later that night, he swam across the crocodile-infested Nile with a knife in his teeth. He killed the four best sheep in town, dragged them back across the river, ate the best meat, sold the rest, and got drunk with the money he made from the sale.

The local authorities banded together and gave chase. His men deserted him, and Moses sought refuge in a monastery. When he saw the monks' life of peace and contentment, his heart was stirred to join them.

Needless to say, he had a hard time adjusting.

Moses was constantly reprimanded for breaking the rules and skipping fasting days. But slowly he came around. One night, four members of his former gang raided his monastic cell, not knowing their former boss had turned monk. Moses had been fasting for seven days but was still immensely strong. He overcame all four, tied them up, and carried them to the elder of the monastery. The father told Moses to free them. When the robbers witnessed Moses' obedience and saw that he had truly changed, they, too, became monks.

Moses suffered from horrible nightmares about his previous life as a marauding bandit, rapist, and murderer. He couldn't shake the dreams, so for seven years he stood awake all night. And then he ended up crippled in bed for a year after that.

Moses struggled to overcome temptation and the desire to sin. He was wracked with guilt and punished himself for his faults. One day his superior took him to the roof at sunrise and said, "Only slowly do the rays of the sun drive away the night and usher in a new day, and so it is with the soul."[1]

Moses eventually found inner freedom and started his own monastery. Seventy-five monks joined him, and together they lived a disciplined life of prayer, service, and love.

When Moses was seventy-five years old, he received word that a group of Berbers planned to attack the monastery. The monks wanted to defend themselves, but Moses ordered the monks to run, saying it was better to be killed than to kill others. Moses stayed behind and was martyred.

There is a great darkness in each of our hearts. An inky blackness mires our souls. It takes discipline to root weeds out of a garden, and it takes hard work to cultivate a loving character. Discipline, especially self-discipline, is difficult. But men like Moses remind us that we have tools to assist in the struggle. Fasting and other spiritual exercises help us work out our faith.

I've done a forty-day fast before. It was horrible. I lost forty-four pounds and was completely depressed. I couldn't sleep but didn't want to get out of bed. I've never felt so weak in my entire life.

But it was worth it. It completely changed the direction of my journey, from a money-hungry young man into someone who tries to seek the common good. As Bill Bright said, "Fasting reduces the power of self so that the Holy Spirit can do a more intense work within us."[2]

Food isn't the only thing we can give up for a season. Daniel gave up meat, alcohol, and hygiene products in Daniel 10:3. The Corinthians gave up sex for a short season. Andrew Bonar suggests that we "abstain from whatever hinders direct fellowship with God."[3] By sacrificing and disciplining ourselves to overcome temptation in the dark things, we open ourselves up to the light of God's grace, in which we can experience transcendent peace like Moses the Martyr did. Light drives out darkness. A new day dawns.

CONTEMPLATION

1. What darkness separates you from friendship with God?
2. Where have you failed in the discipline of character cultivation?
3. What can you abstain from for a season in order to rely more on Christ?

PRAYER

Lord, we have broken our communion with You. Help us in our holy fast, that we may not only say grace but receive it.

BEARD:
THE OTHER
CHEST HAIR.

I MARRIED A BEARDED GOSPEL MAN

BY MICHELLE BROCK*

"I love you so much."

"You look stunning today."

"I'm so glad I get to spend my life with you."

Before I say, "Thanks, I love you too," I sometimes find myself pausing to ensure my husband's words are indeed directed toward me and not the mirror. While I'm disgruntled by the fact that Jay's crumb collector and I are both objects of his affection, I often remind myself that the man behind the beard shows his love for me in many ways, anchored in a belief that he's honed and cultivated through our nearly two decades together:

He's not afraid of my strengths.

Some husbands view their wives as competitors—as if only one is allowed to succeed and thrive and make a difference in the world. Jay sees me as an equal life partner and wants me to be the fullest version of myself that God created me to be. And he doesn't simply tell me this. He shows it through his actions.

First, he actively invests in my career and personal development. Whether it's purchasing an online course I'm interested in, taking me to a conference, or brainstorming together for hours about vision and logistics for an upcoming project I want to undertake, Jay is serious about putting foundations under my dreams.

Second, Jay champions my relationships. Twice a year, he goes to a cottage with his close guy friends—something I've always envied. I was complaining one summer about how this never happens with my girlfriends. A couple months later, Jay and I went to the grocery store and got a feast's worth of food, which he claimed was for an extravagant date, and after he was done cooking, he told me he was leaving for the evening and that I would be joined by a handful of mystery guests. As they trickled in, I realized why he'd asked me a question a few weeks prior: "Who are women you respect that you'd like to have some intentional time with?" Sneaky.

Furthermore, Jay values my contribution. When he was writing his first book, he asked me to do the first edit without letting his ego get in the way when I killed a sentence, tweaked a story, or challenged an assumption. Trusting me to add value makes me feel valued.

Finally, Jay draws out the depth in me. Proverbs 20:5 says that "the purposes of a person's heart are deep waters, but one who has insight draws them out." Jay often asks questions that make me plunge into those deep places within—the places that often hold uncertainty, fear, and insecurity, but also precious morsels of truth that can only be discovered through wrestling and diving in the depths. I am grateful for a husband who helps me reach those places.

I'm at my best when I'm equipped to dream, surrounded by healthy relationships, and encouraged to go deep. Those things allow me to be the fullest version of myself, which also gives me the opportunity to be a strong wife for a man I love so much. As we celebrate and take refuge in each other's strengths, we get to embrace the joys and weather the storms of life as a team. We become stronger together.

I guess Jay's beard can come along for the ride too.

---

* *Michelle Brock is the cofounder of Hope for the Sold and the co-director of* Red Light Green Light *and* Over 18.

CHAPTER 5

D. L. Moody

GOSPEL, MUSIC

BY AARON ALFORD

Meditation: For I am not ashamed of the gospel, because it is the power of God that brings salvation to everyone who believes.

—ROMANS 1:16

Quote of the Day: Would you like to have a song, gentlemen?

—D. L. MOODY

Dwight Lyman Moody was born February 5, 1837, the sixth of nine children, to a working-class Massachusetts family. He and his siblings lived a simple, rural life, provided for by the hard work of his father, Edwin, a brick mason. But when Edwin died unexpectedly at the age of forty-one, everything changed. Dwight was just four years old at the time, and his mother, Betsy, was only a month away from giving birth to twins. Betsy was suddenly a single mother of nine children, with little to no options for income. Creditors came for almost everything she had.

Betsy's family helped however they could, providing firewood in the freezing winter, while the family's pastor assisted with both food and spiritual support. Friends and neighbors urged Betsy to break up the family and place her children in other families' homes. Betsy would hear none of that. The family would stay together. Each sibling did his or her part. When Dwight was eight, he was working for extra money with his brother, aged twelve, at a neighboring farm.

For all the hardship he and his family faced, Dwight was known as a mischievous boy with a love for playing jokes. He might set loose a tomcat in the schoolhouse during a recitation of "Julius Ceasar," or perhaps post signs all over town for an important meeting with a prestigious lecturer, a meeting that half the town shows up for, only to find no such person exists.

He grew up attending church each Sunday and had an old-but-untouchable family Bible in the home, but it was not until he was living on his own that Dwight would encounter God for himself. By the time Dwight was seventeen, he had moved to Boston and was working in his uncle's shoe store. As part of the arrangement with his uncle, he was required to attend church and Sunday school. His Sunday school teacher, a man named Edward Kimball, helped Dwight develop a true curiosity about the Bible and the Christian faith. Until then, he had known Christianity as an external set of rules, advice for living. But something deeper was awakening.

Mr. Kimball appeared at the shoe store one day, and as Dwight was wrapping up a pair of shoes in the back of the building, Mr. Kimball simply told Dwight how much God loved him and how eager God was for Dwight to love Him in return. That was all it took. All at once, the things that had once been done out of moral obligation became life giving, and life changing.

"Before my conversion," he later said, "I worked towards the Cross, but since then I have worked from the Cross; then I worked to be saved, now I work because I am saved."[1]

He immediately had a zeal for reaching out to those in need of the gospel of grace that had changed his own life, particularly those on the margins of society. Within a few years he found himself working in Chicago, where he spent much of his time in saloons, sharing his faith with anyone who would listen. He was frustrated, however, with the way churches did "evangelistic" meetings: "Services are not made interesting enough," he said, "so as to get unconverted people to come. They are not expected to come, and people would be mortified if they did come."[2]

So Dwight decided that he would do things differently. Though lacking in musical talent himself, Moody knew the power of song. A few days later, Moody, an imposing figure with a large build and generous beard, entered a Chicago saloon. But it was who he brought with him that turned people's heads: a bright-eyed choir of young people. With every eye upon him, Moody said cheerfully, "Would you like to have a song, gentlemen?"[3] No one objected, and the young choir sang a patriotic song.

The patrons, delighted in spite of themselves, offered a round of applause. The youth then sang a hymn, and Moody followed it with an earnest word of prayer. There were tears and sniffles, and when he invited them to his meeting (hosted in a converted saloon itself), half the men present followed him to hear more about this gospel.

Moody always had a heart for those who were suffering and downcast. When the Civil War began, he could not in good conscience enlist, saying, "In this respect I am a Quaker."[4] He did, however, see it as his responsibility to care for soldiers, and not just those of the Union. He visited and held meetings for Confederate prisoners "with all the tender love of a brother . . . and they hailed his coming to cheer and comfort, to instruct and evangelize them, with unspeakable delight."[5]

Moody had a spirit of brotherly friendship that reached beyond societal boundaries, and in his preaching he avoided "needless offence to those from whom he most differ[ed] in doctrine."[6]

In his evangelistic campaigns, Moody worked closely with local churches across denominational lines. Great care was taken to host his meetings in neutral spaces, especially where there was any contention between local congregations. In return, "men of all sects and churches honored and trusted him, and were ready to do his bidding."[7]

And wherever he went, there was music. Today when we think of large revival meetings and stadium-sized evangelism, we take for granted the presence of professional musicians and communal worship. But at the time of Moody's meetings, this was a novel idea. For Moody, singing hymns was not simply a reflection of an individual's beliefs, but a path to believing.

"If we can only get people to have the words of the Love of God coming from their mouths," he once said, "it's well on its way to residing in their hearts."[8]

Moody became friends with Ira D. Sankey, a popular (and mutton-chopped) gospel singer at the time, and the two began working together in a partnership that would last for years. They worked on tours that took them from San Francisco to Vancouver, and along the Eastern Seaboard. They sailed to England, Ireland, and Scotland, hosting meetings for thousands of people. Along the way they befriended Charles Spurgeon and Hudson Taylor. *Gospel Hymns and Sacred Songs*, a songbook compiled by Moody, Sankey, and a man named Philip Bliss, reached a circulation of twenty million and took in more than $1 million in royalties, all of which was channeled through a committee to fund various ministries and schools.

Despite his fame, Moody was always known for treating others as better than himself. This likely stemmed from the fact that, despite becoming a prominent Christian leader, he had received only a fifth-grade education. Early in his ministry, he struggled just to read the story of the prodigal son to a child on his knee. But what many would see as a weakness became a defining strength: humility.

"I have no education," he said, "but I love the Lord Jesus Christ, and I want to do something for Him: and I want you to pray for me."[9]

It was this humility that fostered friendship with Christians of various denominations, and this same humility that drew drunkards and gamblers, soldiers and prisoners, the rich and the poor to hear his words about Christ and the gospel. And they came by the thousands.

Moody's last series of meetings was held in Kansas City in November of 1899. Presbyterians and Methodists came together to form a choir of five hundred voices. "They sing famously well," Moody said. "At first, I am told, there was some difference between the Methodists and Presbyterians. . . . The Methodists sang fast, and the Presbyterians sang slow. . . . But we have taught them to pull together pretty well now."[10]

He preached his last sermon to more than fifteen thousand people. He spoke simply and passionately on the parable of the great feast and the marriage supper of the Lamb.

"Tonight, my friends," he said tenderly, "let me say that you are invited, every one of you. . . . God has headed His invitation with 'whosoever,' in great burning letters; and if you will go in, God will receive you tonight."[11]

Just over a month later, three days before Christmas, Dwight Lyman Moody handed in his invitation and joined the feast. The newspapers proclaimed his death, but according to Moody himself, that wasn't the full truth:

> Some day you will read in the papers that D. L. Moody, of East Northfield, is dead. . . . Don't you believe a word of it! At that moment I shall be more alive than I am now. . . . I was born of the flesh in 1837. I was born of the Spirit in 1856. That which is born of the flesh may die. That which is born of the Spirit will live forever.[12]

CONTEMPLATION

1. What might it look like, in your own life, to preach the gospel? Who, in your city, might "like to have a song"?

2. Do you have friendships with Christians outside of your own local church or denomination? How might you "pull together" with Christians who may believe differently, for the advancement of the kingdom?
3. Moody recognized his limitations and worked with people who could do the things he could not. Where are you gifted? In what areas are you lacking? How might you work with others as a team?

PRAYER

Heavenly Father, in everything we say and do, let us speak and act in love, and with a song of praise in our hearts.

My beard is not proof
of my manliness.
My beard is proof
of my patience.

THE BEARDS THAT MIGHT HAVE BEEN

BY AARON ALFORD

Even as we celebrate the Bearded Gospel Men who have gone before us, we cannot help but mourn for the Bearded Gospel Might-Have-Beens—people who, while having the gospel part down, never grew a great mane of manliness. But take heart! What history hath prevented, our imaginations can provide!

C. S. LEWIS (1898-1963)

Oh, Professor Lewis. He wrote so eloquently of the beard. Whether that was Father Christmas in *The Lion, The Witch, and the Wardrobe*:

> He was a huge man in a bright red robe (bright as holly-berries) with a hood that had fur inside it and a great white beard that fell like a foamy waterfall over his chest. . . . He was so big and so glad and so real that they all became quite still.[13]

or Captain Ransom in *That Hideous Strength*:

> All the light in the room seemed to run towards the gold hair and the gold beard of the wounded man. . . . She had, or so she had believed, disliked bearded faces except for old men. But that was because she had long since forgotten the imagined Arthur of her childhood—and the imagined Solomon too. . . . For the first time in all those years she tasted the word *King* itself with all its linked associations of battle, marriage, priesthood, mercy, and power.[14]

Whenever Lewis needed a character who reflected wisdom, strength, and dignity, he knew to give him a beard. One can only hope he has one now in glory!

J. R. R. TOLKIEN (1892–1973)

Of course we couldn't fail to mention Lewis's dear friend, the one who helped him find his way to Christianity, the great J. R. R. Tolkien. Tolkien also wrote beautifully of the beard, giving the entire race of dwarves magnificent beards, not to mention the stately beard of the wizard Gandalf.

THOMAS AQUINAS (1225–1274)

The man who wrote one of the greatest theological works of all time, the *Summa Theologica* (Summary of All Theology), sadly never seemed to find a reason to let those follicles fly. The world can only wonder what wisdom would have been born of an Aquinian beard. Perhaps we would have gotten a sequel to the *Summa Theologica*, the *Summa Barbalogica* (Summary of All Beards).

BILLY GRAHAM (1918–FOREVER, APPARENTLY)

He preached the gospel to millions, famously ending every stadium-filled gospel crusade with the old hymn "Just as I Am." We love you, Billy, just as you are. But a Billy beard! What a sight to behold such a thing would be! Perhaps, however, it was better this way. Thousands would have come forward at your meetings just to get a closer look at the beard and may have caused confusion with the numbers of those getting saved.

MOTHER TERESA (1910–1997)

Okay, Mother Teresa never had a beard, nor should she have. But she was pretty great, wasn't she? Dedicating her life to serving the poorest of the poor and becoming a living example of Jesus' love is simply rad. She was one heck of a Godly Gospel Woman (so much so that she may even have gotten a whole chapter elsewhere in this book about Bearded Gospel Men!).

CHAPTER 6

Daniel Nash

SPIRITUAL NAPALM

BY JARED BROCK

Meditation: This is the confidence we have in approaching God: that if we ask anything according to his will, he hears us.

—1 JOHN 5:14

Quote of the Day: I would rather teach one man to pray than ten men to preach.

—CHARLES SPURGEON

The room was packed with excited children and proud parents. I was six years old, and my Sunday school classmates had worked hard all year for this day, memorizing great swaths of Bible verses.

It was Celebration Sunday, and the table at the front of the room was piled high with treasure. Lollipops. Frisbees. Slinkies. There were bigger things, too, like Super Soakers and skateboards. And then there was the biggest prize of all, a giant green turtle-shaped swimming pool. The room bristled with anticipation.

They started with the small prizes. Pens and stickers for the slackers. Chocolate bars for the sloths. Board games for the mediocre achievers.

I figured I fell somewhere in the Mars bar range. I couldn't recall memorizing any verses, but surely I must have learned at least a few. As the prizes grew larger, I grew more distraught. The prize table emptied quickly. The skateboards rolled away. Soon, only one prize was left, and I was in tears, having been forgotten, or simply dropped from the honor roll. The announcer dragged the giant green turtle-shaped pool to the front of the stage.

"And the winner of the grand prize, for memorizing the most Bible verses, is . . ."

The crowd leaned forward. I slumped back in sorrow.

"Jared Brock!"

The audience erupted.

My parents cheered wildly.

I sat stunned.

My father hoisted me to my feet and gave me a gentle shove. My knees wobbled as I guiltily walked toward the front of the room, carefully avoiding eye contact with the announcer. I even went so far as to duck into a few rows, attempting to hide my shame by becoming invisible among my fellow awardees. I was carefully corralled by my beaming mother, who accepted the prize on my behalf.

Later that afternoon, as my father filled the pool with a green garden hose, I hesitantly asked, "Daddy, what's this for?"

"You memorized the most Bible verses!" he said approvingly.

I'm so grateful he didn't ask me to quote one. I couldn't remember learning a single verse.

Needless to say, I was a terrible Sunday school student. Permanently evicted before the age of ten, I was relegated to the second pew, right side, where I read Hardy Boys books.

Our minister at the time, Pastor Jack, took notice of my reading habits and gave me a copy of a slim volume about a man named

Daniel Nash. Terrible student that I was, I've never forgotten his story.

Author Paul Reno wrote:

> Daniel Nash pastored a small church in the backwoods of New York for six years, and traveled with and prayed for a traveling evangelist for seven more years until his death. As far as we know, he never ministered outside the region of upstate New York during days when much of it was frontier. His tombstone is in a neglected cemetery along a dirt road behind a livestock auction barn. His church no longer exists, its meetinghouse location marked by a historical marker in a cornfield; the building is gone, its timber used to house grain at a feed mill four miles down the road. No books tell his life story, no pictures or diaries can be found, his descendants (if any) cannot be located, and his messages are forgotten. He wrote no books, started no schools, led no movements, and generally, kept out of sight.[1]

In a town of 2,000 people, Nash led 270 people to Jesus but was evicted from his church because—as the official record shows—they wanted "a young man to settle in."[2]

No one saw any use for an aging preacher. But Charles Finney did.

Finney was a young, finely tufted, lawyer-turned-evangelist when the fifty-year-old Nash met him. They teamed up to barnstorm the nation for Jesus. Nash would slip into town a month in advance, find a handful of folks ready to be intercessors on behalf of their community, and start praying. By the time Finney arrived, spiritual fireworks were ready to ignite.

Today we call this the Second Great Awakening, a powerful spiritual renewal that swept the nation. Finney and Nash spent the next seven years together, speaking thousands of times in churches, barns, and any other building.

More than one hundred thousand people came to faith through Finney's preaching and Nash's prayer.

Nash died in 1831, and his neglected tombstone reads, "Laborer with Finney, mighty in prayer."[3]

Charles Finney stopped preaching just four months after Nash's death. He went on to become a fierce abolitionist and the head of Oberlin College, but the fire in his preaching was gone; without his prayer partner, he was unwilling to continue. As one publication reported, "Charles Finney so realized the need of God's working in all his service that he was wont to send godly Father Nash on in advance to pray down the power of God into the meetings which he was about to hold."[4]

CONTEMPLATION

1. Are you praying prayers according to God's will?
2. Who can you ask to regularly hold you up in prayer?
3. What could you accomplish with the power of Christ?

ACTION

This subject is so important that I'm diverting from our template a tad. My wife and I run a charity to fight exploitation, and we need all the backup we can get. Accordingly, we have enlisted about fifty prayer partners who get a regular update from us. I honestly don't know where we'd be without them. Here are ways you can build a Daniel Nash–style spiritual support system:

1. Write a list of people who might be willing to pray for you, and ask them to do so.
2. Never turn down the opportunity to receive prayer. When someone asks if you need prayer, don't take it lightly. Give

that person specific things to pray for, and ask him or her to follow up.

3. Get some on-the-spot practice today: Ask someone, "Will you please pray for me?"

PRAYER

Father who knows our needs, help us pray prayers that You can hear, and send answers in Your time.

SOMEONE HAS TO BE AWESOME.
IT MIGHT AS WELL BE ME!

A BEARDIANITY TIMELINE

c. 195

Clement of Alexandria calls the beard "the mark of a man."

361

Roman Emperor Julian sports a beard to show his break with the shaven Christian emperors before him, and to mark his connection to pagan Roman religion.

c. 411

Euthymius forbids unshaved dudes from entering his Judean Desert monastery.

c. 475

A rule is made that "no cleric should grow long hair or shave his beard."

816

The Council of Aachen requires monks to shave twenty-four times per year. Hermits ignore the rules.

867

Pope Nicholas I writes that Eastern church leaders were critical that "among us, clerics do not refuse to shave their beards."

868

The bishop of Paris writes that Eastern leaders judged the "Latins and Romans because they shave their beards."

868

Ratramnus, a Benedictine monk, opposes the Eastern church leaders who require beards. Lame.

1043

An abbot writes of the German Empire, "The shameful custom of the vulgar French . . . the cutting of beards . . . execrable to modest eyes."

1005

The English Canons of Edgar say no priest should "retain his beard for any time."

1031

The Council of Bourges demands that "all who minister within the Holy Church" should shave (which is why you've never heard of the Council of Bourges).

July 16, 1054

Christianity splits into Eastern and Western factions when a French cardinal excommunicates the patriarch of Constantinople. The list of "heresies" ends spectacularly: "Because they grow the hair on their head and beards."

c. 1060

Otloh of St. Emmeram tells the story of a beardless layman who goes to confession, and the priest points out that he should grow a beard like other common folk. The sinner promises, "Never again shall a razor touch my beard." He then shaves a few weeks later with a sharp knife instead. Otloh was happy to report that, soon after, the man "was captured by his enemies and . . . his eyes were gouged out."

October 5, 1080

While attempting to convert the Greeks on Sardinia, Pope Gregory VII forces the archbishop and the local priests to shave.

1096

The archbishop of Rouen threatens to excommunicate anyone with a beard.

c. 1160

After accidentally insulting some bearded lay brothers, the clean-shaven Abbot Burchard of Bellevaux writes *Apologia de Barbis*.

c. 1170

Pope Alexander III bans beards on priests.

1531

Piero Valeriano Bolzani writes *Pro Sacerdotum Barbis*—a defense of priestly beards—after Pope Clement VII threatened to force priests to shave.

July 6, 1535

On the day of his beheading, Sir Thomas More pushes his beard away from his neck on the chopping block, saying, "This hath not offended the king."

1535

Henry VIII institutes a beard ban. Told you he was a tool.

1547

Thomas Cranmer, archbishop of Canterbury, begins to grow a beard to signal a break with the (beardless) Catholic priests.

1830

Massachusetts pastor George Trask preaches against the "vain" beard of an attendee named Joseph Palmer, insists he shave it off, and denies him communion until he does so. Palmer grabs the cup, takes a swig, and hollers, "I love my Jesus as well, and better than any of you!"[5] He was shaved a few days later by four attackers armed with shears, a brush, soap, and a razor.

March 5, 1864

London satire mag *Punch* runs a block of caricatures displaying different kinds of Anglican clergy beards, and notes that Catholics and Baptists don't even have facial hair. "The Dissenters shave in gloomy silence, leaving this noble field of ecclesiastical adornment to the Clergy of the Establishment."

1942

C. S. Lewis writes in *The Screwtape Letters*: "We have now for many centuries triumphed over nature to the extent of making certain secondary characteristics of the male (such as the beard) disagreeable to nearly all the females."[6]

c. 1970

A handful of Christian colleges ban beards for their association with protesters.

2012

Bearded Gospel Men is founded.

CHAPTER 7

Saint Luka of Crimea

DOCTOR OF THE CHURCH

BY AARON ALFORD

Meditation: The Spirit of the Lord is on me, because he has anointed me to proclaim good news to the poor. He has sent me to proclaim freedom for the prisoners and recovery of sight for the blind.

—LUKE 4:18

Quote of the Day: Guard this truth like the best treasure of the heart, walk straight without looking right or left. Let us not bother with what we hear against religion, losing our bearings. Let us hold on to our faith which is the eternal indisputable truth. Amen.

—SAINT LUKA

The funeral procession was getting out of hand. The Communist government wanted the old man's ceremony and interment to be a quiet affair. The Orthodox priest-physician had been a thorn in their sides for most of his life. His fame would have been a source of pride for the state if he was known only as a physician and surgeon of unparalleled knowledge and skill, but he was much more than that.

He was also an Orthodox bishop, one of profound holiness and astonishing kindness, and he was already being hailed as a saint.

For an atheist government, this was a problem. But try as they might to silence him, to hide him from sight throughout his life and even now in his death, his life was lived too boldly to do so.

Valentin Felixovich Voino-Yasenetsky was born April 27, 1877, in Crimea, on the northern coast of the Black Sea. Although his family was religious, young Valentin did not discover Christ for himself until he was a teen. He received a New Testament as a graduation gift from his principal, and he discovered a love for God and a faith in Jesus he had never known before.

He was a talented illustrator and artist, and he was about to enroll in an art academy, but as his love for God deepened, so, too, did his love for the poor, particularly the sick. He knew his art could, of course, be expressed to the glory of God, but he felt drawn to care for people in a practical way. So he studied medicine, and after graduating with honors, he became a peasant doctor, practicing medicine for those who could otherwise not afford medical care.

In 1904, he met a nurse named Anna Lansky, and the two were married. For the next thirteen years, he practiced medicine in many different small towns and cities, increasing the breadth of his skills to include ophthalmology in order to serve even the blind beggars he encountered on the streets, who often suffered from trachoma, an infectious eye disease. His skill in this area resulted in him pioneering a surgical method that restored the sight of thousands of patients.[1]

"I ought to tell you," he later wrote, "that what God did to me was amazing and incomprehensible. . . . My pursuing surgery completely satisfied the goal I always had to serve the poor and the suffering, to dispose all my strength for the comfort of their pains, and to help them in their needs."[2]

After the First World War, his fame as a skilled surgeon spread, and he found himself teaching medicine as well as performing complex surgeries. During this time, however, Anna became ill with tuberculosis and died at the age of thirty-eight. Valentin held all the more tightly to his faith, studying theology and becoming more involved in his church. At a time when priests and bishops were being routinely executed for their faith, Valentin became an ordained deacon and, soon after, a priest at the age of forty-four.

"I felt it my duty," he said of this time, "to preach in defence of our abused Saviour, and to praise His boundless mercy toward humankind."[3]

In the early 1920s, the newly formed Soviet regime took a keen interest in the Orthodox Church. For the atheistic government, the Orthodox Church was a major problem, and they used every means at their disposal to weaken her. They used outright persecution, including arresting and even executing outspoken church leaders. But they also used shrewder means. When they saw debate happening in the Orthodox Church, especially in regard to how the church should relate to the Soviet government, they also saw an opportunity to bring division and gain some measure of control over the church. From within the church, the Soviet secret services planted agents to help establish what became known as the Living Church, a church that had the form of orthodoxy but was subservient to the interests of the Soviet government.

Around this time Valentin took monastic vows and, as a symbol of consecration, the name of an apostle who was near and dear to his heart: Luke, the physician evangelist. Now known as Father Luka, he was approached by the secret service. He refused to bow to pressure to become an agent within the church. And so, over the next fourteen years, Father Luka would endure a series of exiles and imprisonments, facing unspeakable hardships and even torture. He faced these times with an astonishing grace and profound courage. Rather than breaking him, these sufferings made his faith all the stronger. They "purified" him, and his love for Christ and for his fellow man grew all the deeper.

Even in exile, and in deplorable conditions, Father Luka continued to minister to the spiritual and physical needs of the people in harsh, remote places, such as Krasnoyarsk and Siberia, to which he was sent. He never distinguished his work as a physician from his work as a priest and pastor, and he routinely wore his *ryassa*, a priestly cassock, even as he performed surgery.

"They demand that I remove my ryassa," he said. "I will never do so. It, my ryassa, will be with me to my very death. . . . I help people as a physician, and I help them as a servant of the Church."[4]

At the advent of the Second World War, Father Luka begged to have his exile interrupted in order to tend to the most severely wounded and ill soldiers on the front lines. His request was granted, and he was later awarded a medal for his valiant work.

Father Luka loved each patient to whom he attended as an individual and a unique creation of God. No patient or parishioner was merely a number. With such love and care for each person, he became a bishop in 1944, even while continuing to provide medical help to the poorest of the poor. He practiced medicine for another two years before focusing solely on pastoral work.

He also brought attention to injustices of the government against Christians through multiple hunger strikes. When he angered government authorities, they would forcibly move him to another city in an attempt to silence him. But of course this only served to spread his notoriety and encourage the Orthodox Church. Wherever he went, he was a force to be reckoned with.

Eventually, though, the man who had healed so many wounds,

diseases, and blindness, both physical and spiritual, found his own health declining. Father Luka, the renowned ophthalmologist, eventually lost his vision. In June 1961, at the age of eighty-four, Father Luka, long blind, was granted the gift of faith-made-sight when he passed from this life into the arms of his Savior.

The Soviet government tried to make his funeral proceedings a low-profile affair. This was not to be. Thousands poured through the church to say good-bye to the priest and physician who had been an instrument of healing in body and soul. The funeral procession extended for three kilometers.

The words Father Luka had spoken as a bishop in a time of intense religious persecution resounded still, and the love with which he had spoken them still carried his healing presence:

> Everywhere and in all places, despite the success of atheist propaganda, Christ's little flock has endured, and continues to endure. You, you, all of you who are listening to me, are the little flock. And know and believe that Christ's little flock is invincible, that nothing can be done to it, that it fears nothing, because it knows and always treasures Christ's great words, "I will build My Church, and the gates of hell shall not prevail against it."[5]

CONTEMPLATION

1. Father Luka used his skills as a surgeon to serve the poorest of the poor. How can you use your abilities to serve the needy?
2. Father Luka did not distinguish his work as a surgeon from his work as a pastor, but rather saw all of his work as a way of loving God and loving people. Do you see some of your work as "spiritual" and other work as merely "physical"?
3. How might the two aspects of work intersect?

PRAYER

Heavenly Father, let everything we do be infused with a knowledge of love for You and love for the people in front of us. Let us be healers of heart, mind, and soul.

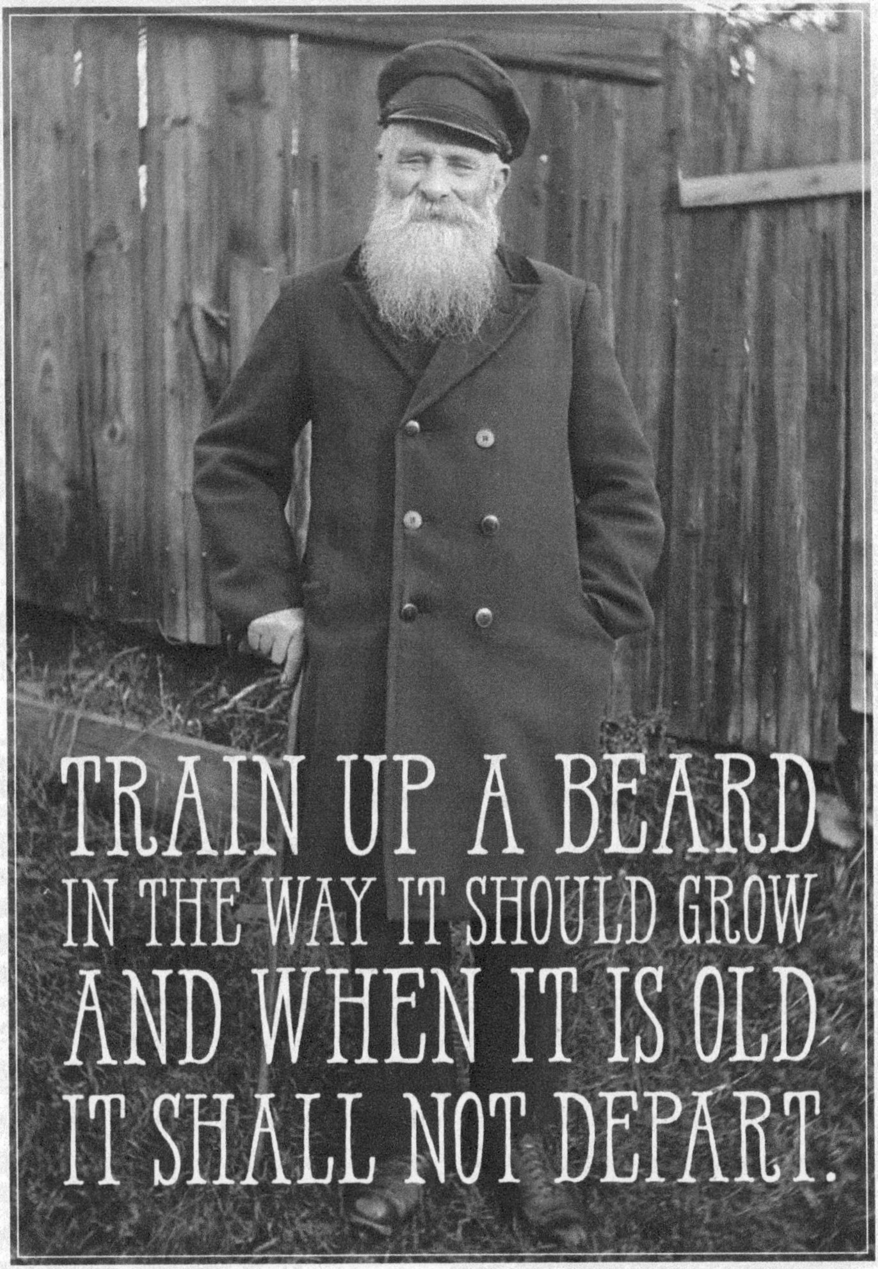
TRAIN UP A BEARD
IN THE WAY IT SHOULD GROW
AND WHEN IT IS OLD
IT SHALL NOT DEPART.

ANGSTROMS, BEARD-SECONDS, AND THE MEASUREMENT OF CHARACTER

BY AARON ALFORD

Ever heard of a beard-second?

As a light-year is determined by how far light travels in the span of one year, a beard-second is determined by how much a beard grows in one second. Nuclear physicists use a measurement called an angstrom, one ten-billionth of a meter, in discussing extremely small measurements. A beard-second is valued at one hundred angstroms per second, scientifically proving G. K. Chesterton's wisdom: "You cannot grow a beard in a moment of passion."[6]

If you want to grow a glorious beard like Father Luka's or Thomas More's, you need only stop shaving off those precious angstroms, because each one of the 86,400 beard-seconds of the day is of vital importance. If you've ever struggled to bring forth a beard, you know the attention that must be given to the smallest of growth.

It's strange, though, how we don't think in these terms when it comes to our character. We forget that every second matters. We forget that each small decision we make throughout the day is a choice to shave off precious angstroms of character, or let it grow.

Maximilian Kolbe, a Christian friar, found himself in Auschwitz, a Nazi concentration camp, during World War II. After three men escaped from the death camp, ten men were randomly chosen to be starved to death. Maximilian was not selected but volunteered to take the place of another man. He and nine others were confined together and starved, and all the while Maximilian led them in prayers and songs of worship. He was the last to die.

We read stories about men like this, and we're amazed at their steadfast faith and strength of character. They died with the gospel on their lips and in their hearts, surrendering their lives for the love of Christ. Perhaps we say things like, "I can only hope I could be so faithful!"

We forget that no one attains this strength of character and love for Christ in a sudden rush of heroism or willpower. Men like Maximilian practiced their martyrdom, the laying down of their own lives for the sake of others, their whole lives. Their last heroic moments were simply a natural expression of who they had always been.

We make small choices every day, and each choice, whether we're paying for our coffees or passing a beggar on the street, is full of meaning and possibility. There are hundreds of choices to be made in a day, big and small, either to step beyond ourselves in selfless love or to play it safe. In these moments, we can either cooperate with God's grace or cut it off.

What does it look like to lay down my life for the girl who's handing me coffee in the morning? Perhaps it's as simple as stepping out of my own thoughts and worries for a moment to actually see her and say a sincere "Thank you, ma'am." What does it mean to lay down my life for the beggar on the sidewalk? Maybe it means stopping for a moment to say hello or taking three minutes to learn his name and show an interest in his life.

These small choices, like beard-seconds, add up. They can determine what I'll make of big choices later on. Of course God can pour out His grace in critical moments, despite how selfish our previous choices have been. He's in the business of redemption. But His grace flows in our lives more freely when we continuously, every day, cooperate with the movements of the Holy Spirit.

We are, in every second, becoming who we will be at the hour of our death. Every choice I make is a choice toward becoming the man I wish to be. When I want to know if one day I'll be the kind of man who would lay down his life for another, I need only ask if I'm laying down my life for another right now.

A man's character, like a man's beard, cannot be grown in a moment of passion, even in a moment of martyrdom. Character is grown and cultivated. Sometimes the growth is nearly imperceptible, just a hundred angstroms a second, but it's happening. As long as I'm cooperating with the grace of God, it's happening. And one day, years from now, like the beard on my face, the result will be glorious.

CHAPTER 8

Frederick Douglass

ABOLITIONIST EXTRAORDINAIRE

BY JARED BROCK

Meditation: The Lord said to him, "Now then, you Pharisees clean the outside of the cup and dish, but inside you are full of greed and wickedness."

—LUKE 11:39

Quote of the Day: One and God make a majority.

—FREDERICK DOUGLASS

You can't talk about the history of American civil rights without mentioning the magnificently bearded Frederick Douglass. Originally named Frederick Augustus Washington Bailey, Douglass was born in Maryland around 1818. Slaves rarely knew their exact birth dates, so Douglass later chose Valentine's Day as his birthday. His father was likely his owner or the overseer, and his mother died when he was young.

Owners forbade their slaves to learn how to read and write—they'd then have the power to write their own passes—but Douglass learned the alphabet from his master's wife at age twelve and later traded food for lessons from neighboring white children. He started reading Bible verses and longed for a father figure in his life.

> I was not more than thirteen years old, when in my loneliness and destitution I longed for someone to whom I could go, as to a father and protector. The preaching of a white Methodist minister, named Hanson, was the means of causing me to feel that in God I had such a friend. He thought that all men, great and small, bond and free, were sinners in the sight of God: that they were by nature rebels against His government; and that they must repent of their sins, and be reconciled to God through Christ. I cannot say that I had a very distinct notion of what was required of me, but one thing I did know well: I was wretched and had no means of making myself otherwise. I consulted a good old colored man named Charles Lawson, and in tones of holy affection he told me to pray, and to "cast all my care upon God." This I sought to do; and though for weeks I was a poor, broken-hearted mourner, traveling through doubts and fears, I finally found my burden lightened, and my heart relieved. I loved all mankind, slaveholders not excepted, though I abhorred slavery more than ever. I saw the world in a new light, and my great concern was to have everybody converted. My desire to learn increased, and especially, did I want a thorough acquaintance with the contents of the Bible.[1]

Douglass continued to read every newspaper or pamphlet he could find. They formed his political views on human rights, and by age sixteen he was teaching the New Testament to a group of forty other slaves. For the rest of his life, he made it clear: "Once you learn to read, you will be forever free."[2]

At age twenty, on his third attempt, and with the help of his soon-to-be wife, Douglass impersonated a sailor and escaped from slavery. The two were wed and took their name from the hero of Sir Walter

Scott's "The Lady of the Lake." Douglass became a preacher the following year. Despite the occasional mob beating, Douglass toured the nation with the American Anti-Slavery Society. He published his autobiography, which became an instant bestseller. He was forced to move to Europe for two years to evade being captured, and eventually bought his freedom.

Douglass published five newspapers and spoke freely about race, rights, and faith. As he wrote in his autobiography:

> Between the Christianity of this land, and the Christianity of Christ, I recognize the widest possible difference—so wide, that to receive the one as good, pure, and holy is of necessity to reject the other as bad, corrupt, and wicked. . . . I love the pure, peaceable, and impartial Christianity of Christ; I therefore hate the corrupt, slaveholding, women-whipping, cradle-plundering, partial and hypocritical Christianity of this land. Indeed, I can see no reason, but the most deceitful one, for calling the religion of this land Christianity.[3]

Douglass believed in equal rights for all people, including black people, women, First Nations people, and immigrants. He was the only African American to attend the first women's rights convention in 1848. He argued that he couldn't accept the right to vote as a black man if women couldn't do the same. He was an adviser to Presidents Lincoln and Johnson on African-American welfare.

After the Civil War, Douglass served as president of the Freedman's Savings Bank, then was US ambassador to the Dominican Republic, and later served as minister-resident and consul-general to the Republic of Haiti. He was the first black man to hold a high-ranking government position, and he was the first African American to appear on a presidential ballot when he was nominated as vice president alongside Victoria Woodhull, the first woman to run for president of the United States.[4] He often remarked, "I would unite with anybody to do right, and with nobody to do wrong."[5]

Frederick Douglass died just a few days after his "birthday," on February 20, 1895.

CONTEMPLATION

1. What is the difference between "the Christianity of this land and the Christianity of Christ"?
2. Are there any areas where your faith might be hypocritical?
3. How are you showing your hatred for corruption and injustice through your actions?

PRAYER

God of all, who made all in Your image, wash away our outer pomposity and inner hypocrisy.

She married me for
LOVE.
She stayed for the
BEARD.

PORN IS THE WORST

BY JARED BROCK

I got an email from an old camp friend. "We need to talk. Can we go for lunch?"

I hadn't seen him in ten years. He knew I was a documentarian, but I had no idea what he wanted to talk about. We went out for lunch, and he cut straight to the point. "I'm a youth worker in my home church," he said. "I'm working with thirty young men, and they all have porn addictions. We need your help."

So, he started raising doc money, and I started asking people: "How old were you the first time you saw porn? What was it? Where were you? How did it make you feel?"

I first saw porn at ten years old. I was babysitting, the kid was asleep, and it was a stormy night. I was watching the NBA All-Star Game. (I used to be quite the baller—I was on my way to the pros when I learned that white boys can't jump.) My hand was nowhere near the remote control. Lightning must have hit the cable box, because all of a sudden I was watching the Playboy channel. And they didn't get the Playboy channel.

So, being a godly, faithful, Christian ten-year-old boy, I immediately turned it off.

Then I ran to the front door to make sure no one was coming before running back to resume watching. I watched for maybe five or ten minutes, not understanding what was going on. Then, suddenly, it switched back to the basketball game.

I didn't see porn again until I was eighteen or nineteen and I had moved out of my parents' house. By then, I was trying to make better choices. And, as I soon discovered, my cerebral cortex was starting to develop in order to protect me against addiction, so I didn't get hooked on porn.

But all that being said, if I'd had porn in my pocket—if I'd had a cell phone with instant access, twenty-four hours a day, seven days a week, to free, unlimited, hardcore pornography—how would I not be addicted to pornography today? How would any kid, with exposure so young and easy repeat access, not get entirely hooked on porn?

So we made a documentary on porn. It's called *Over 18*, and we've already booked hundreds of screenings around the world. The stories we've encountered are grim. The official stat is that 90 percent of boys and 60 percent of girls see porn before age eighteen, and the average boy sees porn for the first time at age twelve. That means for every fifteen-year-old who sees porn for the first time, there's a nine-year-old like Joseph, the young star of our film.

Joe started watching porn at eight years old, after he clicked on a pop-up on a video game he was playing. He was soon addicted to ultraviolent Internet pornography. It's taken years of recovery for Joe to wean off of porn and start to treat women with dignity and respect. Sadly, Joe's story is pretty average.

Every night as we toured our film, we heard stories of kids seeing porn at ridiculously young ages. Most men I meet first saw porn between the ages of seven and eleven. One chicken farmer's eight-year-old son found hardcore porn when he searched for the word *chicks*. We've heard stories of people seeing porn as young as two or three years old from porn-addicted parents, older siblings, babysitters, or the Internet. We've heard multiple stories of kids as young as eight—third graders—having porn parties. It should not come as a surprise to us when young men assault a girl when they make the high school or college football team.

I've never had anyone come up to me at an event and say, "My ten-year porn addiction has been amazing for my marriage," or, "My fifteen-year porn struggle has been brilliant for my faith." But my wife, Michelle, does have women come up to her in tears, describing the violent and degrading sex acts that men request from them, with no difference between the Christians and the non-Christians. We hear countless stories of addiction and divorce. I had a teenage girl come up to me and ask, "What do you do if you know your dad is addicted to pornography?"

I always knew that porn was bad, but now after making *Over 18*, I'm here to report: porn is the worst.

But here's the thing: My wife and I are super pro-sex. We're just convinced that porn is not pro-sex. It commodifies and profits from the human form. It turns people into voyeurs. Digital stimulus is causing addiction, ruining careers, wrecking marriages, creating porn-induced erectile dysfunction, and causing aggression toward women. Committed sex is about loving, giving, and serving. Porn sex is about taking, dominating, and controlling. Sex is like a fire—it's amazing in a campfire, but it's horrible in a forest fire. And our world is on fire.

We need to get serious about implementing meaningful age verification on the Internet as a way to prevent porn addiction in our children. We need to get serious about protecting ourselves with tactics and accountability so porn doesn't ruin our lives too. We need to help one another cultivate intimacy and sexual expression that embodies our beliefs: that people are made in the image of God, that they have value and worth and deserve our respect and love. Porn offers a false image, and we have the opportunity to restore the real picture of God's love to humanity.

CHAPTER 9

John the Baptist

LESS IS MORE

BY AARON ALFORD

Meditation: There was a man sent from God whose name was John. He came as a witness to testify concerning that light, so that through him all might believe. He himself was not the light; he came only as a witness to the light. The true light that gives light to everyone was coming into the world.

—JOHN 1:6–9

Quote of the Day: He must increase, and I must decrease.

—JOHN THE BAPTIST

It's noon on the day of the winter solstice, just a few days before Christmas, and the sun's rays break through the dust of the old California chapel of San Juan Bautista, a mission church built in 1797. Near the altar stands a small statue of John the Baptist, and as the sun's beams come to rest on the figure, it bursts forth in golden light. At no other time of the year does the sun fall so perfectly upon the statue. Just a few hours later, however, the sunlight brilliantly illuminates the altar itself, where Christ is made present in communion.

This is no accident of light in the little church; its builders knew exactly what they were doing, according to archaeologist Ruben G. Mendoza.[1] The Franciscan missionaries sought to communicate something of the mystery of Christ, and even of John the Baptist's relationship to Him, through the architecture of the building where they worshiped. They carefully set the windows in just the right place to achieve this strange and beautiful effect. The sun illuminates John the Baptist, but soon moves on to Christ himself.

"He must increase, and I must decrease."[2]

These are the famous words of John the Baptist, cousin of Jesus, forerunner of the gospel, herald of the Son of God, eater of grasshoppers.

John the Baptist, perhaps the most famously bearded figure of the Bible, would appreciate the symbolism so intentionally built into the mission chapel. Born six months before his cousin Jesus, he was destined to shine as much as he was destined to fade.

John the Baptist is famous for living in the desert like a first-century Grizzly Adams, and many scholars believe he was part of an entire community of desert-dwelling Grizzly Adamses called the Essenes. These men lived austere lives and spent their days studying the Jewish scriptures. It's easy to imagine John reflecting on the strange circumstances surrounding his birth (and the even stranger circumstances surrounding the birth of his cousin) as he carefully read the ancient scriptures. What was it like to realize that these poems and prophecies were written about you? What was it like to realize they were written about your younger cousin, the boy with whom you used to build blanket forts?

However he came to realize it, John knew that he was the one who would prepare the people of Israel for the arrival of their Savior. So, when the time was right, he put on his camel-hair tunic, tied his leather belt around his waist, had a morning bowl of Honey-Nut Locusts, and set forth to tell the world that the Son of God was coming to set the world on fire.

He preached to whomever would listen, and all were welcome to come and be yelled at by the wild-eyed prophet of God. Tax collectors, average Josephs, and even soldiers of the Roman occupiers came to hear him preach. More than that, they came to put their old lives to death and to begin a new life in the waters of the Jordan River. John the Crazy Hermit became John the Baptizer.

Baptism was not an uncommon practice of the day; it was a way of proclaiming that you were leaving an old life behind and beginning a new one. And the kind of life change the Baptizer preached was no simple rearranging of the furniture. It was radical.

"Anyone who has two shirts," he said, his unkempt beard blowing in the breeze, "should share with the one who has none, and anyone who has food should do the same" (Luke 3:11).

If indeed he was a member of the Essenes, the words he preached were only part of his preaching. He was a living example of what he preached. As an Essene, he would have lived a life of radical poverty and community with his brothers, something very close to modern monasticism. For an Essene brother, baptism wasn't something you did once in a lifetime or even once in a while; you were literally baptized every single day. It was a sign of daily repentance and cleansing as you sought to live your life in conformity with the benevolence of God and in unity with your brothers. These men took the law of God seriously. So seriously, in fact, that if you had to, ahem, "express your bowels" on the Sabbath, well, you'd just have to hold it till the sun went down. No pooping on Saturdays! But their fervor for the law included more than bodily functions. They abstained from the ritual blood sacrifices of the time because they believed very literally that the Lord desired "mercy, not sacrifice," and that "a reverent mind was the best offering to God."[3]

Their spirituality was not merely focused on personal purity but included practical acts of charity. They had no possessions of their own and gave to the needy. They cared for the sick with no regard to the patient's religion or creed and even went to great lengths to study natural medicinal aids and cures. They helped the elderly. They welcomed the stranger. We cannot know for certain that John the Baptist was part of the Essene community, but his spirit and spirituality seem to coincide with theirs in interesting ways.

But as radically committed to holiness as he was, he didn't consider himself worthy even to untie the shoes of the One who was to come. He told the crowds, "He will baptize you with the Holy Spirit and fire" (Luke 3:16).

Imagine his shock when Jesus Himself showed up to be baptized. John tried to object. "I'm the one who should be baptized by you!" he said. Jesus refused his objection. Although He had no sins for which to repent, Jesus was beginning a new phase of His life, and He felt it only right to be baptized for all to see.

You probably know the story from here. Jesus, as He rose from the water, John's hand on his back, saw the sky pulled back like a curtain. The Holy Spirit of God descended as a dove, and a voice proclaimed, "This is my beloved Son, with whom I am well pleased" (Matt. 3:17 ESV).

Then the dove was gone. John was standing in the water with his cousin Jesus, who smiled at him with great love.

And just as John knew it should happen, people began to listen to Jesus instead of John. John had done his job. He had gotten people ready to meet Jesus, and it was time for Jesus to begin His new life as a preacher, teacher, and healer. Many of the people who had followed John began to follow Jesus, and like the winter sun in that California chapel, John the Baptist's light began to fade.

He must increase, and I must decrease.

CONTEMPLATION

1. John was commissioned to go before the Lord to prepare His way. How can you prepare the way for Jesus in others' lives?

2. Are there areas of work or ministry in your life in which it may be time to "decrease," like John, so that someone else may "increase," like Jesus?
3. Does your life preach the message that your lips proclaim? Where might you need to make changes to more closely match what you preach with how you live?

PRAYER

Dear Jesus, grant us the boldness and the humility of Your cousin John, and teach us to rejoice in being humbled.

IT'S REAL,
AND IT'S
SPECTACULAR!

CONFESS YOURSELF BEFORE YOU WRECK YOURSELF

BY AARON ALFORD

Alcoholics are some of the coolest people I know.

If you've never been to an Alcoholics Anonymous meeting, I highly recommend attending one at least once in your life, even if you've never tasted a drop. I am not an alcoholic, but I've had the great honor of attending an AA meeting as a guest of a friend. I quickly understood why folks who attend these meetings often say they wish church could be more like AA.

It was only an hour long, but it was filled to the brim with grace. Several people were called on to share about how they were doing. Here's why alcoholics are so cool. With everything that people shared, there was precisely 0 percent "bull pucky." People were not trying to be careful with their words, because they knew they were in a safe place where everyone was on equal ground. Their stories were peppered with salty language, but sometimes such is the price of honesty. People shared with complete candor their thoughts, their struggles, their frustrations, and their need for grace. And through everything, there was a deep, beautiful strain of thankfulness. When you know your need for mercy, you're all the more thankful to have received it.

I left that meeting with a sense of freedom. I felt the freedom to be honest, the freedom to confess my failings and to receive grace. I was put in mind of James 5:16: "Therefore confess your sins to each other and pray for each other so that you may be healed. The prayer of a righteous person is powerful and effective."

The Devil loves a secret, and he's terrified of truth. He likes to make us think our sins are so great, so horrible, that they must never be confessed to another human. One of his favorite things to tell us when it comes to our sins is that "it's just Jesus and me." And we wonder why we stay trapped in the same cycles of sinful behavior! This "just Jesus and me" mentality is about as destructive to a Christian as idol worship, causing us to completely shut out the family of God we are intended to live within.

Will God forgive you if you contritely confess your sins privately to Him? Of course He will. He loves forgiving sins. He's eager to forgive sins. But if you want to be healed, to receive the grace you need to change these sinful patterns, you'll need to confess your sins to a person. That's one of the many reasons the Father gave us the gift of the church. "That you may be healed."

Anyone in AA knows exactly what James was writing about. When we come together in Jesus' name, Jesus has promised to be there with us, and in that divine presence, God will pour out His grace. It is our humility, our willingness to be completely honest with ourselves before at least one other person, that creates a kind of receptacle to receive what God wants to give.

Grace just can't fit into anything less.

CHAPTER 10

Dirk Willems

ANABAPTIST LIFEGUARD MARTYR

BY JARED BROCK

Meditation: Do not be overcome by evil,
but overcome evil with good.

—ROMANS 12:21

Quote of the Day: I do not believe that persecution
will fail to come. . . . I hope to God that He
will grant the medicine of patience.

—CONRAD GREBEL

The sixteenth-century Anabaptists of Europe were pacifists who led the way for today's Mennonites and Amish. At least fifteen hundred were tortured and killed for their faith. Men were usually burned alive and women were usually drowned—often on the grounds of not believing in infant baptism, but let's be honest, it was because Anabaptists also opposed the highly profitable state use of usury, military service, and control of the church.

Dirk Willems was arrested in his hometown of Asperen one winter day and was tried as an Anabaptist by the Duke of Alva during a time when Spain inexplicably ruled the Netherlands. The court document outlined his crimes:

> Dirk Willems, born at Asperen, at present a prisoner, has, without torture and iron bonds (or otherwise) before the bailiff and us judges, confessed that at the age of fifteen, eighteen or twenty years, he was re-baptized in Rotterdam, at the house of one Pieter Willems, and that he, further, in Asperen, at his house, at divers hours, harbored and admitted secret conventicles and prohibited doctrines, and that he also has permitted several persons to be re-baptized in his aforesaid house; all of which is contrary to our holy Christian faith, and to the decrees of his royal majesty, and ought not to be tolerated, but severely punished, for an example to others; therefore, we the aforesaid judges, having, with mature deliberation of council, examined and considered all that was to be considered in this matter, have condemned and do condemn by these presents in the name; and in the behalf, of his royal majesty, as Count of Holland, the aforesaid Dirk Willems, prisoner, persisting obstinately in his opinion, that he shall be executed with fire until death ensues.[1]

His property was confiscated and he was locked in a makeshift prison until execution day.

Knowing what fate awaited him, our bearded hero escaped from the palace through a window, down a rope of knotted rags. Guards gave chase. Willems dropped to the ice that covered the castle moat and started to run.

The moat led to a large pond called the Hondegat—translated "the Dog Hole"—which was upward of thirty feet deep. It was covered with a thin sheet of ice, barely a frost. Having survived on prison rations, Willems was light enough to skitter across the pond, but one of the guards fell through in pursuit. He struggled for shore and cried for help, but the ice kept breaking and he started to drown.

Dirk Willems froze. His response was reflexive. His conscience compelled him to turn. His faith compelled him to love at all costs. Willems helped the man escape from his icy fate.

In gratitude for saving his life, the guard was about to let Willems go when the chief magistrate arrived at the other side of the pond. He reminded the soldier of his duty and ordered him to arrest the escapee. The guard reluctantly seized the prisoner and dragged him back to a more secure prison cell above the bell in a church tower.

Four days later, on May 16, 1569, Willems was burned at the stake outside of town. A strong wind blew from the east and prevented the smoke from causing Willems to faint from inhalation. His death was excruciating, and his cries of anguish were heard for miles. The neighboring town heard him scream seventy times, "O my Lord; my God!"[2] The judge was filled with sorrow and demanded the executioner to end it quickly.

CONTEMPLATION

1. Where are you currently being overcome by evil?
2. What can you do to overcome evil with good?
3. How can you serve your enemies?

PRAYER

God of good, by Your power help us to overcome evil by practicing Your presence and bearing Your image; grant us the medicine of patience in the hour of persecution.

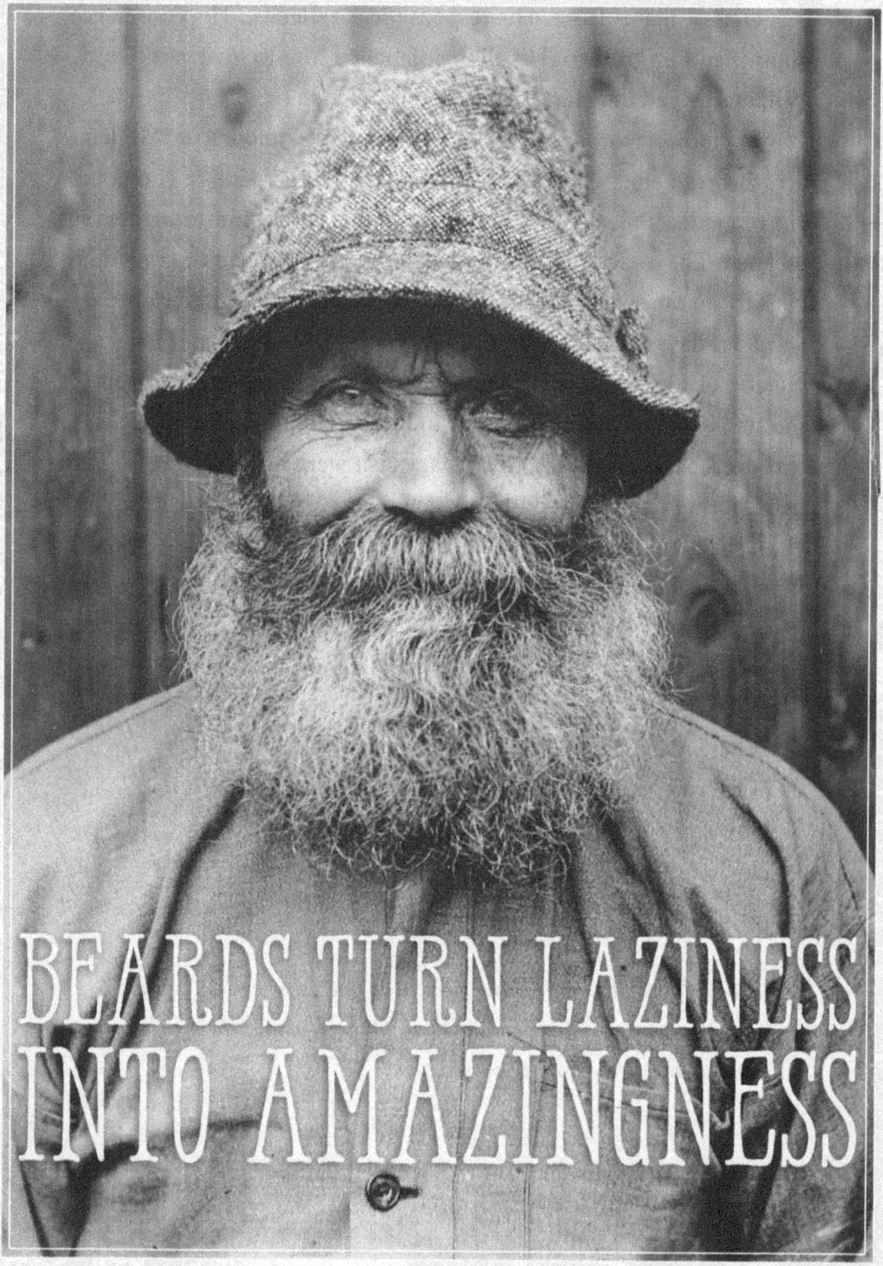
BEARDS TURN LAZINESS
INTO AMAZINGNESS

CHAPTER 11

Sir Thomas More

THE BEARD HATH COMMITTED NO TREASON!

BY AARON ALFORD

Meditation: I am the resurrection and the life. The one who believes in me will live, even though they die; and whoever lives by believing in me will never die. Do you believe this?

—JOHN 11:25–26

Quote of the Day: I die the King's good servant, and God's first.

—SIR THOMAS MORE

He knelt before the wooden block, his hands tied tightly behind his back. Long had he lay forgotten and neglected in prison. His frame was emaciated, his bones fragile, his beard long and wild. His death by beheading, upgraded from mere hanging, was moments away. The gates of heaven would open for him, and he would see face-to-face the Christ whom he'd served so faithfully.

The black-hooded executioner placed a hand on his shoulder.

"Please, sir," came the boyish voice from behind the mask, "please forgive me."

"Friend," the prisoner responded, "be not afraid of thy office.

Thou sendest me to God." Then the prisoner's eyes flickered with a merry light. "My neck is short, though," he added. "Take care not to strike it awry!"

The executioner blurted a chuckle in spite of himself. Then the prisoner laid his head on the chopping block. He was ready to go to God, and no earthly care could touch him now. Except that there was a certain scratch at his soon-to-be separated Adam's apple, and he realized there was one last thing that must be made right before his passing. He lifted his head, and, with a nod, shifted his long beard away from his neck.

"This hath not offended the king."

The executioner's ax did not strike his neck awry, and Sir Thomas More's head (and his wholly intact beard) landed with a thump in the basket below.[1]

Sir Thomas More was one of the most highly respected men of his time (sixteenth-century England) and, like his beard, he had committed no treason. But sometimes being true to your convictions can cost you your life.

More was a lawyer, a man who loved order in his home, in his politics, and in his faith. He also valued knowledge and learning, and he insisted that his three daughters receive as thorough an education as his son at a time when such consideration for women was nearly unheard of.

But his love for order and erudition was not at the cost of joy, and he was known for an infectious sense of humor. His friend Erasmus of Rotterdam once said Thomas's face was "always expressive of an amiable joyousness, and even an incipient laughter . . . better framed for gladness than for gravity or dignity."[2]

His skill and reputation as a lawyer grew and eventually led him to become a member of Parliament and to a position in King Henry VIII's inner circle. As Protestantism spread through England, Henry called on Sir Thomas to write theological letters of response to Luther's critiques. It was a time of unprecedented turmoil within the church, and More was asked to enforce anti-heresy laws. The government and the church were so closely entwined in matters legal and spiritual as to be almost inseparable, and More was a man of his time. He did everything in his power to stamp out what he believed to be heresy wherever it was found.

More found great favor with King Henry and was one of the king's most loyal subjects. King Henry was known to come unannounced to More's home, strolling through the gardens with his hand amicably wrapped around Sir Thomas's neck.

More, however, knew that friendship with a king such as Henry should be held lightly, as the king did not have much of a reputation for temperance or stability. "If my head," he once wrote to his son-in-law, "should win him a castle in France, it should not fail to go."[3]

It was this quality of unpredictability that eventually led Henry to demand a church-sanctioned annulment from his first wife, Catherine of Aragon, so that he could marry his mistress, Anne Boleyn. (Anne, too, would eventually be separated from her head by Henry. But that's another, beardless, story!) After the Roman Catholic Church refused to condone such an annulment, Henry simply proclaimed himself to be the head of the church in England, essentially extending his kingly power to things heavenly as well. He created the Act of Supremacy, declaring that the king was "the only supreme head on Earth of the Church of England."[4]

Thomas had always counted the letter of the law to be his friend, and had, up to this point, remained tactfully silent on the matter of King Henry's annulment and subsequent scandalous marriage. He had remained loyal to the king, foolish as the king was. "I never saw a fool yet," he later wrote, "that thought himself other than wise."[5]

But soon Henry created the Treasons Act, which made not signing the Act of Supremacy an act of treason punishable by death. Thomas refused to sign, and for this, he was arrested and taken to the infamous Tower of London, where he was held for many months. A prison cell is not unlike a monk's cell, and Thomas, who had almost became a monk himself, dedicated his time to prayer, fasting, study, and writing.

A trial was eventually held in which a former colleague named Richard Rich (yes, Richard Rich!) perjured himself in order to secure a guilty verdict. More was headed for the executioner's block. But Sir Thomas did not beg or plead for his life, nor did he rail against the injustice done to him (though he spoke plainly of Rich's deceitfulness). He simply remained true to his beliefs, to himself, and to his God.

On the morning of July 6, 1535, Sir Thomas More was led up the scaffold to his execution. But that sense of wit, humor, and good-naturedness remained with him, even in the moments before his death. He joked as he ascended the rickety scaffold, "Pray, Sir, see me safe up; and as to my coming down, let me shift for myself!"[6]

At the scaffold, he prayed aloud the Fifty-first Psalm, a psalm that begs God's mercy on a sinner:

> Have mercy on me, O God,
> according to your unfailing love;
> according to your great compassion
> blot out my transgressions.
> Wash away all my iniquity
> and cleanse me from my sin.
> For I know my transgressions,
> and my sin is always before me. . . .
> Cleanse me with hyssop, and I will be clean;
> wash me, and I will be whiter than snow. (vv. 1–3, 7)

He then forgave his executioner and, after he had safely tucked his long beard away from the path of the blade, said this: "I die the King's good servant, and God's first."[7]

Thomas More died for his convictions, but he did not die in a blaze of defiant anger. He did not die with vengeance and hatred in his heart. He died as a man who was deeply aware of his own sin and need for grace, and he died with the joy of a humble man who knows his Savior.

Thomas wrote to his daughter not long before his execution: "I do nobody harm, I say none harm, I think none harm, but wish everybody good. And if this be not enough to keep a man alive, in good faith I long not to live."[8]

Many of us might find it easy to die for our convictions or to be martyrs for our beliefs, even if that only goes as far as proclaiming them on Facebook and suffering an "unfriending" or two. But how many of us can do so wishing "everybody good"? It's one thing to suffer for your convictions, but it's another thing entirely to do so with joy in your heart and peace on your lips. Sir Thomas did that. May his example steady our convictions with humility, grace, and love.

CONTEMPLATION

1. Have your convictions ever led you to being falsely accused of wrongdoing? How did you respond?
2. How do you think Sir Thomas was able to face his death so confidently?
3. What do you think your last words would be in a similar situation? Would they reflect bitterness and anger, or forgiveness and humor?

PRAYER

Father, grant us the grace to be steadfast in our convictions, and let us do so with no ill will toward anyone.

HAVING A BEARD
doesn't make me better than you.
JUST BETTER
LOOKING.

AHM YO BAH

BY JIMMY SUSTAR*

The ethnic regions of Burma, governed by a broken form of democracy and controlled by a military junta, was a violent and dangerous place to live.

Refugee camps along the Thai border were overflowing, and the powers that be did not allow any more people to obtain refugee status. Those needing to flee war, poverty, extortion, and slave labor crossed into Thailand to live illegally, often working in slave labor conditions or as undocumented migrant workers. Children of these families were left vulnerable to many types of exploitation, including slave labor, sex trafficking, and a severe lack of provisions and education.

It was 2011, and I was working as a missionary in a garbage dump where around three hundred undocumented displaced people lived. The focus of our work was relational medical relief, as a means of building a safe community.

One day we set up two mats on top of the rotting garbage and sat down with forty-five little kids and their mothers. We colored pictures with them. The children intently beautified those black-and-white pages exactly the way they wanted. They were creating beauty in the midst of chaos, stink, and filth.

Flies feed and lay their eggs on rotting organic matter. Imagine a cluster of flies at the bottom of your trash can. That is what rested on the bodies and faces of the toddlers as they sprawled across our mats to share crayons and markers.

One baby boy struck me with the reality these people lived in. He was ten months old and was sleeping on his mother's shoulder. Wearing only a T-shirt, he rested as flies covered his snot-plastered face, repeatedly entering his mouth.

His mother colored. It was an escape for her. A moment of peace.

The boy woke up fussing, so she laid him on the ground near her. As I watched him, I discovered he couldn't roll over or sit up on his own. He was severely delayed in his development, unable to move. He was helpless. His mother motioned to me that there was something wrong with this child's brain.

"Ma kaun boo," she said, and returned to her coloring. *Not well.*

I asked his mother his name.

"Ahm Yo Bah," she said.

Suddenly two older kids approached and began fondling his genitals and kicking him on his body and on his head. He could do nothing to protect himself and erupted in screams and cries while his mother did nothing. She was afraid to. This was shame doing its deep and ugly work.

I rebuked the perpetrators and picked up the frightened little baby. I held him and wept.

He stared at me with a blank face, limp in my arms. Heartache, anger, and fear flooded my soul as I asked God, "What does the future look like for this boy? What can I do? Where is the kingdom of God?"

I gave him water, and I spoke his name. "Ahm Yo Bah." I held him, whispering into his ear all of the beautiful truths that get me out of bed every morning, while holding my whiskered face against his. I kept saying, "I love you. Jesus loves you." I didn't know what else to do.

After fifteen minutes of this, he thrust his feet into my lap and stiffened his back as he smiled into my eyes. He came alive as he bounced up and down. I sat him down on the mat. He sat up on his own, and then he ran off to his mother's arms.

A miracle? Sure.

The deepest part, and the piece that changes me and gives me a glimpse into the glory of God, is the Emmanuel we both experienced in the middle of degradation and despair.

When referring to God-With-Us, Frederick Buechner said that the "Ultimate Mystery [was] born with a skull you could crush one-handed."[9]

God's vulnerability, solidarity, and love for a broken mess is the only thing that can change anything in this world. The only thing that makes holiness and wholeness happen. Ahm Yo Bah and I met Jesus together on a floor mat in the middle of rotting trash, flies, and stench.

We met together in simplicity, humanness, need, and love. We met Emmanuel.

** Jimmy Sustar is a bearded musician and missionary with Youth With A Mission. He and his family currently work in Wooster, Ohio, in the area of community development.*

CHAPTER 12

Charles Spurgeon

CIGAR-CHOMPING PRINCE OF PREACHERS

BY JARED BROCK

Meditation: Why do you look at the speck of sawdust in your brother's eye and pay no attention to the plank in your own eye?

—MATTHEW 7:3

Quote of the Day: I am perhaps vulgar, but it is not intentional, save that I must and will make people listen. My firm conviction is that we have had enough polite preachers.

—CHARLES SPURGEON

Probably the most famous Christian smoker in the world, Charles Haddon Spurgeon was born in England on June 19, 1834, as one of seventeen children born to his mother.

He converted to Christianity as a teenager and started preaching in a barn at age sixteen. Despite his lack of education, he became a pastor the next year, and quickly earned the nickname "The Boy Preacher."

Though he never attended seminary—he missed his interview after a servant girl accidentally showed him into the wrong room—his private library contained more than twelve thousand books when he died, and he claimed to read six books per week. He'd already preached more than six hundred times by the time he took over New Park Street Chapel at age twenty, where he earned a new nickname: "The Prince of Preachers."[1]

Attendance grew to more than ten thousand people. The church constructed the vast Metropolitan Tabernacle to accommodate the crowds, which included Florence Nightingale, the prime minister, and members of the royal family. Spurgeon published more than two thousand sermons, and they were so popular that they literally sold by the ton—at one point selling more than twenty-five thousand copies per week. His sermons were published on Mondays in the *London Times* and often reached the *New York Times* as well, before being translated into another twenty languages. One woman came to faith after reading a single page of one of Spurgeon's sermons, which had been wrapped around some butter she'd purchased.

But back to cigars. Spurgeon was an aficionado, but he smoked less than one per day and argued he wasn't addicted. He believed that smoking a cigar wasn't technically a sin, because unlike smoking cigarettes he didn't have to inhale and so theoretically wasn't hurting his body. At that time people didn't understand the negative health effects of smoking, and Spurgeon's doctor even recommended them to the great orator. On his horse-drawn carriage rides to church, he would often enjoy a morning cigar as a way to prepare his throat for preaching.

The real smoking controversy began when a visiting minister, a man with the delightful name Dr. George F. Pentecost, climbed into Spurgeon's pulpit and railed against the perceived vice. As the *Daily Telegraph* reported on September 23, 1874:

> Last Sunday evening, at the Metropolitan Tabernacle, the deservedly popular, unquestionably benevolent, and eminently shrewd

> Mr. Spurgeon was preaching a sermon on the sinfulness of little sins. . . . At the close of his useful sermon the minister introduced an American clergyman who, he said, was anxious to address a few words to the congregation. This reverend gentleman "improved the opportunity" by inveighing fiercely against the sin of smoking tobacco, especially in the form of cigars, and told his hearers how he had struggled and fought against the pernicious habit, and how at last, by the blessing and with the assistance of Providence, he had conquered his addiction to the weed. Then uprose Mr. Spurgeon and, with quiet humour, remarked that he would not allow the congregation to separate without telling them that he did not consider smoking to be a sin, and that, by the grace of God, he hoped to enjoy a good cigar before going to bed that night.[2]

Christian World printed more of Spurgeon's wily rebuttal in their magazine two days later:

> Well, dear friends, you know that some men can do to the glory of God what to other men would be sin. And notwithstanding what Brother Pentecost has said, I intend to smoke a good cigar to the glory of God before I go to bed to-night. If anybody can show me in the Bible the command, "Thou shalt not smoke," I am ready to keep it; but I haven't found it yet. I find ten commandments, and it's as much as I can do to keep them; and I've no desire to make them into eleven or twelve. . . . Therefore I mean to smoke to the glory of God.[3]

When it predictably started a firestorm, Spurgeon wrote to the *Telegraph*'s editor to confirm his theological position. He admitted that the phrase "smoking to the glory of God" didn't sound stellar, but then struck at the greater church issue of the day: "There is growing up in society a Pharisaic system which adds to the commands of God the precepts of men; to that system I will not yield for an hour.

The preservation of my liberty may bring upon me the upbraidings of many good men, and the sneers of the self-righteous; but I shall endure both with serenity so long as I feel clear in my conscience before God." In a letter to an American correspondent, he further wrote, "There is no liberty left us by these spiritual prudes."[4]

But his detractors may have had a point. After Spurgeon's declaration, British advertisers began to market the famous preacher's cigars with his image and quotes. Stores had signs that nicknamed them "Spurgeon smokes." Parents from the church complained that their kids defended their smoking habits by saying, "But Spurgeon does."[5]

Still, he carried on. There's an enduring myth that Spurgeon repented of his hobby. Even modern conservative Christians such as the Gospel Coalition's managing editor Trevin Wax have tried to make the case that he finally quit smoking, but it doesn't hold up to historical fact. Spurgeon died in France while trying to recuperate from ill health, and according to his great-grandson, Spurgeon smoked Francisco Perez del Rio Cubans to the very end, and he has his ancestor's half-finished cigar case to prove it.

When Spurgeon's body returned from France to England, almost sixty thousand people paid their respects during his wake, and one hundred thousand people lined the street for his two-mile funeral procession. His tombstone likeness contains no cigar, but it does sport a rather sizable beard.

The truth is, Spurgeon isn't the only famous Christian dude to smoke: J. R. R. Tolkien, G. K. Chesterton, Karl Barth, C. S. Lewis, and Malcolm Muggeridge all smoked tobacco of various kinds. We now know that smoking is a terrible idea and that it's not an ideal substance for the temple of the Holy Spirit. Understanding it the way we do now, perhaps Spurgeon would have tried to quit or maybe smoked privately to keep others from stumbling. We don't know, but we need to follow the Spirit's conviction in our own lives.

Spurgeon's greater truth remains: we are happy to judge and

point out the specks of sawdust in others while remaining completely blind to the thundering river logs in our own. As the handsomely goateed Philip Yancey put it, "Christians get very angry toward other Christians who sin differently than they do."[6]

In fact, smoking was probably one of Spurgeon's smallest challenges. The great preacher endured an immense amount of sorrow and suffering. The slander and scorn he endured for his preaching was often unbearable. He once wrote, "Down on my knees have I often fallen, with the hot sweat rising from my brow under some fresh slander poured upon me; in an agony of grief my heart has been well-nigh broken."[7]

Spurgeon's physical condition was rough, at best. He contracted gout at age thirty-five and was bedridden for several weeks or months each year while trying to recuperate from various physical ailments. Spurgeon was rarely free of pain after age thirty-seven, when he developed rheumatism and chronic kidney inflammation. Spurgeon's wife, Susannah Thompson, also became an invalid at age thirty-three and rarely attended her husband's preaching.

The sheer weight of Spurgeon's work was heavy. Not only did he write sermons for his 5,311-member church, but he also wrote books, ran an orphanage, oversaw a Bible college, and answered five hundred letters every week. Even preaching itself caused immense anxiety, with Spurgeon declaring that "there was scarcely ever an occasion, in which [my deacons] left me alone for ten minutes before the service, but they would find me in a most fearful state of sickness." Yet that didn't keep him from accepting invitations to preach, and he sometimes preached as many as ten sermons in one week.

By age fifty Spurgeon had founded and managed sixty-six organizations. By the time he died, he'd written sixty-three volumes of sermons. Weighing in at more than twenty million words, the series is the largest set of books ever produced by a single author in Christian history.

Detractors dogged Spurgeon's ministry. During one packed evening service when he was just twenty-one years old, a handful of hooligans started a stampede for the exits by screaming that the building was on fire and that the balconies were about to give way. Seven died, and twenty-eight were seriously injured. Spurgeon collapsed; the incident broke him for days. In fact, Spurgeon almost quit, saying, "It might well seem that the ministry which promised to be so largely influential was silenced for ever."[8]

Depression dogged Spurgeon for decades. In the autumn of 1858, he missed almost a full month of preaching. But Spurgeon believed his stormy cloud would bring glory to God.

Despite all the dark heaviness he carried, Spurgeon's generosity and passion shone through. By the time he died at age fifty-seven, his church was the largest independent congregation in the world. Spurgeon preached to almost ten million people over the course of his life, founded an orphanage for fatherless boys, and started a college—at age twenty-two—that trained nearly nine hundred pastors and planted almost two hundred churches in his lifetime. The Bible college and ministry he started more than 150 years ago continues to thrive to this very day.

CONTEMPLATION

1. Where do you judge others but keep a false standard for yourself?
2. What do you do that might be causing others to stumble?
3. Are you doing everything for the glory of God?

PRAYER

God of grace, keep us from judgment. Help us see our sin and know all that You can do in us as we seek to give You all that we are.

THE UNKNOWN

BY ERIC FUSILIER*

I'm less than two weeks away from planting a church, and I have no idea what's about to happen. I don't know all the next steps. I don't know why God asked me, of all people, to do this. I don't know what happens if it fails. As Christians, we often dismiss our fears. In the church we tend to gloss over feelings like this in the name of faith, but the truth is, there is so much that God doesn't reveal to us, and it can be incredibly scary when He asks us to do something difficult or painful. I know God can do amazing things—He does all the time—but I don't know what God will do. And sometimes living in the unknown is terrifying.

A few years ago I was in a worship band, and none of us expected things to take off like they did; by the end of our first year touring all over the United States on the tail of a hit single on Christian radio, we were exhausted. I'm a huge music fan, and I've always dreamed of playing in a band and touring. I've also always had a strong belief in the importance of songs in the life of the church as a means of worship. So, the fact that our little worship band was given the opportunity to tour and sing with churches all over North America was mind-blowing.

Then, just as we got home for Christmas, we found out that we were going on another, even bigger tour in the new year.

Early in December I came down with a cold. It wasn't anything big, but I was pretty wiped out. My wife asked me to go see the doctor, but I had no interest. Christmas came and went, but I wasn't feeling any better. And with a massive tour right around the corner, I figured I should probably get the lingering cold checked out. After a quick check-in with the doctor, I went home to pack.

At midnight, while I was still packing, I got a call from the on-call doctor, and he told me to get to the closest emergency room immediately. I woke up my wife, and we left right away. At four in the morning, after hours of waiting and several tests without any updates or information, a doctor walked in, looked at her charts, and without looking up, said, "It's cancer. You have leukemia."

I sat there stunned. The weight of that word. *Cancer.* I had so many questions. And the doctor had no answers. I started treatment right away and spent the better part of the next two years in and out of the hospital, where the answers were few and far between. It was more painful than I can describe, but the worst part was not knowing if I was going to live or die. I knew that God could heal me, but I didn't know if He would heal me. I was desperate to be healed, desperate to go home, desperate to end the pain, desperate to hear from God.

Dwelling in the darkness of the unknown, in that hospital room, I had several profound experiences of God. He became more real to me in that desperate place than ever before. I felt a kinship with Jesus in my own suffering, knowing that it paled in comparison to His. And I clung to those experiences. The darker things became, the more I needed to hold on to the profound, intimate moments where God met me, comforted me, changed me.

Ultimately, despite the statistics stacked against me, God oversaw my healing. The unknown of those years shook me. But it was in the unknown that I saw God's goodness firsthand. If we can be honest enough to admit it, we really don't know a lot. But being caught up in the terrifying unknown gives us the opportunity to truly trust God and rely on Him in a deeper way. That's the beauty of the unknown.

I don't know why I was allowed to get sick, and I don't know why God chose to save me from cancer. I don't know why God asked me to plant a church, and I don't know what God's plans are. But I'm 100 percent certain that God will meet me in the unknown, no matter the outcome. Because that's who He is. And He's the only one with the power to do something in our unknown.

---

* *Eric Fusilier is a bearded church-planter-in-residence at Reunion Church in Ontario.*

CHAPTER 13

G. K. Chesterton

FRENEMY

BY AARON ALFORD

Meditation: You have heard that it was said, "Love your neighbor and hate your enemy." But I tell you, love your enemies and pray for those who persecute you, that you may be children of your Father in heaven.

—MATTHEW 5:43–45

Quote of the Day: The Bible tells us to love our neighbors, and also to love our enemies; probably because generally they are the same people.

—G. K. CHESTERTON

In every sense of the word, the famous writer and apologist G. K. Chesterton was a very large man. Magnanimous, six feet four inches tall, and built like a wine cask, his presence could be as cheerful as a fine vintage of old port. He never grew a full beard, but who could imagine that mirthful grin without a mouthful of moustache? For this reason, we are happy to include him in the hallowed ranks of Bearded Gospel Men.

Born in London in 1874, Gilbert Keith Chesterton grew up in the Christian faith. He aspired to be an illustrator and enrolled in a college of art. He took classes in literature, and although he never completed a degree in the field, he did show great proficiency as a journalist and critic.

In 1908, at the age of thirty-four, he published *Orthodoxy*—a book that, along with C. S. Lewis's *Mere Christianity*, remains one of the best crash courses in the basics of Christian belief ever written. Speaking of Lewis, we almost certainly would not have the venerable C. S. without the inimitable G. K. Chesterton's ability to express profound philosophy and deep theology with a sense of whimsy. It was something a young atheist named Clive Staples Lewis found very appealing. Lewis cited Chesterton's follow-up to *Orthodoxy*, *The Everlasting Man*, as instrumental in his own conversion.

This affable sensibility was perhaps the greatest part of who Chesterton was as a man. He delighted in debate, but not as someone who merely takes pleasure in besting an opponent or proving himself correct. He delighted in debate the way an artist delights in painting a canvas; he found it immensely rewarding, and when he engaged in public discussions with well-known atheists of his era, such as H. G. Wells, he did so in a way that endeared his ideological enemies to him as friends. Wells once wrote to Chesterton's wife, Frances, "Of all the joys in life nothing would delight me more than a controversy with G. K. C., whom indeed I adore."[1]

He is also famous for having the wonderful ability to express paradox and mystery, things which some of us modern Christians are very uncomfortable with. We often prefer to have an airtight theology that keeps God safe and secure within our own notions of how things should be. For Chesterton, however, a sense of mystery and paradox was at the heart of the Christian faith. Indeed, it was what drew him and secured him to the Christian faith. God was not an equation to be solved but a mystery to be lived in. He thought of paradox as "truth standing on [its] head,"[2] and he wrote of "the thrilling romance of Orthodoxy."[3] For Chesterton, there was a wildness in tradition, an excitement at the heart of theology, and this sense of wonder was ever present when he wrote about his faith.

But Chesterton's influence on the world around him was not limited to matters of religion. His writing was staggeringly prolific, and in his hundred books, two hundred short stories, plays and novels, and more than four thousand newspaper essays, he touched on just about every topic one could think of. His intellectual and ideological influence on the twentieth century is not often discussed but is nevertheless tremendous. Mahatma Gandhi, as one example, was inspired to work for India's independence from the English (and to do so in a peaceful "Indian" way) by reading an essay Chesterton had written for the *London News* in 1909. And of course his influence in literature is almost immeasurable. From Ernest Hemingway to Neil Gaiman, Orson Welles to J. K. Rowling, Chesterton's literary influence is admitted by some of recent history's most brilliant writers.

The extent of his influence points to his willingness to be influenced, for Chesterton did not sequester himself inside his Christianity but allowed himself to live in the wider world. He wore his faith simply and as a matter of fact, and defended it without ever seeming defensive. "There is no such thing as fighting on the winning side," he once wrote; "one fights to find out which is the winning side."[4] His fiercest ideological critics were also among his closest friends, because the charm with which he spoke and wrote was not something merely put on, a mask of politeness to cover disdain, but an aroma that followed him like the scent of his ever-lit cigar (though far more pleasant!).

Although he may well one day be declared a saint, Chesterton wasn't perfect. He wore his intemperance, for example, for all to see in his eventual four hundred pounds. (He is quoted as saying privately, "One pint is enough, two pints is one too many, three pints isn't half enough."[5]) But he was never duplicitous, even if he was somewhat of a paradox himself. He was a man of staggering genius and would often get lost on the train home. He could construct a complex political ideology (Distributism), but could not tie his necktie. And as wonderfully as he could satirize others, it was himself whom he deemed most worthy of humorous derision. Once, when he became stuck in a car door, he said it reminded him of something an old woman had said: "Why don't you get out sideways?" "I have no sideways."[6]

And the affection with which he held his friends was as true as the affection with which he held his foes, and they were often the same person. Chesterton speaks to us today as an example of someone who stood firm for truth, but did so in a winsome way that fostered friendships more than inflamed hostilities. Of his friend and foe George Bernard Shaw, he said, "It is necessary to disagree with him as much as I do, in order to admire him as much as I do; and I am proud of him as a foe even more than as a friend."[7]

After Gilbert Keith Chesterton's death in 1936, H. G. Wells, another close enemy and an even closer friend, wrote in a letter, "From first to last he and I were very close friends. . . . I never knew anyone so steadily true to form as G. K. C."[8]

CONTEMPLATION

1. Is there a sense of whimsy or mystery in your relationship with God? Where might God be speaking in unexpected places?
2. How do you respond to people who disagree with you in politics or religion? Do these disagreements bring you closer to those with whom you disagree, or farther apart? How might a disagreement with someone bring you closer to each other rather than create division?
3. Think of someone with whom you've had a disagreement, either in person or on social media. How might you foster a better friendship with that person?

PRAYER

Heavenly Father, help us not only to love our enemies, but to have true affection for them; teach us to live our faith in a winsome way.

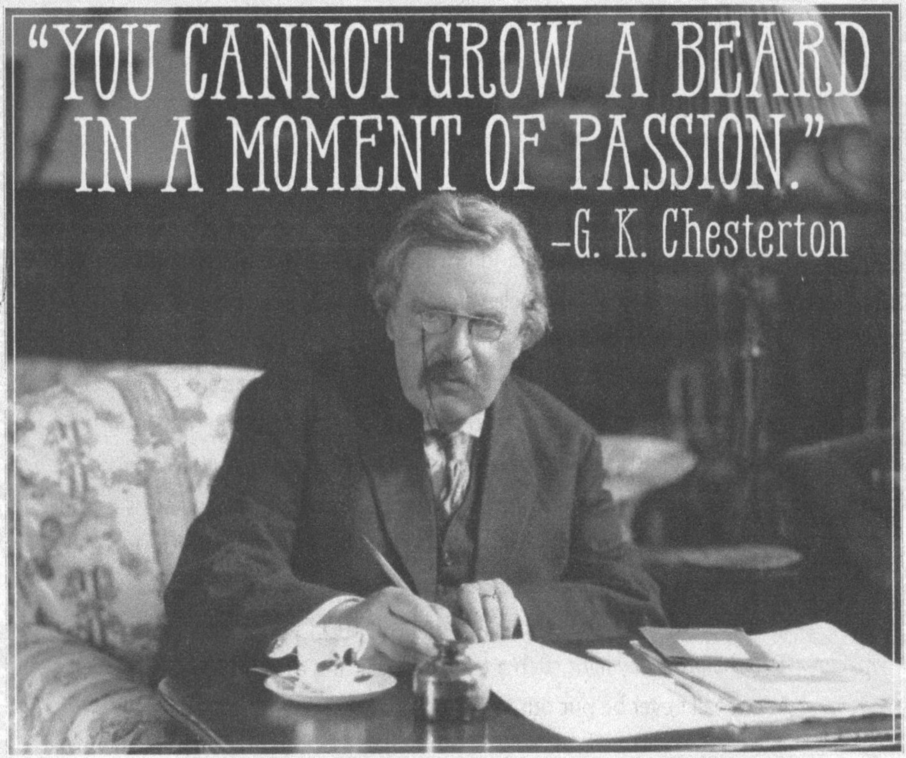
"YOU CANNOT GROW A BEARD
IN A MOMENT OF PASSION."
–G. K. Chesterton

THREE HEROES

BY MALCOLM GUITE*

This little *jeu d'esprit* rings out the praises of three bearded heroes of mine, and since their biographies don't appear elsewhere in this volume, I will introduce them briefly here.

Hugh Latimer (1487–1555) was the greatest preacher of his age. At the dawn of the Reformation, he discovered for himself the relief and release of salvation by faith and not works. He fearlessly preached a gospel of grace for all who believe, often illustrating his sermons with wonderful everyday images. In the sermon of the card, he says we are like people who are losing our souls to the Devil in a card game gone wrong. The Devil wins us over piece by piece, playing our sins like cards against us, but Christ Himself comes and tells us that love conquers all; hearts are trumps. He trumps sin with grace and wins back our souls by the offer of His own heart of love opened for us on the cross.[9] When Bloody Mary came to the throne, Latimer was arrested and burned at the stake for his faith. His last words were, "We shall this day light such a candle in England as I trust by God's grace shall never be put out."[10]

Alfred Lord Tennyson (1809–1892) was the greatest poet of the nineteenth century. He suffered from depression and was, as a younger man, tormented by doubt after his best friend died suddenly. But instead of abandoning faith, he worked through his doubts in the great poem "In Memoriam," which concludes with a faith in Christ that has been deepened and strengthened by the journey through doubt.

George MacDonald (1824–1905) was a Scottish poet, novelist, and preacher who was a powerful inspiration to C. S. Lewis, J. R. R.

Tolkien, and G. K. Chesterton. He wrote magical fantasies for both children and adults, which fill their readers with a deep desire for God's goodness and a longing for their home in heaven.

A Paen in Praise of Three Heroes

Who are the saints I've most revered?
You ask, I sagely stroke my beard
And wait until my mind has cleared.
I see them now and I am cheered;
The three bright stars by whom I've steered;
Three sages, each blessed with a beard.

First of the three, and not the least,
A scholar, preacher, and a priest.
Hugh Latimer whose words still burn
With zeal and love, would have us learn
That when the Devil plays us foul,
And tries to win our perjured soul,
Then Christ alone will pay the cost;
His grace will win the souls we've lost.
Christ stands with us and takes our part,
Lays down for us His loving heart,
Decrees that hearts are trumps indeed.
(The only trump we'll ever need!)
When deeds were dark and times were hard,
He preached his "sermon of the card,"
And faced the flame of martyrdom
To bring his gospel preaching home.
I think of him, my soul is cheered,
God bless him and his flowing beard!

My second bearded hero shines
Through every poem's flowing lines;
For sometimes, when my spirits droop,
Depression threatens faith and hope,
Then Tennyson comes to my aid,
An honest doubter unafraid.
He faced and then outfaced his doubt
And turned the skeptics inside out,
He drank depression's deadly dram
And still wrote "In Memoriam,"
He saw his hopes all fall to dust
But grew through grief to deeper trust,
And rang the bells so wild and free
For Christ who is and is to be.
Beyond "the bourn of time and place"
He met his Pilot face-to-face
And triumphed over all he'd feared,
God bless his hat and cloak and beard!

And now, my highland hero, hail,
Imagination's Holy Grail,
Third of my bearded trio, come
And draw me to my heavenly home.
Like Lewis I have been inspired,
And my imagination fired,
By George MacDonald's magic tales.
Princess Irene never fails
To spin the yarn and set the skein
That draws me back to Christ again,
Her childlike vision helps me name

The roses in the holy flame.
His phantasies still cast a spell
That whispers "All, all will be well,"
As his transfigured visions glow
To re-enchant the world we know.
His grace and wisdom I've revered
As free and flowing as his beard!

God bless them each and every one,
These bearded saints who guide me on;
Now praise the Father, praise the Son,
And Holy Spirit, three in one.
My song is sung, my writ is run,
My rhyme is rung, my tale is done.

---

* *Malcolm Guite is an Anglican priest, poet, and author of eight books, including* Faith, Hope and Poetry, Parable and Paradox, *and his most recent book,* Mariner: A Voyage with Samuel Taylor Coleridge.

CHAPTER 14

C. T. Studd

MUSTACHIOED GOSPEL CRICKETER

BY JARED BROCK

Meditation: Teach us to number our days,
that we may gain a heart of wisdom.
—PSALM 90:12

Quote of the Day: Some wish to live within the sound of church or chapel bell; I want to run a rescue shop within a yard of hell.
—C. T. STUDD

As you can guess from the above quote, C. T. Studd was a straight shooter who ignored societal expectations and conventions, encouraging fellow Christians not to "care a damn"[1] about the way of the world.

Charles Thomas Studd was the son of a wealthy British indigo planter who'd retired to a large country house where he could hunt and race. Studd's older brother was a cricket player, and the competitive youngster was determined to outdo him. Through hours of practice, Studd eventually became high school cricket captain at Eton College. He went on to captain the Cambridge University cricket team and soon became a household name throughout Great Britain. In 1882 he played for England against Australia in the first of the legendary matches called the Ashes. Studd is considered the Michael Jordan of cricket, and he played at a time when cricket was the nation's most popular sport.

Studd had accepted Christ as a young man, but had spent the next six years indifferent to his faith. His older brother became deathly sick, and C. T. was forced to question himself: "What is all the fame and flattery worth when a man comes to face eternity?"[2] He wrestled with the question until he heard D. L. Moody preach in 1883. Moody's preaching lit his soul on fire, and he decided to give up cricket. Every person around him counseled against it, but he defended his decision: "I knew that cricket would not last, and honour would not last, and nothing in this world would last, but it was worthwhile living for the world to come."[3] He accepted the call to missions, along with six of his schoolmates. They became known as the Cambridge Seven. The young men made headlines across Edwardian England for turning their backs on a life of privilege for a life of purpose.

Within two years, Studd was on a boat to China with Hudson Taylor. The young men dressed like the locals, ate the local food, and learned Mandarin. He even went so far as to shave his head and face.

Studd's father died, and his will stipulated that Studd should receive his inheritance on his twenty-fifth birthday. Studd contemplated how to spend the money. As he read and prayed, he became convinced: "If Jesus Christ be God and died for me, then no sacrifice can be too great for me to make for Him."[4]

On January 13, 1887, before even knowing how much he'd inherit, Studd wrote a five-thousand-pound check to D. L. Moody, two checks totaling five thousand pounds to George Müller, and an additional fifteen thousand pounds to various organizations, including George Holland's Ragged School, General William Booth's

Salvation Army, and Thomas Barnardo, a fellow Bearded Gospel Man whose orphanages cared for almost sixty thousand children.

Studd ended up receiving an even larger inheritance than expected, the equivalent of tens of millions of dollars today, so he gave away several thousand pounds more and then gave the remaining £3,400 as a wedding present to his new bride, a young Irish missionary. Priscilla Livingstone Stewart was not impressed.

"Charlie, what did the Lord tell the rich young man to do?" she asked.

"Sell all," he replied.

"Well then," she said, "we will start clear with the Lord at our wedding."[5]

They gave it all away. This, of course, meant they had no money, but time and time again, God came through. On one occasion, Studd remarked, "Funds are low again, hallelujah! That means God trusts us and is willing to leave His reputation in our hands."[6]

Studd served as a missionary for a decade in China and then another six years in India. He suffered several heart attacks and numerous sicknesses along the way, and was eventually forced to return to England. One rather honest friend, Dr. A. T. Wilkinson described him as "a museum of diseases."[7] But Studd refused to retire. "How could I spend the best years of my life in living for the honors of this world, when thousands of souls are perishing every day?"[8]

Studd was broke, having been dropped by a group of businessmen who had promised to support him but didn't think he was fit to continue. He gathered the group together and declared, "Gentlemen, God has called me to go, and I will go. I will blaze the trail, though my grave may only become a stepping stone that younger men may follow."[9] And then he sailed alone to Sudan and Congo—the largest unevangelized region in Africa at the time. He believed that his voyage was more than his final mission trip: "This journey is not just for Africa but for the whole unevangelised world."[10]

While in Sudan, Studd founded the Worldwide Evangelization for Christ organization and started sending missionaries around the globe. Studd stayed in Africa for twenty-one years until his death on July 16, 1931. His last word was "Hallelujah."[11]

Today WEC International has more than eighteen hundred mission workers serving around the world. Their mission is simple: be the church where there is no church.[12]

According to biographer Norman Grubb, "C. T.'s life stands as some rugged Gibraltar—a sign to all succeeding generations that it is worthwhile to lose all this world can offer and stake everything on the world to come. His life will be an eternal rebuke to easygoing Christianity. He has demonstrated what it means to follow Christ without counting the cost and without looking back."[13] According to Grubb, the mission never asked for money, never took up offerings, didn't guarantee their missionaries' salaries, and refused to take on debt, and all funds received were divided equally among them.[14]

Sometimes you have to give up fame and fortune and realize there's a bigger game at play. Sometimes you have to trade a career for a calling. Sometimes you have to cut off your beard for the sake of the mission.

As Studd once said:

> Too long have we been waiting for one another to begin! The time of waiting is past! The hour of God has struck! War is declared! In God's Holy Name let us arise and build! "The God of Heaven, He will fight for us," as we for Him. We will not build on the sand, but on the bedrock of the sayings of Christ, and the gates and minions of hell shall not prevail against us. Should such men as we fear? Before the world, aye, before the sleepy, lukewarm, faithless, namby-pamby Christian world, we will dare to trust our God, we will venture our all for Him, we will live and we will die for Him, and we will do it with His joy unspeakable singing aloud in our hearts. We will a

> thousand times sooner die trusting only our God, than live trusting in man. And when we come to this position the battle is already won, and the end of the glorious campaign in sight. We will have the real Holiness of God . . . we will have a masculine holiness, one of daring faith and works for Jesus Christ.[15]

CONTEMPLATION

1. How much of your life's work, so far, will last for eternity?
2. What are some ways you can continually be aware that you have only one short life to live?
3. What can you do for Christ that will stand the test of time?

PRAYER

God, our Father, make us, Your sons, princes of peace and warriors of hope.

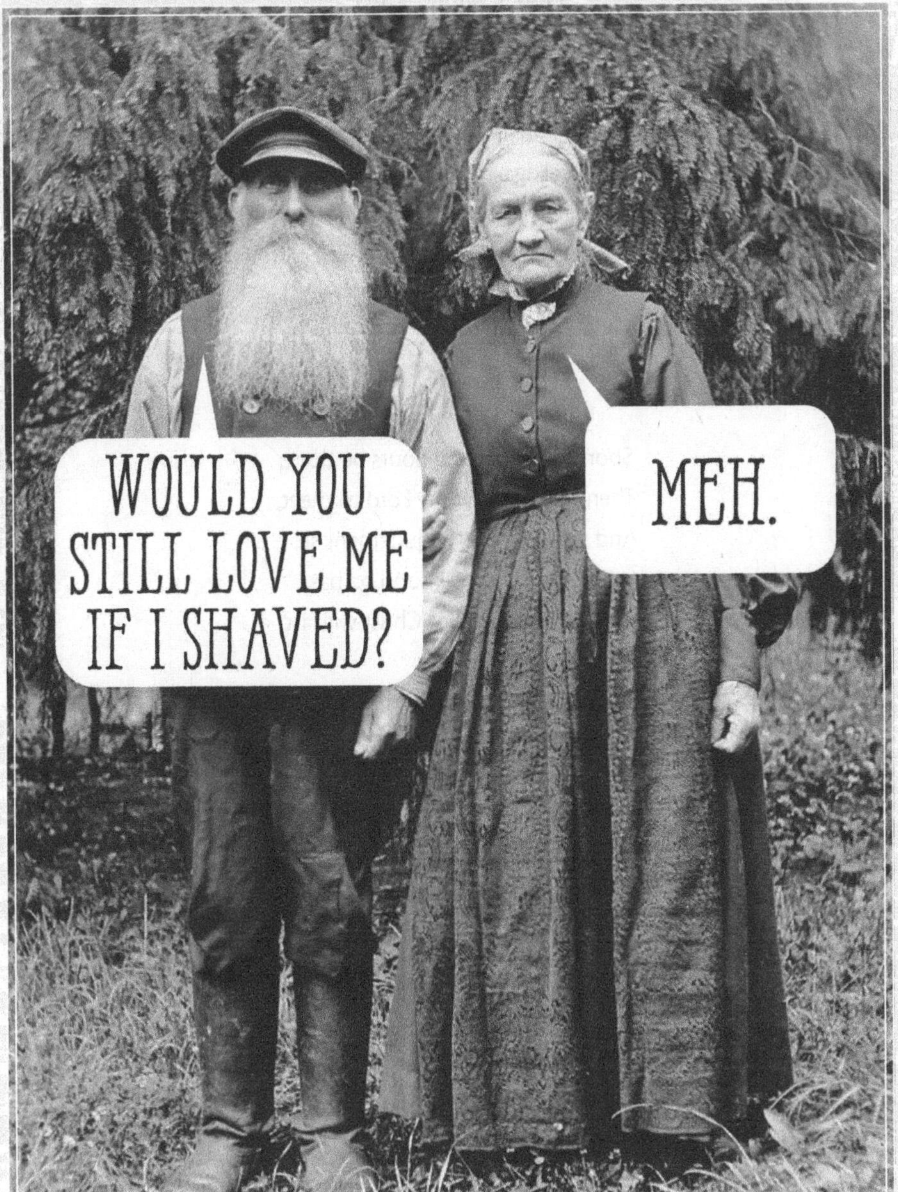
WOULD YOU STILL LOVE ME IF I SHAVED?
MEH.

ONLY ONE LIFE

BY C. T. STUDD

Two little lines I heard one day,
Traveling along life's busy way;
Bringing conviction to my heart,
And from my mind would not depart;
Only one life, 'twill soon be past,
Only what's done for Christ will last.

Only one life, yes only one,
Soon will its fleeting hours be done;
Then, in "that day" my Lord to meet,
And stand before His judgment seat;
Only one life, 'twill soon be past,
Only what's done for Christ will last.

Only one life, the still small voice,
Gently pleads for a better choice
Bidding me selfish aims to leave,
And to God's holy will to cleave;
Only one life, 'twill soon be past,
Only what's done for Christ will last.

Only one life, a few brief years,
Each with its burdens, hopes, and fears;
Each with its clays I must fulfill,
living for self or in His will;
Only one life, 'twill soon be past,
Only what's done for Christ will last.

When this bright world would tempt me sore,
When Satan would a victory score;
When self would seek to have its way,
Then help me Lord with joy to say;
Only one life, 'twill soon be past,
Only what's done for Christ will last.

Give me Father, a purpose deep,
In joy or sorrow Thy word to keep;
Faithful and true what e'er the strife,
Pleasing Thee in my daily life;
Only one life, 'twill soon be past,
Only what's done for Christ will last.

Oh let my love with fervor burn,
And from the world now let me turn;
Living for Thee, and Thee alone,
Bringing Thee pleasure on Thy throne;
Only one life, 'twill soon be past,
Only what's done for Christ will last.

Only one life, yes only one,
Now let me say, "Thy will be done";
And when at last I'll hear the call,
I know I'll say "'twas worth it all";
Only one life, 'twill soon be past,
Only what's done for Christ will last.

Only one life, 'twill soon be past,
Only what's done for Christ will last.
And when I am dying, how happy I'll be,
If the lamp of my life has been burned out for Thee.

CHAPTER 15

Zacchaeus

OF CAMELS AND TREES

BY AARON ALFORD

Meditation: "How hard it is for the rich to enter the kingdom of God! Indeed, it is easier for a camel to go through the eye of a needle than for someone who is rich to enter the kingdom of God." Those who heard this asked, "Who then can be saved?" Jesus replied, "What is impossible with man is possible with God."

—LUKE 18:24–27

Quote of the Day: Zacchaeus was a wee little man, and a wee little man was he. He climbed up in a sycamore tree, for the Lord he wanted to see.

—*TRADITIONAL*

Zacchaeus was a little man. Little as in petty. Little as in greedy. Little as in low. He was a deputized extortionist, a servant of the foreign occupiers, and he made a killing by being as greedy and as petty and as little as he could be. The city in which he lived, Jericho, was a prosperous one, famous for its production of balsam. Balsam wood was in great demand, popular for both its medicinal qualities and aromatic scent. Taxes would have been high in Jericho, and its tax collectors would have been wealthy. Zacchaeus, however, was not only a tax collector, but a chief tax collector, one of the richest of the rich.

But of course, wherever there is great wealth, there is also great poverty. The working poor of the city, many of them laborers in the balsam trade, would have suffered the worst from high taxation. Zacchaeus, from his lofty position, would seldom if ever have to interact with such people. He was twice removed from them: removed by his wealth and by his association with the Roman government, a scandal to his Jewish countrymen.

All of this makes the story of Zacchaeus, as recorded in the gospel of Luke, even more amazing, and more than a bit ridiculous. We don't know what sparked the tax collector's interest in the rabbi Jesus. Perhaps he'd heard about Jesus' harsh words against the Pharisees, the holier-than-thou teachers who would have been a thorn in his own side. Perhaps he'd heard about the miracles Jesus performed. Whatever it was, when Zacchaeus heard that Jesus was passing through Jericho, he became consumed with one thought: seeing him.

But, as we know from the gospel, there was one thing Zacchaeus's great wealth could not buy him: height. Zacchaeus was a wee, little man, and with the entire city of Jericho filling the streets, he had little hope of catching a glimpse of this Jesus whom he so desperately wanted to see. But a mind that was adept at thinking of creative ways of fudging numbers and defrauding people of their hard-earned cash could also come in handy for creative problem solving. He decided to run ahead of the crowd and climb a tree.

He must have known how ridiculous he'd look. Wealthy people don't usually have to do something so unbecoming as climbing a tree to see a celebrity; they usually have a backstage pass. But off he went, climbing a sycamore-fig tree in his three-piece business suit (or the New Testament equivalent of a three-piece suit) to catch a glimpse of the itinerant rabbi. We know what happened from there, of course. Jesus happily called the rich man down and invited Himself over for dinner. Suddenly the man Zacchaeus only hoped to catch a glimpse of was a guest of honor at Zacchaeus's dinner table.

Zacchaeus, deeply moved by the presence and love of Jesus, stood up and made an announcement: "Look, Lord! Here and now I give half of my possessions to the poor, and if I have cheated anybody out of anything, I will pay back four times the amount" (Luke 19:8).

One can hardly overstate how big a deal such a statement really is. It encompasses both an immense generosity borne of thankfulness ("I will give half of my possessions to the poor!") and penitential joy. Paying back four times the amount was the maximum penalty for theft under Jewish law.

Another interesting thing about Zacchaeus is that we know his name. The rich young ruler who appeared just one chapter previous didn't get a name and left the disciples asking, "Who then can be saved?" (18:26) when Jesus made His statement about rich people and camels and needles. Modern biblical scholars posit that when a character in one of the Gospels is given a name, it's probably because he or she did not just fade into the background after his or her encounter with Jesus, but became a known and upstanding member of the early church. These people told their stories publicly, and as a result these stories became part of the historical Gospels. Zacchaeus is mentioned by name because it is entirely likely that it was Zacchaeus himself who told Luke his story.

There is even more evidence of Zacchaeus's involvement in the early church in an ancient document called the *Apostolic Constitutions*. Though it can only be dated to about AD 375, it purports to have been written by some of the first leaders of the church, and it contains fascinating insights regarding the early bishops of various cities. It includes this statement: "Now concerning those bishops which have been ordained in our lifetime, we let you know that they are these: . . .

Of Cæsarea of Palestine, the first was Zacchæus, who was once a publican."[1]

When stories such as Zacchaeus's become familiar and quaint and have cute little songs written about them, we can forget that they are about real people. Zacchaeus wasn't just a winsome little fellow who provides a bit of comic relief in the story of Jesus. He was a real person who showed that the impossible was possible. A rich man could enter the kingdom! A person could, in fact, give up all he owned to radically follow Jesus. (And yes, I'm pretty sure "half of my possessions" plus "four times the amount" he owed anyone comes out to approximately everything he owned!) The man who extorted the poor willingly became poor himself, a slave of Christ and a servant of the church.

The man who climbed a tree just to catch a glimpse of Jesus was seen by Jesus, and Jesus saw all that this petty little man could be. Zacchaeus, famous for being short, would be a giant in the kingdom because he made himself small enough to pass through the needle's eye.

CONTEMPLATION

1. Have you ever wronged anyone, even unintentionally? How might you make that right today?
2. Is there anything in your life that might be obstructing your view of Jesus? How might you see past these things to catch a glimpse of Jesus?
3. Is there anything Jesus may be asking you to give up, specifically in regard to material possessions or money?

PRAYER

Jesus, we want to see You. Teach us the joy of repentance and giving.

I WOKE UP LIKE THIS.
FLAWLESS.

BEARDLY'S BEARDLIEVE IT OR NOT!

(You probably should not.)

BY AARON ALFORD

- A single beard hair has a prehensile strength comparable to Spider-Man's webs and can lift over one metric ton. Beard hair has been used by craftsmen for centuries in the creation of nearly indestructible rope.
- In 1866, an assassination attempt was made on the bearded King Pedro II of Brazil. His quick-thinking beard deflected the bullet and later apprehended the bare-faced suspect.
- Contrary to popular belief, the infamous Rasputin was completely clean-shaven and unable to grow a single whisker. He wore a fake beard made of yak hair.
- The modern safety razor was invented by Dumbsley Stupidsworth III, Lord of Idiotston. He died while on safari in Africa, attempting to shave a lion.
- NASA has never had a bearded astronaut. The moon landing was faked.
- A 1991 study found that unbearded men were six times more likely to listen to the music of New Kids on the Block, wear Hammer pants, and list the TV show *Cop Rock* as their "all-time favorite."
- A complete lack of facial hair is the number one cause of beardlessness.

CHAPTER 16

Saint Valentine

PATRON SAINT OF LOVERS (AND BEEKEEPERS)

BY JARED BROCK

Meditation: Do not conform to the pattern of this world, but be transformed by the renewing of your mind. Then you will be able to test and approve what God's will is—his good, pleasing and perfect will.

—ROMANS 12:2

Quote of the Day: Let your religion be less of a theory and more of a love affair.

—G. K. CHESTERTON

Ah, Valentine's Day. That bittersweet day where we brave the winter weather to spend our hard-earned money on overpriced folded paper, price-fixed flowers, and (hopefully fair trade) chocolate. What few people know is that it's not even an official religious holiday.

The tradition of sending gifts started in fourteenth-century France and England because medieval people believed that birds paired off to mate on February 14th. The very first Valentine's Day card was sent in 1415 by Charles, the Duke of Orleans, to his wife while he was held prisoner in the Tower of London.

Valentine's Day didn't become popular until Esther A. Howland embossed paper lace cards at her father's stationery store in Worcester, Massachusetts, in 1847. Hallmark Cards of Kansas City began mass-producing cards in 1913, and the dead of winter has never been the same. The rose and chocolate industries quickly pounced on the trend, as did the diamond jewelers and restaurateurs. Today we send around one billion Valentine cards annually and spend around twenty billion dollars on the day.

So what is the real Valentine's Day story?

Well, it's complicated. Pope Gelasius I declared February 14 as the Feast of Saint Valentine around 498, adding him to a list of people "whose names are justly reverenced among men, but whose acts are known only to God."[1] This should give you an idea of just how little we actually know about Valentine. In fact, the Catholic Church removed Valentine's Day from its official holiday calendar in 1969, in an effort to prune back the number of saints' days with dubious origins.

There are about a dozen saints named Valentine, three of which were martyrs who died on February 14. In addition to being the patron saint of engaged couples, Valentine is also the patron saint of beekeepers, epilepsy, travelers, and a dozen other things.

If there was a real Valentine, our bearded man's name was actually Valentinus, and he was a Christian priest (or possibly bishop) in Italy sometime in the third century.

According to Jacobus de Voragine's *Golden Legend* of 1260, the emperor at the time, Claudius Gothicus—who won most of his fights with the Germans and the Goths before losing to smallpox—ordered Valentinus to deny Christ, and he refused. While awaiting execution—compelled by love, even for his enemies—Valentinus miraculously healed the jailer's daughter, who was deaf and blind.[2]

In the *Nuremberg Chronicle*, published in 1493, the text suggests that Valentinus was arrested for marrying Christian couples in a time when the emperor was persecuting Christians. A more oddly specific version suggests that Claudius wanted an all-bachelor army, thinking they'd fight better if single, and that Valentine wed young couples as a way to help them avoid going to war.[3]

In the Nuremberg version, Valentine was dragged into court and Claudius took a liking to the prisoner, but quickly changed his mind when Valentine tried to convert him to Christianity. The emperor ordered Valentine to renounce his faith, under threat of being clubbed to death. When he failed to do so, he landed in prison.

The day of execution arrived, whereupon he left a note for the jailer's daughter, signed, "From Your Valentine."[4] The priest was beaten with clubs. He somehow survived the bludgeoning and was stoned. He survived that, too, and was finally beheaded outside the Flaminian Gate on February 14 in either AD 260 or 273.

His supposed remains can be visited at St. Valentine's Reliquary in Whitefriar Street Church in Dublin, Ireland. Alternately, you can visit his flower-adorned skull in the Basilica of Santa Maria in Cosmedin in Rome, or various bits of his skeleton in the Czech Republic, Scotland, England, or France.

What are we to make of this muddled tale of Saint Valentine?

The truth is, committed love in the time of Rome was dangerously close to extinction. Polygamy and incest were rampant, and a ban on marriage was undermining the family unit. Like Easter, Halloween, and Christmas, Valentine's Day was the church's attempt to redeem a sinful pagan holiday. In fact, Valentine's Day replaced two of the most sexually perverted festivals in history: Lupercalia and Juno Februata.

Lupercalia was celebrated on February 15, in honor of the Roman god of fertility. It was a festival of sexual license—complete with vestal virgins, blood-soaked priests, and dog sacrifices. Women would line up in a row while the men, drunk and naked, would flog them with the dead dog carcasses as a way to ensure fertility.

Juno Februata was celebrated on February 14, in honor of the goddess of feverish love. Small pieces of paper, each containing the name of a teenage girl, were placed in a jar. Roman boys would choose a name at random, and the two became a couple for a series of erotic games, which took place at feasts and parties across the capital. When the festival ended, the couple often remained sexual partners for the rest of the year.

Imagine the broken hearts.

Imagine the venereal diseases.

Imagine the unplanned pregnancies, the potential orphan crisis, the trauma.

The church transformed the sexual lottery by filling a box with names of saints—parishioners picked a name and were supposed to emulate that virtuous person for a year. They unseated the Roman gods of fertility and sex and enshrined Valentine as a symbol of faithful love. They changed the culture.

Scientists tell us that the male species is wired for novelty and newness. Society tells us that marriage no longer matters, that family isn't important, that commitment should last only as long as it feels right. But that isn't the way of love. Valentine refused to bend to the prevailing cultural winds. He understood the way of love. The way of love speaks truth to power. The way of love goes against culture. The way of love commits for life.

CONTEMPLATION

1. What is God's plan for sex and love?
2. How have you conformed to the pattern of this world when it comes to sex?
3. How can you show God's love to people far from Him?

PRAYER

God of purity, keep us from sinning with our thoughts, our eyes, and our actions. Help us to love others as You have loved us.

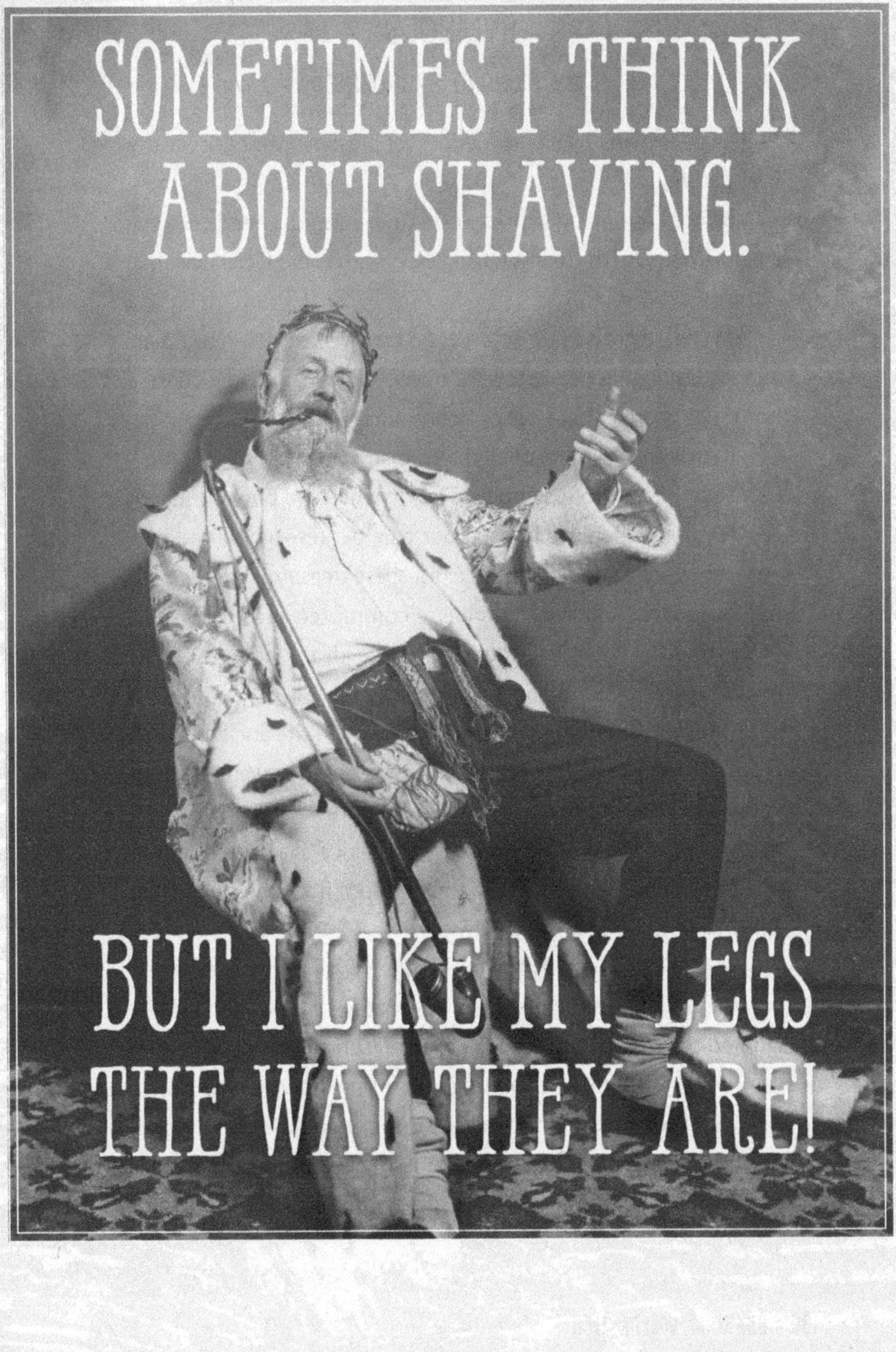
SOMETIMES I THINK
ABOUT SHAVING.
BUT I LIKE MY LEGS
THE WAY THEY ARE!

SYMBOLS

BY RICHARD SAUNDERS*

The beard is man's true best friend. Ever present. Ever trustworthy. Ever faithful.

Before continuing with my ode to the beard, I need to come clean—there are thirteen-year-old boys with more facial hair than I have.

My beard growth trajectory is on the five-years-to-never plan, and it's leaning Pisa-style toward never. With that off my chest—not much there either—we can continue.

Beards are a symbol of all that is manly.

So let's talk about symbols. They're where we bury our deepest treasures, where we lock up our true desires—good and bad. So is the beard a good placeholder for these treasures? Being genetically deprived, you might think I'm committed to the downfall of the beard. But I actually don't mind the idea of holding up the mighty beard for admiration.

Paul did something similar with crowns. In the ancient world, crowns were powerful symbols. They represented power, authority, and victory. Paul used the crown to illustrate what Christians are to chase after. Victory over sin, against injustice, against selfishness. The crown represented victory and freedom from the things that kill—namely, sin. Chase the crown.

But crowns also had other meanings in Paul's day. For example, crowns symbolized the power to do whatever you want. Paul just ignored that use of crowns. Followers of Christ don't do whatever they want. They follow their King's marching orders—God's will.

Paul took a common and powerful symbol from his world, used the wise bits, discarded the foolish pieces, and held it up as something for Christians to chase after.

Maybe we can swap the beard into that kind of role, holding it up where it points to the good and true and discarding the rest. What if we not only chased a spiritual crown but also a spiritual beard?

What are the good qualities we see in the beard? You know that sense of safety, security, and faithfulness that comes from having a legitimate beard? Maybe that's where we start.

Are you safe to be around? Or does your temper or desire trample the safety and security of your spouse or friends or family? Do your actions match your words? Do your words match reality? Are your thoughts, words, and actions brought into submission of your King? We know it's likely that Christ rocked a miraculous beard. But more important, we believe that He was perfectly faithful.

But let's not get too excited about symbols. Why do we pursue a spiritual crown or beard?

The prophet Isaiah tells us that our Savior would experience the ultimate shame, and he frames it in terms that people in his time would understand: body beaten and exposed, beard plucked out. Naked in every way. Jesus on the cross—another powerful symbol—relinquishes all His security, safety, and faithfulness in exchange for our unfaithfulness.

Our physical beard—that symbol of faithfulness—should act as a reminder to emulate the most manly man that ever lived, our Lord Jesus Christ.

---

* *Richard Saunders, MDiv, is pastor at Stone Ridge Bible Chapel, where he often massages his chin in an attempt to stimulate beard growth.*

CHAPTER 17

Joseph of Cupertino

THE BEARD WHO COULD FLY

BY AARON ALFORD

Meditation: Those who hope in the LORD will renew their strength. They will soar on wings like eagles.

—ISAIAH 40:31

Quote of the Day: Pray to God: "You are the spirit and I am only the trumpet, and without your breath, I can give no sound."

—JOSEPH OF CUPERTINO

Try as he might to study hard like the other kids in his class, book learning didn't come easily to little Joseph. It didn't help that, even as a boy of eight, he found himself enraptured and daydreaming at the thought of Jesus. At the sound of church bells, Joseph would drop his books and stare off into the sky, his mouth agape. The other children gave him a nickname: Open-Mouth Joe.

Born in Cupertino, Italy, in 1603, Open-Mouth Joe was a somewhat difficult child. As much as he loved Jesus, he had a quick temper, and his poor mother often found she was at the end of her wits dealing with a boy who was alternately getting into fights and daydreaming about Jesus for hours on end.

As he grew to be a teen, he would still find himself daydreaming at the sound of a hymn, or even the mention of Jesus' name. He never did learn to read or write very well, and when his mother arranged for him to be a cobbler's apprentice, he found he couldn't even cobble so good.

With his obvious love for God, however, his mother thought that perhaps working at a Franciscan friary would be a better fit. He tried working in the kitchen. Several broken dishes later, he was politely asked to find some other people to help. So he found another order of Franciscans and at last found work for which he had a knack: shoveling horse poop. He worked in the stables, looking after the horses and mules, where it was harder for him to break things.

He had grown into a tall, broad-backed young man with "a long, heavy beard, which originally black turned grey in later life, as did also his hair."[1] The friars came to admire Joseph, and it was obvious that although ol' Open-Mouth was not the brightest candle in the chapel, his love for God was deep and true.

He eventually took vows as a Franciscan and was often sent into town to ask for donations and alms for the friary. With his earnest smile and his frumpy Franciscan habit, the townspeople couldn't help but love him, and they gave generously.

Because of his deep sense of love and devotion, he was eventually allowed to become a priest, even though he barely (some say miraculously) passed the scholarly requirements to do so.

And just as it had when he was a boy, the mere mention of Jesus' name would send Joseph into a spiritual ecstasy. This happened especially in times of worship and prayer, so much so that people swore they saw him floating in the air, his face a picture of pure, enraptured joy.

These weren't isolated reports, either. His earliest biographers say that his literal flights of fancy happened over seventy times! He might lift off during communion or at times of corporate prayer—and at other times when you would least expect it (not that one would ever expect it!).

One Christmas Eve, when Joseph invited a group of flute-playing shepherds to church to celebrate the birth of the Christ child, he was so taken with their music and his love for the baby Jesus, he flew through the air about forty feet to the altar. He stayed up there for about fifteen minutes while "the shepherds marvelled exceedingly."[2]

His superiors found all this floating around and "marveling exceedingly" a little too distracting, however, so they eventually made a special little chapel in Joseph's room, where he could receive communion and float around as much as he liked.

It's hard to keep human flight under wraps, however ("It's a bird! It's what in the future will be called a 'plane'! It's a Franciscan man!"), and in spite of himself, Joseph was becoming famous. But he never thought very highly of himself. Joseph said he was "but an ignorant man and a poor sinner," and if he "had aught of good, it came from God, who generally made use of the greatest sinners to perform great things."[3] He had an honest view of himself and often referred to himself as Brother Ass. (For more on being an ass, see page 16, "On Being a Bible Donkey.")

Ignorant as he may have been, Joseph also became renowned for a wisdom that surpassed his lack of scholarly knowledge. Learned men and women came from far and wide to hear the simple wisdom of Open-Mouth Joe.

But Joseph's life was not just a succession of dopey-faced visions and aeronautic ecstasies. He also went through a profound dryness in his spiritual life. For several years, his prayers and songs seemed to fall flat, and he couldn't feel the presence of God like he had before. He was, as one biographer put it, "oppressed by a deep gloom."[4] In faith, however, he pressed all the more into Christ's heart, praying "that God take my heart, my whole heart."[5]

At the age of sixty, Joseph became ill. He was feverish and weak, and the last flight of Joseph of Cupertino had landed long ago. He knew his time to meet Jesus was soon at hand. But in his heart, he was still a little boy called Open-Mouth Joe. At his bedside, one of his friends began to speak to him about the love of God, and Joseph began to laugh with delight. "Say that again, say that again!" he said. He died with his mouth agape and smiling.[6]

Even after Joseph died, he had one last little miracle to perform, one which we here at Bearded Gospel Men especially appreciate. Joseph's body was taken for embalming and laid on a sheet, and somehow that sheet caught fire. The flames engulfed his corpse, but when the fire was extinguished, no harm had come to him, and "the beard and hair were not even singed."[7]

In our postmodern age of cynicism with our desperate need to rationalize and explain away any sense of whimsy, it's been suggested that Joseph was simply a very nimble gymnast. Of course, it could arguably be considered just as much a miracle to perform a back layout with a half twist in a cassock. But the most important aspect of Joseph's life is not his incredible hang-time. It's his profound humility and his openness to Christ. Joseph knew he wasn't smart, and he knew he was a sinner, but he also knew that the love of God surpassed every human limitation. He knew that Jesus could take any willing soul, no matter how sinful, no matter how stupid, and make it soar.

CONTEMPLATION

1. Do you ever feel inferior to those around you? How do you think God sees you?
2. Have you experienced a time of spiritual dryness, as Joseph did?

What brought you through this time? What might bring you through such a time in the future?

3. How might you cultivate a sense of wonder in your spiritual life?

PRAYER

Lord, in Your presence we are filled with wonder. Give us the grace to have a sense of Your presence wherever we go.

I SUFFER FROM
MALE PATTERN
MAGNIFICENCE.

CHAPTER 18

Festo Kivengere

THE BILLY GRAHAM OF AFRICA

BY JARED BROCK

Meditation: You will keep in perfect peace those whose minds are steadfast, because they trust in you.

—ISAIAH 26:3

Quote of the Day: Peace is not automatic. It is a gift of the grace of God. It comes when hearts are exposed to the love of Christ. But this always costs something. For the love of Christ was demonstrated through suffering, and those who experience that love can never put it into practice without some cost.

—FESTO KIVENGERE

I'm a very big fan of Billy Graham, so it's my great pleasure to introduce to you a man considered by many to be the "Billy Graham of Africa."[1]

His name was Festo Kivengere, and he was an absolute bearded gospel boss. Born in 1919, just a few months after Billy Graham, Kivengere grew up among semi-nomads on the rural plains of southwest Uganda. He came to faith in Christ in his early twenties, after contemplating suicide and struggling with alcohol misuse.

Kivengere became a gifted evangelist, and his honesty was disarming. He didn't shy away from sharing his flaws with his listeners or readers. He talked openly about the times he'd fought with his wife or daughters, or had been jealous of a fellow preacher, or had experienced spiritual doubts. He made it easy for audiences to acknowledge their own faults and failures.

At the same time, the decidedly beardless Idi Amin—an Islamic polygamist with five wives and forty-three children—considered himself God's gift to mankind. He officially called himself "His Excellency, President for Life, Field Marshal Al Hadji Doctor Idi Amin Dada, VC, DSO, MC, Lord of All the Beasts of the Earth and Fishes of the Seas and Conqueror of the British Empire in Africa in General and Uganda in Particular."[2] To be clear, he won exactly none of the awards he listed, but he did give himself an honorary doctorate. He also insisted he was the uncrowned king of Scotland.

Initially backed by Israel and the American CIA, the former boxing champion quickly transformed into a totalitarian dictator, exterminating as many as five hundred thousand Ugandans. Amin was a fearful despot who silenced his critics with force. "There is freedom of speech," he once said, "but I cannot guarantee freedom after speech."[3]

But Kivengere was fearless about speaking truth to power, no matter what. He challenged his fellow bishops, some of whom had become state spies in exchange for bribes. He became an international spokesman for the Ugandan church and denounced human rights violations in his home country. He spoke out against state favoritism between Catholics and Protestants, knowing it was little more than a political wedge to foster disunity among Christians. He even challenged armed guards and the president himself.

While Kivengere became the Billy Graham of Africa, Idi Amin became known as the Adolf Hitler of Africa. It was only a matter of time before their paths would cross.

The occasion that warranted their meeting occurred in 1973 when three men from Kivengere's diocese were tried on false charges and sentenced to death by firing squad:

> February 10 began as a sad day for us in Kabale. People were commanded to come to the stadium and witness the execution. Death permeated the atmosphere. A silent crowd of about three thousand was there ready to watch. I had permission from the authorities to speak to the men before they died, and two of my fellow ministers were with me. They brought the men in a truck and unloaded them. They were handcuffed and their feet were chained. The firing squad stood at attention. As we walked into the center of the stadium, I was wondering what to say. How do you give the Gospel to doomed men who are probably seething with rage?
>
> We approached them from behind, and as they turned to look at us, what a sight! Their faces were all alight with an unmistakable glow and radiance. Before we could say anything, one of them burst out: "Bishop, thank you for coming! I wanted to tell you. The day I was arrested, in my prison cell, I asked the Lord Jesus to come into my heart. He came in and forgave me all my sins! Heaven is now open, and there is nothing between me and my God! Please tell my wife and children that I am going to be with Jesus. Ask them to accept him into their lives as I did." The other two men told similar stories, excitedly raising their hands, which rattled their handcuffs.
>
> I felt that what I needed to do was to talk to the soldiers, not to the condemned. So I translated what the men had said into a language the soldiers understood. The military men were standing there with guns cocked and bewilderment on their faces. They were so dumbfounded that they forgot to put the hoods over the men's faces! The three faced the firing squad standing close together. They looked toward the people and began to wave, handcuffs and all. The people waved back. Then shots were fired, and the three were with Jesus.[4]

Kivengere and his fellow bishops wrote a letter to the dictator in protest. Amin summoned them to his quarters. They bravely appeared before the State Research Bureau and were questioned, but all were eventually permitted to leave except the archbishop, Janani Luwum. They waited patiently outside, but he never joined them.

The next day, Radio Uganda reported that Luwum had died in a car accident after he tried to overpower the driver in an escape attempt. When the archbishop's body was returned to his relatives, it was riddled with bullets. Uganda's minister of health, Henry Kyemba, wrote about it after he escaped the country: "The archbishop had been shot through the mouth and at least three bullets in the chest."[5]

Later that week, despite threats from Amin's regime, almost fifty thousand people gathered at the Anglican cathedral in Kampala to honor Kyemba. Kivengere was not in attendance. "One dead bishop is enough," his friends insisted.[6] The bishop and his wife drove as far as they could, and then the local church helped them walk the hills all night until they reached Rwanda. He eventually made it to America, where he preached and raised funds for ministry work in his home nation. God went to work on his heart, too, and he penned a book with a breathtaking title: *I Love Idi Amin*.

Imagine if Billy Graham, in his midtwenties in 1944, had published a book titled *I Love Adolf Hitler*.

Kivengere was asked to translate Billy Graham's sermons into Swahili. Graham grew to trust his African brother so much that he said, "Don't bother to translate literally. You know what I mean, get that across."[7] They became lifelong friends and spoke at each other's revival tours.

When Amin was overthrown and forced to flee to Saudi Arabia, Kivengere returned to Uganda. Corruption was widespread, and ethnic divisions had deepened. The population was militarized, and economic inequality created immense tension. Western materialism began to take root, and pastors were using faith as a way to reap cash rewards.

So Kivengere got to work. He formed the African Evangelistic Enterprise and preached widely. He put his money where his mouth was, living modestly and helping the poor. He helped thousands of refugees when it was unpopular and dangerous to do so. By the time he died of leukemia in 1988, he was the Anglican bishop for all of Uganda, Rwanda, Burundi, and modern-day Congo.

CONTEMPLATION

1. When have you remained silent when you should have spoken truth to power?
2. Who has wronged you that you need to forgive?
3. What has your faith cost you?

PRAYER

God of truth, do not allow us to be silent in the face of darkness. Where there are lies, let us speak Your words—and in doing so, hear Your voice.

As for the man whose hair
has fallen from his head,
HE IS BALD,
BUT HE IS CLEAN.
Leviticus 13:40

BEARD LOVE—A MAINTENANCE GUIDE

BY JARED BROCK

In the grand scheme of things, I'm quite new to the world of bearding. I started shaving at age eleven, but didn't get my connectors until my midtwenties. I've been able to grow a full beard for the past three years or so, but I still have some weak spots.

So I reached out to Taylor Welden, officer at the Austin Facial Hair Club and the 2015–2016 winner of Best in Show at the US National Beard and Moustache Championships. Here are his top five tips for cultivating top-notch facial foliage:

1. #DontShave

   Wise words.
2. Don't overthink it.

   "It will grow on its own," Welden explained. "The best thing to do is nothing. See item #1. Have fun with it."
3. Oils and conditioners—don't use too much.

   We at BGM couldn't agree more. Resist the urge to shampoo every day so that you don't wreck the natural oils. I recommend a weekly shampooing, something super moisturizing, especially in the winter. Coconut oil also does the trick. You can add a leave-in conditioner if you're feeling classy. Immediately after exiting the shower, rub a generous amount of beard oil into your skin and gently comb or brush your beard. But don't overdo it. "Beard oils and beard conditioners can help maintain healthy hair," Welden advised. "Don't use too much."
4. Hair is not alive.

   "The hairs are made of dead cells," Welden explained. "Trimming the ends does not make a beard grow longer after a trim. But sometimes trimming can help make your beard stronger, by eliminating split ends for example." We suggest a monthly trimming.

5. All facial hair is valid.

   "All facial hair is valid," Welden encouraged. "Even if you cannot grow facial hair. Having a beard does not make a man or woman (yes, I know women with actual long beards) better than a man or woman without a beard. A long beard is not better than a shorter beard or a moustache or a cleanly shaven face."

   As firm believers in the brotherhood of all, we agree. The central idea of BGM is the gospel.

   Thanks, Taylor!

CHAPTER 19

Keith Green

YOU PUT THIS LOVE IN MY HEART

BY AARON ALFORD

Meditation: But while he was still a long way off, his father saw him and was filled with compassion for him; he ran to his son, threw his arms around him and kissed him.

–LUKE 15:20

Quote of the Day: When I die I just want to be remembered as a Christian.

–KEITH GREEN

Keith Green quietly walked up to the piano. His hands hovered over the keys while the drummer counted off. A moment later, his fingers hit the ivories and the song was off and running. His fingers did not so much dance across the keyboard, but expertly slapped the notes into a rock 'n' roll samba. The young man whose life and music would impact a generation and change the lives of thousands was confident and at ease as he lifted his eyes to his audience and began to sing.

He sang a really dumb song about a girl.

Keith Green was eleven years old. He had just signed a five-year recording contract with Decca Records, one of the biggest labels of the time. Here he was on a national television show, his hair bleached blond to maintain a cherubic look, singing a song called "We'll Do a Lot of Things Together." Little Keith Green was going to be the next pint-sized, family-friendly Jerry Lee Lewis.

After his first TV appearance, Keith began showing up on variety shows and teen magazines all over America. He was on his way to teeny-bopper stardom, or so it seemed. But somewhere along the way, things began to sputter out for Keith, and a little Mormon boy named Donny Osmond soon stole the hearts of young girls everywhere. Keith Green was a washed-up rock 'n' roll star by the age of thirteen.

Keith continued to write songs, however, playing and singing anywhere he could. By the early 1970s, he was all grown up, newly married and working hard to court fame in Los Angeles. He had a few close brushes with stardom, but nothing came together. He was unwilling to compromise when a proposition seemed the least bit shady, which cost him some potentially lucrative deals.

But Keith's hunger for fame was strong and was matched only by his hunger for a meaningful spiritual experience. He and his wife, Melody, experimented with various religious experiences and philosophies, and Keith had tried a plethora of drugs along the way in a desperate search for connection with God. In all his searching, there was one figure he could not set aside: Jesus. Keith didn't know if this Jesus was God, as the Jesus freaks claimed, but on December 16, 1972, Keith wrote something significant in his personal journal: "Jesus, you are hereby officially welcomed into me. Now only action will reveal your effect on me."[1]

To say this was the day Keith "got saved" would be an oversimplification. Keith, and with him, Melody, continued to experience a process of conversion that messily unfolded over time, with the Holy Spirit calmly, consistently, persistently, patiently drawing them to

God. It involved reading the Bible, arguing with each other, arguing with friends, watching the popular Jesus-centric films of the time, such as *Jesus Christ Superstar*, and even having "Jesus" himself over for dinner—actor Ted Neeley—to talk about his experiences. In fact, Keith began playing Christian gigs with his friend Randy Stonehill well before he fully understood the divine nature of the Jesus he was falling in love with. Several songs that he would later record on his Christian albums, such as "Run to the End of the Highway," "The Prodigal Son Suite," and "On the Road to Jericho," were written during this time of journeying.

Eventually, though, the grace of faith took full effect in Keith's and Melody's lives, and they came to belief in the godhood of Jesus. Together they pursued Jesus with all the passion and fervor with which Keith had previously pursued fame, a pursuit that inspired them to do something risky for the sake of sharing the love of Jesus. He and Melody opened their home to single moms, recovering addicts, and people struggling to make sense of life. They weren't, at this point, trying to start a ministry. They wanted to make a place where broken people could receive love.

Keith's faith also became a deep well for music, and Keith wrote songs borne of the love God had put in his heart. In 1977, Jesus freaks in bell-bottomed jeans walked from the theater where they'd just seen *Star Wars* to the Christian bookstore to pick up a copy of Keith's first album, *For Him Who Has Ears to Hear.* He toured, often doing concerts in churches that had never seen a bearded hippy like Keith before, let alone one playing rock songs for the Lord.

"I just wanna say that God works in mysterious ways, and I am one of his mysterious ways. I know you haven't seen this much hair up on the pulpit before, but God doesn't look on the outside to see what kind of Christian you are. He looks on the inside."[2]

Keith's career took off while his and Melody's house expanded with loners, losers, and beautiful souls. On stage and at home, Keith was brash, opinionated, and sometimes over the line. But he was always, always honest. No one was safe from this honesty, least of all Keith.

He challenged everything, from Christian consumerism to the way his own music was distributed. He decided that all his concerts, which looked more and more like revival meetings, should be free, and he offered his music on a pay-what-you-can basis. It didn't take long for people to start calling him a prophet, and Keith accepted the mantle.

But the crushing weight of legalism, which pervaded his own walk with God, began to cripple him. He admitted at one point that he wasn't even sure God loved him at all.

Things began to change for Keith when he forged friendships with two men from the missionary organization Youth With A Mission: Loren Cunningham and John Dawson. Loren, the founder of YWAM, became like a father for Keith, and John Dawson like a brother. Keith was no longer a lone wolf, and an awakening of grace began to take hold of him through these grace-filled friendships.

He wrote personal letters of apology to people he'd hurt and alienated. He rejected the title of prophet, explaining in an article that "whenever someone is brash, obnoxious, or loud, we label him a 'prophet.'"[3] He had a deeper peace than he had ever known. Through the grace of friendship, legalism was turning to compassion, and Keith's "prophetic" voice turned to encouraging young men and women toward the mission field.

Keith and Melody, along with Loren Cunningham, began to plan a concert tour to mobilize young people into missionary service. Sadly, this was never to be. At least not in the form that any of them could have anticipated.

In July of 1982, Keith and two of his young children, along with nine others, died when their small plane crashed almost immediately after taking off. Melody was devastated, and along with her, thousands of people who had been touched by Keith's life and music. Melody wept and prayed with Loren and John, and eventually they decided that Keith's planned tour should still happen.

Using footage from one of his last concerts, Keith posthumously toured the country with his challenge to missionary service. Approximately three hundred thousand young people heard the message through the Keith Green Memorial Concert Tour, and both Youth With A Mission and Operation Mobilization reported huge increases in staff and students coming into the mission field.

Keith had sought success since he was a little boy, and when he finally found it, he ended up completely redefining what it meant. Keith seemed to have experienced two landmark spiritual moments in his adult life: one when he found Jesus, and another when the Father found him. The little boy became a young man with a mission, and when he sat at the piano in 1982, there were lights and cameras, but not a rock 'n' roll star in sight. Just a man who'd finally found the affirmation he'd always been seeking, as a child of the Father.

CONTEMPLATION

1. Are you "brash and opinionated"? Do you think God may want to temper these aspects of your character with grace? How?
2. Are you shy and withdrawn? Might God be calling you to be more outspoken? In what areas?
3. Keith had a breakthrough in his relationship with God through his friendships with Loren and John. Do you have brothers and fathers in your life? How can you cultivate such relationships?

PRAYER

Holy Spirit, teach us prophetic boldness and prophetic humility. And teach us most of all to live as sons of the Father.

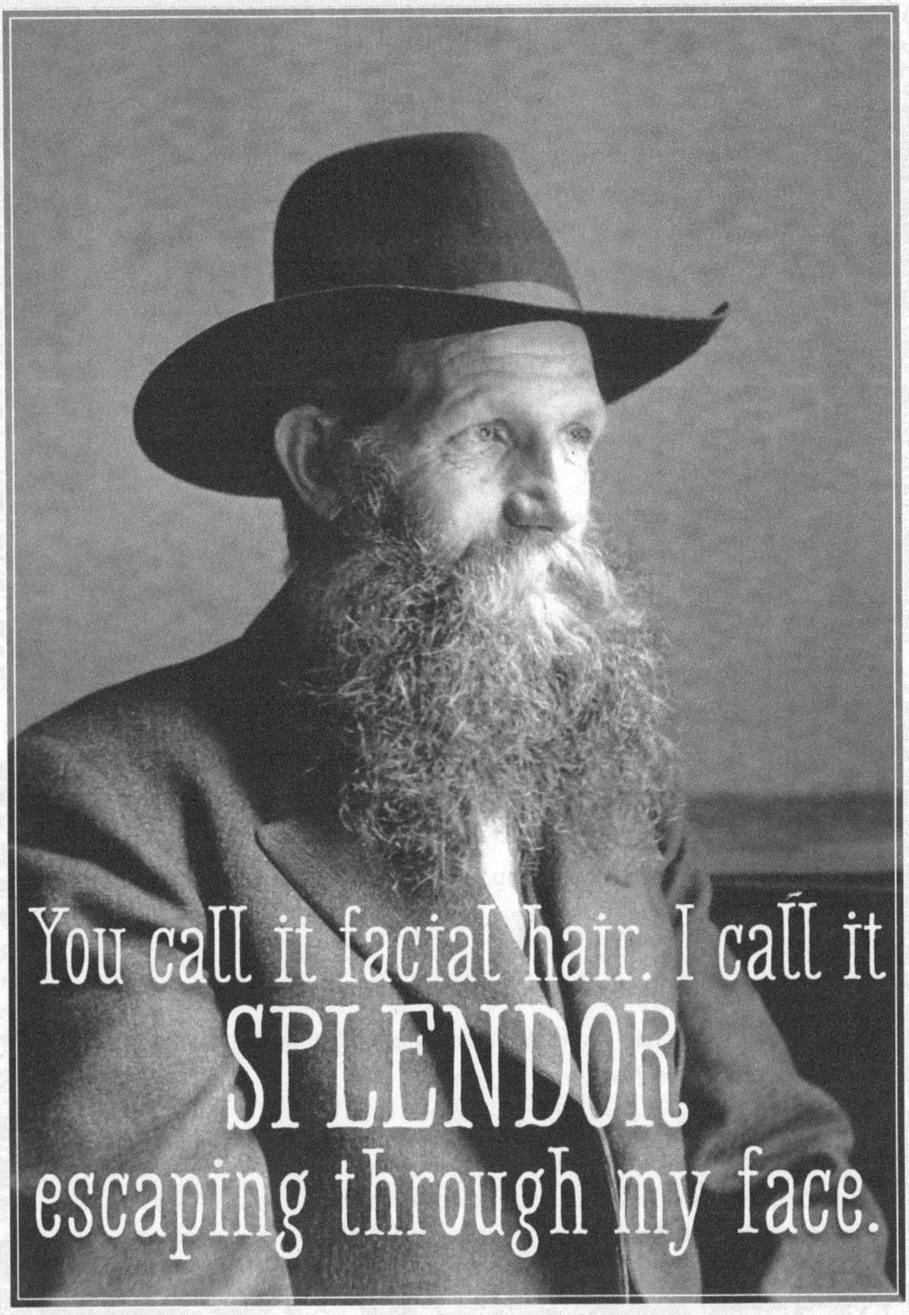
You call it facial hair. I call it
SPLENDOR
escaping through my face.

IL BARBONI

BY AARON ALFORD

The man on the street held out a cup, hoping for change. Providing the standard "Sorry, dude" shrug while not wishing to be unkind, I almost kept walking. I was in Rome, Italy, an expensive place to be, and I was on a tight budget. But as I tucked my hands into my pockets, I realized I did have something to offer. I rarely smoked cigarettes, but for some reason I had purchased a pack that day.

"Smoke?" I asked, along with the universal charades action for smoking. He nodded.

I fished out a few cigarettes and handed them to the man. I asked him his name.

"Franco," he replied.

He was perhaps in his early sixties. He seemed to keep himself as clean as he could, and his black hair was combed back neatly. He had thoughtful eyes, and he asked where I was from.

"Canada," I said, "but I live in California."

We chatted a little longer, and I learned that he was from Sicily. I told him a little about my life, and finally I shook his hand.

"It was good to meet you, Franco. Ciao," I said, and smiled.

"Ciao," he said.

The next day I saw Franco again. I greeted him with a handshake and asked him if he wanted a coffee.

"Sure, si, yes!" he said. "Espresso!"

I strolled over to the coffee shop and soon returned, hot espressos in hand. I hunkered down next to him.

"*Grazie!*" he said, taking a sip.

I sat with him for a while, sipping on espresso and people-watching on the busy street. There were businessmen having Very Important Conversations, smoking cigarettes. There were teenage girls, giggling and smoking cigarettes. A few priests (some of these also smoking cigarettes). And a lot of large, middle-aged people in socks and sandals, holding tourist maps and pointing.

Some people smiled apologetically toward Franco's begging cup. A few looked disgusted. Most walked quickly past, ignoring his outstretched hand. A few stopped and gave change. When someone stopped and gave *me* change, I realized that my beard must have helped me blend in.

"You are *Barboni*," Franco said, smiling and shaking his head. "It mean, 'Bearded One.' 'Tramp.' You looka like tramp, like me!"

I smiled. "It's an honor!"

I handed the change to Franco, and he took a coin and held it between his fingers.

"Where is this from?" he asked.

I looked at it closely. "Australia."

"Australia?" He reached behind him and pulled out a plastic container. "I collect these."

He opened the lid and handed me the collection. There were coins from all over the world. They had made their way from every part of the globe to this dusty butter container on a street corner in Rome. They were of no value here, but Franco treasured them as mementos from places he had never been.

He placed the coin in the container. We sat quietly for a while, and I searched for a topic of conversation.

"Franco, do you like music? You have a . . . a favorite music?"

The corners of his mouth went up a little. "Opera," he said as his eyes met mine. "I love opera!"

"Really? Do you have a favorite opera?"

His eyes showed a spark. "*La Traviata.*" And he smiled a smile of rapture and memory. "Very beautiful."

"What's it about?" I asked.

And he began to tell me the story of *La Traviata*, of the nobleman who fell in love with a woman who strayed. He didn't sing, but I don't think there is any music that could sing the story better than his eyes did. They were alive with the sadness and the joy of the telling. I felt each moment of love and heartbreak, like a song; I was present at the lovers' first kiss and their last embrace. When the story came to its end, my own eyes were as misty as the storyteller's.

Franco smiled, and the song stayed in his eyes. He shook his cup of change to the passersby. I sat with him a little longer, two *barboni* on the streets of Rome, and I would forever be a lover of opera.

CHAPTER 20

Agnes Bojaxhiu

IS THAT EVEN A DUDE'S NAME?

BY JARED BROCK

Meditation: Even though I walk through the darkest valley, I will fear no evil, for you are with me.

—PSALM 23:4

Quote of the Day: The more we receive in our silent prayer, the more we can give in our active life.

—MOTHER TERESA

How's this for a mixed-up situation? Agnes Bojaxhiu (pronounced Anya Boya-jew) was born in Macedonia in 1910 to Albanian parents. At age twelve she visited Kosovo and felt called to missions. At age eighteen she joined a community of Irish nuns in India and took a new name in honor of a French nun. By the time she died, she'd had seven nationalities and spoke five languages. Why is a beardless woman named Agnes being mentioned in a book called *Bearded Gospel Men*? Because this book has less to do with beards and men and everything to do with the gospel, and Agnes Bojaxhiu ranks so high in the world of Beardless Gospel Women that she rightfully deserves coverage in this book.

Agnes worked for seventeen years as a high school teacher in Calcutta, but the poverty outside the school's walls broke her heart. In 1948—the same year Gandhi was murdered—she started an open-air school for slum kids. She didn't have any money, but she convinced the local government to donate an abandoned building. Volunteers and money quickly followed. At age forty, she started the Missionaries of Charity.

Today Mother Teresa's ministry comprises four branches and forty-five hundred nuns that serve the poorest of the poor in 133 countries. In Calcutta alone, they have nineteen homes for orphans, lepers, and the sick. Globally, the order has more than six hundred mission foundations and more than one million volunteers. Mother Teresa won the Templeton Prize, the Nobel Peace Prize, and the Presidential Medal of Freedom. She donated the prize money for every award.

On August 31, 1997, the news broke that Princess Diana had died in a tragic car accident. Six days later, Mother Teresa died, just a day shy of Diana's global funeral. Mother Teresa was completely overshadowed.

And I can't help but think little Agnes would have liked it that way.

Because Mother Teresa lived her entire life in a secret shadow.

Come Be My Light, a collection of letters from Teresa to her spiritual advisers, was never supposed to be public material. In fact, she asked that her letters be destroyed. Sensing they'd prove helpful to others, the advisers ignored the request, and the letters were compiled and published after her death.

Mother Teresa's secret letters show that she spent almost five decades without sensing the presence of God in her life.

"In my soul I feel just that terrible pain of loss, of God not wanting me—of God not being God—of God not existing."[1]

"Darkness is such that I really do not see—neither with my mind nor with my reason. The place of God in my soul is blank. There is no God in me."[2]

"When I try to raise my thoughts to heaven, there is such convicting emptiness that those very thoughts return like sharp knives and hurt my very soul."[3]

"As for me—the silence and the emptiness is so great that I look and do not see, listen and do not hear."[4]

It certainly doesn't sound much like the great woman we saw on the news, does it?

Mother Teresa had even more secret struggles. She suffered for years with kidney problems. She endured two heart attacks, a battle with pneumonia, a broken collarbone, a bout with malaria, and she had a pacemaker for the last decade of her life. Her "dark night" lasted for almost forty-nine years and only lifted near the very end of her life.

For Mother Teresa, silence was the key to healing. Silence was the key to service and action too: "The fruit of silence is prayer. The fruit of prayer is . . . faith. The fruit of faith is love. The fruit of love is service. The fruit of service is peace."[5]

But life is busy, isn't it? We live in the age of a thousand commitments, a million apps, and a billion advertisements. But what is more important than one word from God? We must fight for silence. We must find a place where we can go and listen. Because it's in those quiet times that we hear the still, small voice of God.

CONTEMPLATION

1. Have you ever had a dark night of the soul?
2. How can you prepare for the times when God feels distant and quiet?
3. How can you and those closest to you serve one another during those dark nights?

PRAYER

Father of light, You know the darkness in our hearts and the darkness in our world. Send the light of Christ to show the path. Illuminate our hearts and minds that we may see You.

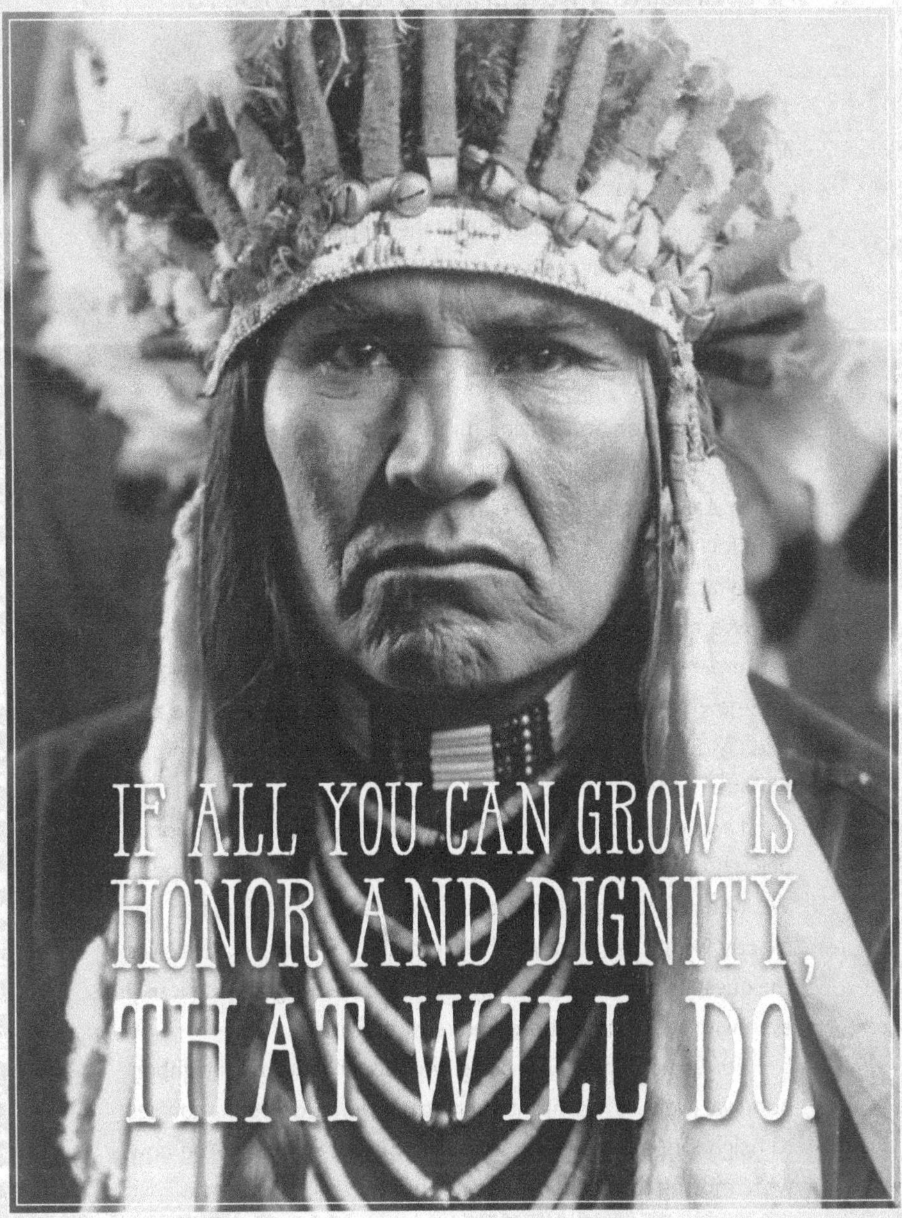
IF ALL YOU CAN GROW IS
HONOR AND DIGNITY,
THAT WILL DO.

RAISING PRE-BEARDED GOSPEL BOYS

BY CATHERINE GREENE*

I'm the mother of four boys, the oldest of whom is six. Most people think we are a little mad, but we love the madness.

Parenting has shown me that kids are your best critics. Leave it to them to tell you exactly what they think, whether it's appropriate or not. Like at the grocery store when one son pointed and loudly asked why the man beside us was so large. Or when another one told a stranger that sometimes Mommy cries in the shower. In my defense, crying in the shower is not a regular occurrence.

Kids are also an amazing mirror for seeing the places where we fall short. We pray with our children every night before bed, which is always an adventure, as their prayers range from thanking God for Wii video games to praying about not punching babies in the face.

We told our boys what was happening in Syria and tried to explain what a refugee is. We prayed that all of these people would find new homes. After we finished, my oldest looked at me and said, "Mom, if they don't have homes, can't they live in our home with us?"

I was convicted. We had taught our boys many times about being hospitable and how God wants us to take care of the poor. We were teaching our kids the principles of the Bible, but not exactly living them out. My husband and I had to ask ourselves the question, what does it really mean to take the gospel seriously even with four kids, a house, and responsibilities?

For us, this has meant being intentional about the neighborhood we live in. It has meant opening our home, delivering cookies to neighbors, and being very active in our local church. And now we're moving to Uganda.

We're taking a season and giving up our home and community to move across the pond to serve young orphans in Uganda. Or in the words of my four-year-old, "to take care of the boys who don't have mommies." It's slowly dawning on us that if we want our kids to live kingdom-centered lives, we need to live kingdom-centered lives. Raising gospel kids starts by being gospel parents.

---

* *Catherine Greene is a follower of Jesus, wife of a bearded gospel man, and mother of four boys.*

CHAPTER 21

Saint Augustine

EARNEST, ACTIVE, VIGOROUS, BEARDED

BY AARON ALFORD

Meditation: How good and pleasant it is when God's people live together in unity! It is like precious oil poured on the head, running down on the beard, running down on Aaron's beard, down on the collar of his robe.

—PSALM 133:1–2

Quote of the Day: You have made us for yourself, O Lord, and our hearts are restless until they rest in you.

—SAINT AUGUSTINE

He was a lazy, dishonest thief, feeble in any resistance to temptation, and quick to capitulate to his own lusts. He was a sad excuse of a man. Each night, his mother wept for him and prayed for the conversion of his sorry soul.

Thank God for stalwart mothers.

Augustine was born in AD 354 in Hippo, a city in modern Algeria. If the boot that is Italy were to kick a small stone, it might land here. His mother was a dedicated and pious Christian, while his father, though he loved and respected his wife, was a pagan with a propensity for philandering. Unfortunately, Augustine took after his father.

By the time he was sixteen, Augustine had become a brilliant student who excelled in writing, grammar, and the art of oration. And with his friends egging him on, he also excelled in all the sins born of idleness and boredom. He would later reflect on a time when he and his friends decided to steal pears from a farmer's tree. It was a minor incident, one that most would easily cast aside as harmless teenage mischief, but Augustine saw in it the depths of his own sin and depravity. He realized he did not steal the pears for any other reasons than for the acceptance of his friends and "having no temptation to ill, but the ill itself. It was foul, and I loved it."[1]

It was also during these reckless years that he would father a child out of wedlock, named Adeodatus ("gift of God"). Augustine and the boy's mother never married, though they carried on a tumultuous romance for several years. Eventually it was she who would end their relationship and leave their son in his care.

Throughout this time, Augustine's skill as a writer, professor, and public speaker grew, and he became enraptured with the philosophies and teachings of the Manichaeans, a religious sect that tried to synthesize all religions (including Christianity) and essentially taught that all matter was evil. To be perfect, all physical desires and attachments had to be overcome by sheer willpower. Eventually, however, Augustine found their philosophies to be empty and their high-minded moralizing to be bereft of true character. "They destroy everything and build up nothing."[2]

Augustine discovered the writings of Plato and became enamored of Platonic philosophy. Here he found enough truth to whet his appetite for more, while realizing that there were two things philosophy lacked: "I had begun to desire to seem wise . . . but rather was puffed up with knowledge. For where was that charity building upon the 'foundation' of humility, 'which is Jesus Christ'? Or, when would these books teach me it?"[3]

It was this desire for truth that would eventually help to lead him fully into Christianity. Augustine's conversion was no mere act of intellectual assent, but was informed in a tangible way by a living example of friendship and humility. When Augustine moved from Rome to Milan to accept a professorship, he still saw Christianity as a simple-minded religion full of empty stories. But then he was introduced to the bishop of Milan, a man named Ambrose—a man who would change his life. Augustine wrote of him later:

> That man of God received me as a father, and showed me an Episcopal kindness on my coming. Thenceforth I began to love him, at first indeed not as a teacher of the truth (which I utterly despaired of in Thy Church), but as a person kind toward myself. And I listened diligently to him preaching to the people.[4]

As Augustine listened, he noted not just the sincerity of Ambrose's words, but their truth. He eventually decided to become a candidate for entrance into the Christian church. Throughout this time of preparation for being received into full communion, a process that was common for all new Christians at the time, he remained tossed about by doubt and the desires of his flesh.

Discouraged and despairing of his inability to conquer his lusts, Augustine wept alone one night in the garden of his home. Then he heard a child's singsongy voice, perhaps carried from a neighbor's house, perhaps solely in his spirit. Whatever the case, it sang, "Take up and read! Take up and read!"[5] He went inside, picked up a copy of the book of Romans, and opened it randomly to this passage:

> Let us behave decently, as in the daytime, not in carousing and drunkenness, not in sexual immorality and debauchery, not in

> dissension and jealousy. Rather, clothe yourselves with the Lord Jesus Christ, and do not think about how to gratify the desires of the flesh. (Rom. 13:13–14)

Something in this brought immediate peace to his heart, and every doubt evaporated. Months before she would pass away, Monica, the mother who had prayed tirelessly for her son's conversion, saw her son received into the church. He was baptized by Ambrose, the bishop whose preaching and whose living example of Christ had been instrumental in his conversion.

Augustine turned every talent and energy he had previously poured into his worldly pursuit of scholarly adulation into the teaching and defending of the Christian faith. He sold his possessions, gave the money to the poor, became a priest and later a bishop of the church. He preached and wrote, refuting the many heresies and unworthy philosophies of his time, and he did so with grace, humility, and passion. The cumulative influence of his theological writings, his highly personal account of his conversion, *The Confessions*, and his other writings on the church and Western thought in general is so great as to be almost incalculable. It's from one of these writings, a short reflection on Psalm 133, that we derive one of our favorite quotes here at Bearded Gospel Men:

> "As the ointment on the head, which descended to the beard, to Aaron's beard, which descended to the fringe of his garment." What was Aaron? A priest. Who is a priest, except that one Priest, who entered into the Holy of Holies? . . . The ointment is on his head, because Christ is one whole with the Church . . . and the Holy Spirit came from the head. Whither? To the beard. The beard signifies the courageous; the beard distinguishes the grown men, the earnest, the active, the vigorous. So that when we describe such, we say, he is a bearded man.[6]

Augustine died at the age of seventy-six, after nearly forty-five years of service to Christ and His church. Far from the lazy, dishonest, carousing thief of his youth, Augustine was courageous. He was earnest. He was active. He was vigorous.

He was a bearded man.

> Late have I loved you, O Beauty ever ancient, ever new, late have I loved you!
>
> You were within me, but I was outside, and it was there that I searched for you.
>
> In my unloveliness I plunged into the lovely things which you created.
>
> You were with me, but I was not with you.
>
> Created things kept me from you; yet if they had not been in you they would have not been at all.
>
> You called, you shouted, and you broke through my deafness.
>
> You flashed, you shone, and you dispelled my blindness.
>
> You breathed your fragrance on me; I drew in breath and now I pant for you.
>
> I have tasted you, now I hunger and thirst for more.
>
> You touched me, and I burned for your peace.
>
> —ST. AUGUSTINE, *THE CONFESSIONS*

CONTEMPLATION

1. Is there someone you love who seems far from God? Consider remembering him or her in prayer each day, entrusting that person to the heavenly Father.
2. In what way were you lost? How and when did God break through your deafness and dispel your blindness? How might you share your story, your "Confessions" with others?

3. Was there someone who faithfully prayed for you during a particularly difficult or straying time in your life? Consider sending him or her a word of thanks.

PRAYER

Heavenly Father, grant us patience and persistence in prayer for those people in our lives who have wandered far from You; let their restless hearts find their rest in You.

BEARDS
THE ONE THING
MEN ARE ALLOWED
TO COMPLIMENT
ABOUT EACH OTHER

THE GIFT OF ENEMIES

BY AARON ALFORD[7]

Your closest friend betrays you. A long-trusted colleague spreads malicious gossip about you. A stranger lashes out at you in anger. As a Christian, you know you're supposed to forgive that person, but in the midst of the moment, or even in the memory of such a moment, a hot rage descends over your eyes and all you can see is injustice. Forgiveness seems like a distant, abstract idea meant for some other situation.

Perhaps you really have forgiven the one who hurt you, at least to the best of your ability, but the wound he or she left still aches. You remember Jesus' command to love your enemies and pray for those who persecute you, but it seems impossible to do so. Just forgiving that person can be a daily struggle, let alone loving and praying for him or her. How can I pray for someone who has hurt and betrayed me? And why would God let that person injure me this way?

You may not see it, but in that injury, God has given you a gift. He has given you the gift of an enemy. How is this a gift? Because by the wounds you receive, you are uniquely capable of praying for the one who wounded you. The way in which that person hurt you reveals his or her own hurt. It has revealed to you the place in one's heart where love is lacking, where he or she most needs the Father's healing touch. In lashing out at you, that person has bound himself or herself to you, and your Father in heaven has entrusted a piece of that person's soul to yours.

What's more, you have been given the grace of seeing something of your own heart and its broken places. With that gift of revelation, you have an opportunity to invite the Father's healing presence into a chamber of your heart that may previously have been closed to Him. Like a man who goes to the hospital for a stomachache only to find he has a more serious illness, the wound itself can reveal the deeper things that need fixing.

Remember, too, that you may be the enemy someone is praying for. "Therefore, if you are offering your gift at the altar and there remember that your brother or sister has something against you, leave your gift there in front of the altar. First go and be reconciled to them; then come and offer your gift" (Matt. 5:23–24).

We often get that scripture backward, thinking that I'm the one who can't have something against someone else. While it's true that we should always be seeking God's grace to forgive our enemies, that is not the point Jesus is making here. He wants us to remember our own failings, and to do what we can to be in right relationship with those we may have injured.

It may or may not be possible to be reconciled to your enemy, but at the very least you can love him or her through your prayers. And when you pray from this place of recognizing your own brokenness, and of having gained insight into the place of your enemy's brokenness, the Holy Spirit can do a work of healing in both of you. Some scars may remain, but God's gifts are always good. And like the wounds in the hands of Jesus, they can be made beautiful.

CHAPTER 22

Johannes Kepler

BEARDED SPACE MAN

BY JARED BROCK

Meditation: The heavens declare the glory of God; the skies proclaim the work of his hands.

—PSALM 19:1

Quote of the Day: The ways by which men arrive at knowledge of the celestial things are hardly less wonderful than the nature of these things themselves.

—JOHANNES KEPLER

In typical scientific fashion, his NASA profile page reports that Johannes Kepler was born (unbearded at the time) two days after Christmas in 1571 at about one o'clock in the afternoon. Kepler was born in Weil der Stadt, a free imperial city of the Holy Roman Empire.[1] As his birthplace suggests, political Catholicism was in its heyday. At the time of Kepler's birth, the church controlled half of Italy, parts of France, most of Germany, and about a dozen other countries. But the Kepler family was Lutheran.

Kepler's family was poor and unsettled. His father was a mercenary who was often gone for years at a time. When Kepler's mother joined his father behind the battle lines, little Johannes went to live with his grandparents. He was a small, weak boy who barely survived a battle with smallpox at age three. His grandfather was a devout Christian and encouraged the little boy to explore his faith as well as his intellect. Despite being a sick child, Kepler was incredibly smart. His grandfather enrolled him in school, and he soon caught the attention of his teachers.

According to the Internet (though we can't find a reputable source), Kepler observed both the Great Comet of 1577 when he was six and the 1580 lunar eclipse, events that no doubt fueled his curiosity and enthusiasm for science.[2] When Kepler's parents returned from war and built an inn, they forced the boy to leave school so they could use him as free labor. His father turned to drink, the inn soon tanked, and the boy was no longer needed.

Sponsored by the Duke of Württemberg, Kepler continued his schooling and won a scholarship to the University of Tübingen. He studied Latin, Hebrew, and Greek along with the Bible, mathematics, and astronomy. At the time, most scholars still believed that the earth was the center of the solar system, but his astronomy teacher, Michael Mästlin, was one of the few professors who agreed with Copernicus's ideas. It wasn't the only belief that kept Kepler on the outside of society.

The young man was excluded from the sacraments of the Lutheran faith because he wouldn't sign their statement of faith. He lost his teaching job during the Counter-Reformation because he was Lutheran, but since he wouldn't sign the Catholic statement of faith either, he had no protection during the Thirty Years' War between the two.

Kepler went to work in Prague with the Danish astronomer Tycho Brahe, Emperor Rudolf II's court mathematician, and took over his post as imperial mathematician when Brahe died. Using Brahe's remarkably accurate data, Kepler discovered the shape of Mars's orbit. He published his findings in 1609, in a book called *Astronomia Nova*. It contains Kepler's first two laws of planetary motion. According to Harvard professor emeritus of astronomy Owen Gingerich, "It is the first published account wherein a scientist documents how he has coped with the multitude of imperfect data to forge a theory of surpassing accuracy."[3] Today we call it the scientific method.

Despite not fitting into a denominational box, Kepler held a great reverence for the heavens and their Creator. He frequently prayed, "O God, I am thinking Thy thoughts after Thee."[4] According to the Institute for Creation Research, "In Kepler's view, the universe itself was an image of God, with the sun corresponding to the Father, the stellar sphere to the Son, and the intervening space to the Holy Spirit."[5]

Kepler's work was his offering and his form of worship. He opened his groundbreaking book, *Harmonices Mundi*, with this introduction: "I commence a sacred discourse, a most true hymn to God the Founder, and I judge it to be piety, not to sacrifice many hecatombs of bulls to Him and to burn incense of innumerable perfumes and cassia, but first to learn myself, and afterwards to teach others too, how great He is in wisdom, how great in power, and of what sort in goodness."[6]

Despite his frail body, constant war around him, and general societal ignorance, Kepler's accomplishments were astounding. In the time of Galileo and Shakespeare, Kepler was the first person to correctly explain planetary motion. His thinking laid the groundwork for Newton's work on gravity. He is considered the founder of modern optics: he explained depth perception, formulated glasses for far- and nearsightedness, and studied how pictures were created with pinhole cameras. He invented the word *satellite*. He wrote the first science fiction story. He discovered a supernova. He was the first person to explain how a telescope works and then made significant improvements to it. One of his books formed the basis for integral calculus, inspiring the hatred of high school math students around the world. He was the first to explain that ocean tides are caused by the moon. He even used space math to derive the birth year of Jesus, which is now universally accepted. Today Kepler is considered one of the founders of modern science.

Kepler's life was not easy. He was forced to flee Prague three years into his post, when the Lutherans were forced out. He was constantly on the run due to his beliefs, which ran scientific and sympathetic to Calvinism. He lost a wife, two sons, and two daughters to sickness. He had financial problems. He had to defend his mother in court against charges of witchcraft. Kepler died in 1630, and his grave was demolished two years later because of the war.

The great scientist never saw a conflict between Scripture and science. Kepler was just as much a theologian as a scientist. "I had the intention of becoming a theologian . . . but now I see how God is, by my endeavours, also glorified in astronomy, for 'the heavens declare the glory of God.'"[7]

Kepler remained steadfast in his faith throughout his life, and incredibly humble despite his achievements, even going so far as to say, "Let my name perish if only the name of God the Father is thereby elevated."[8]

Kepler's life work was a prayer, which he summed up at the close of *Harmonices Mundi*:

> Purposely I break off the dream and the very vast speculation, merely crying out with the royal Psalmist: Great is our Lord and great His virtue and of His wisdom there is no number: praise Him, ye heavens, praise Him, ye sun, moon, and planets, use every sense for perceiving, every tongue for declaring your Creator . . . to Him be praise, honour, and glory, world without end. Amen.[9]

CONTEMPLATION

1. What hardships have kept you from worshiping Jesus?
2. What work are you doing that most people don't see as a way to praise God?
3. How can you turn your work into worship?

PRAYER

Father of creation, we stand in awe at the works of Your hands. May we come to know You better as we discover Your creation.

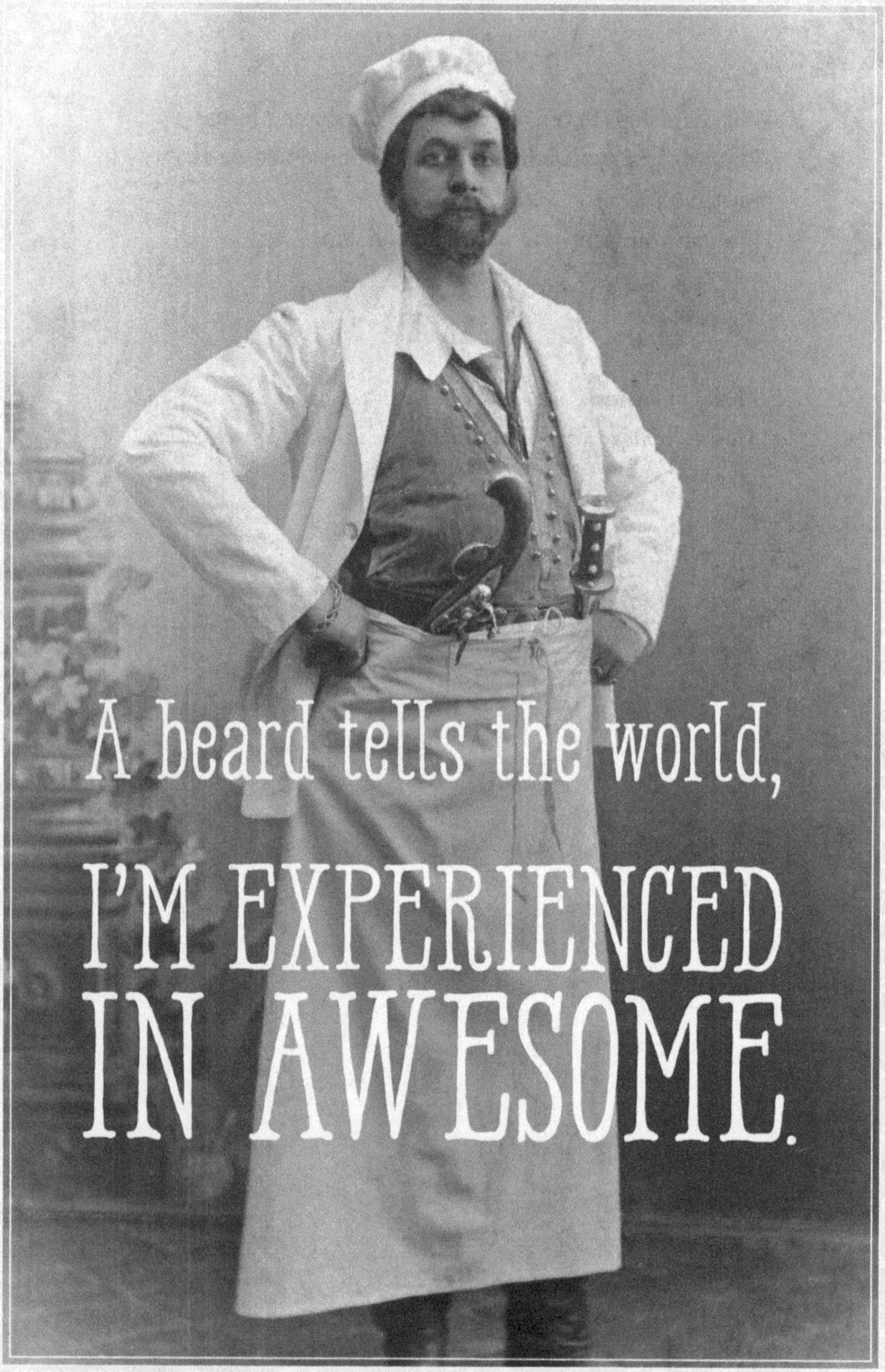
A beard tells the world,
I'M EXPERIENCED
IN AWESOME.

STAY

BY CHRIS WIGNALL*

After more than twenty years of professional ministry experience and a decade focused on philanthropy and developing leaders for the nonprofit world, I often get into conversations about how to know if all the work we're doing is actually worthwhile. The large majority of us don't have the time, training, or priority to become experts in community change. So how can we approach trying to make a difference in the world without making everything worse?

I'm still an amateur in this field, but as a former pastor, I know you can speak to almost any topic with diligent preparation, prayer, a decent concept, and the mighty power of alliteration.

So here's my take:

STAY HEARTBROKEN

With so many issues and injustices all around us, knowing where to start is difficult. The things that make us sad or angry are often indicators of where we should get involved. Have the courage to pray the dangerous prayer of Bob Pierce, founder of World Vision: "Let my heart be broken by those things that break the heart of God."[10]

STAY HUMBLE

We are rich, but we are stupid, and we usually don't know it. Our privilege often blinds us to our inadequacies. Impactful people ask questions, challenge their own assumptions, and constantly seek to improve their work and themselves. There is an endless amount to learn if we want to do anything significant.

STAY HUMAN

Some of us tend to function at a theoretical level, removed from the front lines of difficulty, but the biggest changes are often small changes multiplied by a lot of people. It is always personal.

STAY HELPFUL

Constantly check that what you're doing is still making the difference you desire. Ask the people you are there to serve if what you are doing is the best way to help. Things change constantly. Our strategies have to change too, or we end up trying to address new problems with old solutions that don't work anymore.

STAY HONEST

We all want to believe that our sincere effort is enough, but service in a troubled world is no place for naive sentimentality. Rigorous commitment to the truth and a relentless focus on results is the only way to be sure we aren't wasting our work and resources. We have to be able to show the impact we're making with real outcomes, not just a few touching stories.

STAY HEALTHY

Helping is hard, and it will test every aspect of who you are. Too many people burn out along the way, with devastating results for themselves, their family and friends, and those they were trying to help. You can't care for others for long unless you are also taking care of yourself. Rest, reflection, recreation, and relationships are not optional.

STAY HERE

This might be the toughest one for a lot of us. Most of us tend to move on too soon and never experience the personal growth and lasting outcomes that come only through persevering over a long period. The result is unfinished projects and immature leaders. Having a meaningful impact takes time.

STAY HOPEFUL

The sheer volume of injustice and need in this world is overwhelming. The distinct advantage of people of faith is that we know something better is coming. We need to frequently remind ourselves and one another that the old hymn gets it right; "Tho the wrong seems oft so strong, God is the ruler yet."[11]

Maya Angelou gave probably the best advice for anyone who wants to be part of making the world a better place: "Do the best you can until you know better. Then when you know better, do better."[12]

---

* *Chris Wignall is executive director of the Catalyst Foundation.*

CHAPTER 23

Saint Denis

HEADS ABOVE THE REST

BY AARON ALFORD

Meditation: But you, LORD, are a shield around me, my glory, the One who lifts my head high.

—PSALM 3:3

Quote of the Day: If you strike me down, I shall become more powerful than you can possibly imagine.

—OBI-WAN KENOBI

Denis walked down the streets of the city, his beard rustling in the breeze. It was an easy walk, a downward slope descending from the highest hill in town, and as he walked, he did what he always did. He preached. Loudly, passionately, and for all who had ears to hear. Denis loved to preach and had become known for being one of the best gospel preachers around. Hundreds had come to faith in Jesus by his preaching.

Denis was especially ardent in his preaching today. Perhaps it was because he knew he did not have much time left, that this would be his last sermon. His public speaking was always effective, but today every soul within earshot of his sermon stopped to stare and listen with rapt attention. Some did more than stop and stare. Some stopped and screamed. While there is nothing terribly unusual about a preacher walking through town and preaching repentance, there was something very unusual about this preacher.

It may have had to do with the fact that he was carrying his own decapitated head in his hands.

A good preacher can preach a sermon off the top of his head. A great preacher can preach a sermon with his head off completely. Saint Denis was just such a preacher. This Bearded Gospel Man would hardly let something as inconsequential as decapitation keep him from preaching the gospel.

But more on all this headlessness later.

Born in Italy in the third century, Denis was a missionary bishop, which meant he was both an overseer of pastors and a proclaimer of the gospel, not unlike the apostle Paul before him. Denis, along with two companions, one a priest and the other a deacon, was sent to evangelize Gaul. Gaul, modern France, was part of the vast and formidable Roman Empire. Christianity had taken root there, and the church had even enjoyed a certain level of comfort for a time under Emperor Phillip I, who may have been a Christian himself.

But all this changed with the rise of Emperor Decius. Decius saw himself as a reformer of the glorious Roman religion and its political system, and he saw Christianity as a threat to the integrity of Rome. Christians, who had been around for more than two hundred years, did not worship the Roman gods, nor did they offer sacrifices on behalf of the gods. They did not even hail Caesar as king of kings! Instead, they spoke of Jesus as King of kings and called themselves subjects of His kingdom. Decius had had quite enough of that. He wanted citizens who were unquestionably faithful to gods and country, and clearly, the first loyalty of Christians was to neither.

Under the persecution of Decius, the average Christian was given an opportunity to renounce his or her religion and keep his or her life, but priests and bishops were summarily executed. This persecution, preceded as it was with a time of relative ease, took a great toll on the church, and many recanted. The church in Gaul was dwindling, and it was suffering.[1]

Along with his missionary brothers, Denis bravely went forth, eventually arriving in Lutetia, modern Paris. These friends powerfully communicated the gospel, and many came to believe in the Christ about whom Denis preached, the one true Lord and King. The love and fearlessness these friends displayed brought new life to the church of Gaul, so much so that they built a church on a small island on the River Seine, in the heart of the city.

But these conversions did not sit well with the local pagan priests, and soon Denis and his friends were reported to the Roman authorities. They were taken into custody, and by some accounts the three were scourged, racked, and thrown to wild animals. Surviving these ordeals but still true to their King and His kingdom and unwilling to bow to the empire and its gods, Denis and his companions at last faced the Roman sword.

The three friends were dragged to the top of the highest hill, what is now known as Montmartre, to make sure everyone could see just what happens to anyone who defied the empire and her gods. One can only imagine what was going through Denis's mind as he watched his friends meet their deaths. Evidently he may have been thinking, *This would be a perfect time to preach a sermon!*

Odds are pretty good that this was exactly what he was thinking, for it seems that even decapitation could not keep Denis from preaching the gospel.

Legend says that when the executioner's sword separated his head from his body, Denis calmly picked up his head, carried it in his arms, and started preaching. He walked down the hill through the streets of the city, proclaiming a message of repentance to everyone who would listen. Needless to say, people listened. Finally, after about a six-mile sermon, Denis finished his preaching, set down his head, and died. About two hundred years later, a chapel was built in honor of Denis on the same site. The Basilica of Saint Denis, built on that chapel's foundations, still stands today.

Perhaps the legend of his headless preaching comes from the reality that Denis's message lasted well beyond his actual death. Perhaps it comes from the way that his life was a sermon that continued to be heard after his martyrdom; the fame of this great Christian spread across France almost immediately after he died. Or perhaps the legend came to be because he actually picked up his head and walked around town preaching! We'll have to ask him when we see him.

What's more amazing than his headless preaching, though, is that despite being born a couple of hundred years after the last book of the New Testament, Revelation, was written, Saint Denis is mentioned in it:

> I saw thrones on which were seated those who had been given authority to judge. And I saw the souls of those who had been beheaded because of their testimony about Jesus and because of the word of God. They had not worshiped the beast or its image and had not received its mark on their foreheads or their hands. (Rev. 20:4)

Denis and his companions did not bow to the beast that was, in this case, the Roman Empire. Their allegiance was to Jesus and His kingdom, a kingdom not of tyranny nor the earthly power the Roman emperors held on to so desperately, but of righteousness, peace, and joy. This kingdom was bigger than the Roman Empire could ever be, for it was alive and active in every place its King was present. At a crucial time when the church had suffered from the effects of both comfort in the empire and persecution from the empire, Denis boldly proclaimed Jesus as Lord, the only true King, and the only means of salvation.

CONTEMPLATION

1. What does it mean to proclaim Jesus as Lord in your culture?
2. Is there a distinction between love of country and love of the gospel in your culture? Is it difficult to distinguish them?
3. In what ways might you need to defy the empire today?

PRAYER

Jesus, teach us always and before anything else to be true to You, our King, and to Your kingdom.

THE ONLY THING
THAT GETS CAUGHT
IN MY BEARD
IS
GREATNESS!

A CALLING TO FALL

BY BRADFORD LOOMIS*

People often seem to follow God's call when the benefits are obvious. It's more difficult to follow when they are not. Pastoring a church in Beverly Hills is an easier call to answer than becoming a martyr! When I felt my calling to pursue pastoral training, it seemed overwhelming, humbling, yet somehow perfect.

Since middle school, I have known that I would struggle focusing on much else besides music. When we took those aptitude tests in high school, it was no surprise that my strengths were teaching, counseling, and the creative arts.

As the years went by, however, I never knew how to make the leap of pursuing music. I knew after barely making it through high school that I couldn't handle college, and I wandered aimlessly for years. Then I met the woman who would eventually be my wife. We got married and had a family, and the dreams of my youth grew more and more distant. I periodically worked a few barely tolerable jobs, but my wife most often was the primary breadwinner.

When I was saved, I got really involved in the church. I made friends, and we served God's people together. Some of those friends were starting a new church and, though I was new to the faith, they needed a worship guy. None of us had ever done anything like this before, but my apprehensions about my inadequacies in education and spiritual giftings were eased with assurances that I would receive the needed training. It seemed that being a worship pastor was a perfect fit and a blend of the three professions I was drawn to back in school.

So we jumped.

Embarrassed about the poor decisions I had made in the past, I was eager to redeem myself and so thankful that God was giving me the opportunity to give back to Him. We bought a house in the community where the church was, and I got a great job that would give me the flexibility to pursue my training in ministry. I poured myself into the work relentlessly. I went through the curriculum; I studied theology, administration, ecclesiology; I led ministries; I wrote song after song; I learned how to write out music; and I learned how to shepherd. And I learned what it meant to follow a calling.

As my training went on, however, it became clear that I would never be the type-A, alpha male the church was looking for. Overwhelmed and heartbroken, and realizing how naive I had been, I bowed out of ministry. Right after that, I lost my job, and shortly after that we lost our house. We were stunned. It was soul crushing.

"How did I get here?" I asked myself. I knew that God had called me to this ministry. I believed it with every fiber of my being. Slowly, something dawned on me. He called us to jump off that cliff. We never discussed the landing. I had always assumed I would succeed, but success is not always part of the equation.

Sometimes you're called to fall.

Eight years later, though, I'm a full-time musician, and every day I use the skills I learned through that painful experience. And should God call us to something else? My wife and I will jump then too.

---

* *Bradford Loomis is a singer and songwriter whose albums include* Bravery and the Bell *and* Into the Great Unknown. *He is a little tired of people telling him he looks like Hagrid from the Harry Potter series, even though he totally looks like Hagrid from Harry Potter.*

CHAPTER 24

Francis Schaeffer

FUNDAMENTALIST FOR JESUS

BY JARED BROCK

Meditation: Do not forget to show hospitality to strangers, for by so doing some people have shown hospitality to angels without knowing it.

—HEBREWS 13:2

Quote of the Day: I dare you. I dare you in the name of Jesus Christ. Do what I am going to suggest. Begin by opening your home.

—FRANCIS SCHAEFFER

Francis August Schaeffer was born in January 1912 in Pennsylvania. He was educated in Maryland and Virginia, pastored in Missouri, received honorary doctorates in California and Massachusetts, and died in Minnesota. This Bearded Gospel Man got around.

In his early twenties, Schaeffer married the daughter of a missionary who had served with Hudson Taylor as the assistant editor of China Inland Mission's magazine *China's Millions*. They met in a strange fashion: they first caught each other's eye when they both stood at a youth meeting to defend Christian orthodoxy. The girl's Chinese name was Mei Fuh—meaning "beautiful happiness"—and she is now considered one of the top one hundred women who shaped twentieth-century Christianity.

Schaeffer became a Presbyterian minister, but he was a separatist at best. He fought battle after battle on theological issues, and it began to wear on him. Schaeffer soon realized that his growing cadre of fundamentalists weren't very loving, and his own spiritual life was brittle and dry. After a two-year spiritual struggle in which a fearful Edith/Mei Fuh prayed without ceasing, Schaeffer came to this conclusion:

> The local church or Christian group should be right, but it should also be beautiful. The local group should be the example of the supernatural, of the substantially healed relationship in this present life between men and men. . . . How many orthodox local churches are dead at this point, with so little sign of love and communication: orthodox, but dead and ugly! If there is no reality on the local level, we deny what we say we believe.[1]

When the Presbyterians didn't totally accept this notion, the Schaeffers resigned and moved to Huámoz, Switzerland, in 1955. Rather than start a ministry, recruit a board, or ask for money, Francis and Edith Schaeffer decided simply to open their home to those seeking answers to life's tough questions. They called their retreat L'Abri—the French word for "the shelter." They didn't advertise or market. They just prayed and opened their doors. Their eldest daughter started bringing home friends from college on the weekends, and soon word spread that L'Abri was a safe place. "This was and is the real basis of L'Abri," Schaeffer insisted. "Teaching the historic Christian answers and giving honest answers to honest questions."[2]

Thanks to Edith's warm hospitality and Francis's listening ear and thoughtful wisdom, they were soon hosting dozens each weekend in addition to teaching weekday classes in Switzerland and Italy. But it wasn't all angels and glory: "In about the first three years of L'Abri all our wedding presents were wiped out. Our sheets were torn. Holes were burned in our rugs. Indeed once a whole curtain almost burned up from somebody smoking in our living room. . . . Everybody came to our table. It couldn't happen any other way. Drugs came to our place. People vomited in our rooms."[3]

Many of the visiting students were well versed in humanist philosophy, and while they schooled him with post-Christian thought, Schaeffer watched the toll it was taking on their lives. They didn't know the difference between right and wrong. Their lives were meaningless. They were self-destructing. All this drove Schaeffer to deepen his understanding of modern culture.

Half spiritual community and half philosophy seminary, Schaeffer wanted to provide a space for people to find satisfying answers to highly intellectual questions. He believed that "biblical Christianity can be rationally defended."[4] Thousands of young people came to visit—some for weeks, others for years—including Os Guinness, the Christian author and great-great-great-grandson of the founder of the namesake Dublin brewery. Even LSD guru Timothy Leary made an appearance.

It's hard to put Schaeffer in a box. He was a fundamentalist preacher who ran a student commune and dressed like an Alpine hiker when lecturing. He wore his hair long and white, with a beard to match. He went head-to-head with theologian Karl Barth, but preferred art museums and cinemas. He rarely quoted from the Bible, but insisted on its wholesale inerrancy.

Yet Schaeffer's work among young people in Switzerland had a profound impact, and by the time his message reached America, it shook the nation. According to *Christianity Today*:

> Perhaps no intellectual save C. S. Lewis affected the thinking of evangelicals more profoundly; perhaps no leader of the period save Billy Graham left a deeper stamp on the movement as a whole. Together the Schaeffers gave currency to the idea of intentional Christian community, prodded evangelicals out of their cultural ghetto, inspired an army of evangelicals to become serious scholars, encouraged women who chose roles as mothers and homemakers, mentored the leaders of the New Christian Right, and solidified popular evangelical opposition to abortion."[5]

Audiences sat spellbound as Schaeffer railed with reason against compromise in the church and idiocy in the world. Historian Arlin Migliazzo remembered the encounter with the small, fifty-two-year-old Swiss preacher: "Schaeffer showed me that Christians didn't have to be dumb."[6]

Schaeffer influenced a generation of conservative Christian leaders, including Jerry Falwell, Pat Robertson, Tim LaHaye, and Chuck Colson, but he also influenced hippie-types like musician Larry Norman and Jesus People organizer Jack Sparks. He also found time to write twenty-seven books in all. One of his more audacious works was *A Christian Manifesto*. Written as a counter to the *Communist Manifesto* and the *Humanist Manifesto*, it laid out proposals for how Christians should live in an increasingly secular society. The book sold 290,000 copies in its first year in print.

Yet unlike his politically motivated counterparts, Schaeffer railed against the evangelical church, even telling them to get rid of American flags in their buildings, saying, "Patriotic loyalty must not be identified with Christianity."[7] Schaeffer was far more cultured and nuanced than the Moral Majority, and though conservative, he wasn't part of the establishment.

Starting from their humble beginnings in a Swiss cabin overlooking the Rhone Valley, today the L'Abri community boasts seven chalets with a towering view of the Alps, plus additional study centers across eight countries on three continents. L'Abri became a home for thousands of spiritual pilgrims, whose all-night conversations with their bearded host often left them transformed. As D. A. Carson put it: "In the aeons to come, there will be hundreds, perhaps thousands, of redeemed men and women who will rise up and call him blessed for helping them to escape from various intellectual and moral quagmires."[8]

And it all started by opening his doors.

> You don't need a big program. You don't have to convince your session or board. All you have to do is open your home and begin. And there is no place in God's world where there are no people who will come and share a home as long as it is a real home.[9]

CONTEMPLATION

1. What do you believe that is unpopular but biblical?
2. How can you turn your house into a gospel home?
3. What small start can you make toward impacting the church and the world?

PRAYER

Father of truth, we long for Your wisdom. Guide us in the way we should go. Correct our paths, that we may walk in Your truth.

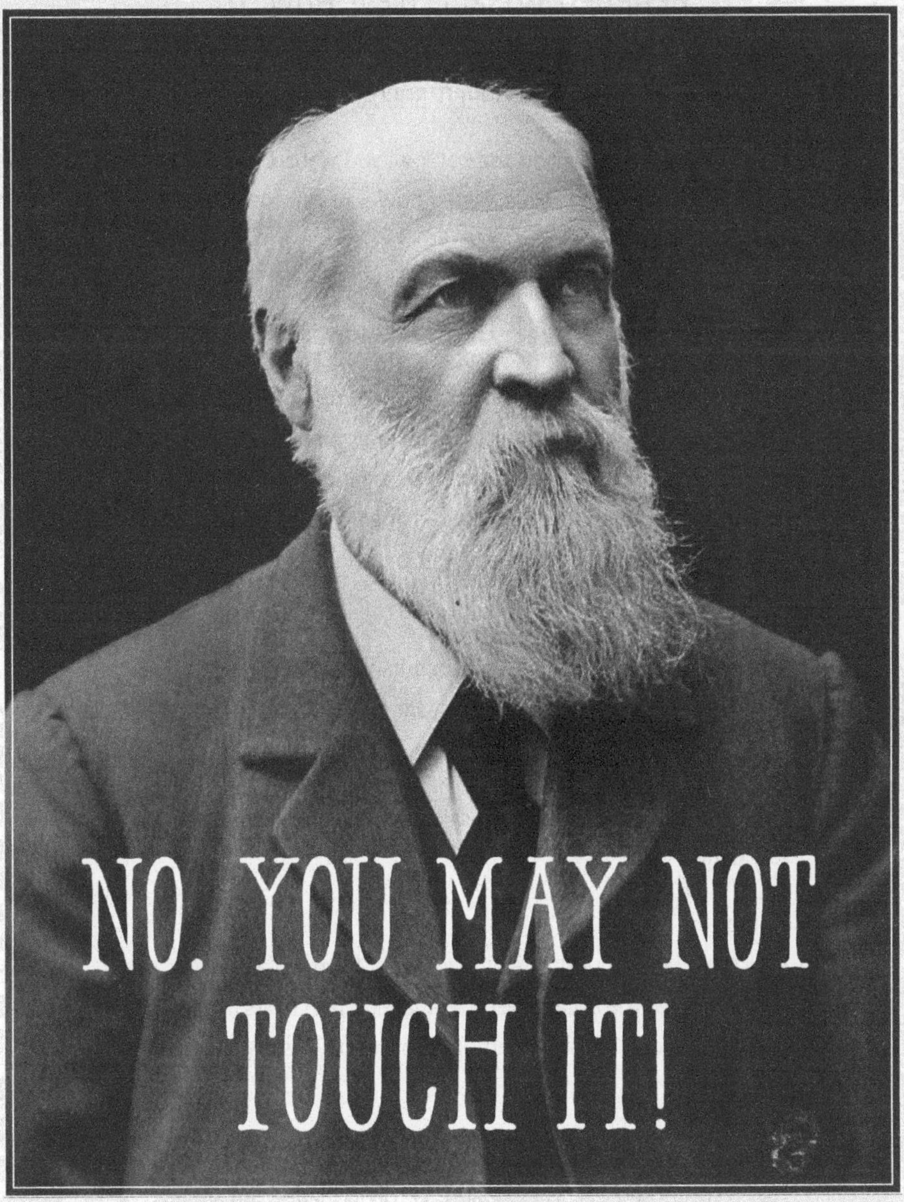
NO. YOU MAY NOT
TOUCH IT!

BEARDED GOSPEL DIET: HOW TO EAT FOR BEARD GREATNESS

BY JARED BROCK

You can brush and oil and stare at it all you want, but true beardliness starts from the inside. Here's how you can eat your way to a better beard:

BOOST TESTOSTERONE

You can promote beard growth by boosting your testosterone. Don't get crazy with this, because super-amped testosterone can elevate your risk of a heart attack. For creation-care purposes I'm recommending you generally avoid meat (beef especially), but there are plenty of other ways to get protein:

Tofu
Scared? Don't be. Get the extra-firm organic stuff, slice it thin, and braise it with buffalo or barbecue sauce.

Beans and Lentils
Any kind. There are hundreds. I love black beans and chickpeas and red lentils.

Salmon
Delicious and nutritious. Get it line-caught from Alaska. Failing that, shoot for the Pacific over the Atlantic. Fresh beats frozen. To keep those good fats from getting damaged, try it slow-baked or poached.

Eggs
Hair is composed mainly of keratin, a protein made from amino

acids. We can't make our own aminos, so we need protein. Get free-range organic eggs, and cook them ever so lightly in order to keep that fatty yolk undamaged. Try soft boiled, barely over easy, or my favorite, poached with lox and avocado.

IN ADDITION TO PROTEIN . . .

Supplements

Don't have time to create a totally balanced diet? Grab a high-performance multivitamin and add B12, biotin, and fish oil.

Pumpkin Seeds

Hair loss is often linked to low zinc levels, and these delicious green snacks are full of zinc. Get 'em raw and organic.

Cinnamon

Killer antifungal/viral/oxidant that improves circulation to follicles. Add to desserts or stir into oatmeal or coffee.

Orange Stuff

Vitamin A maintains skin tissue. You need vitamin A. Beta-carotene converts to vitamin A in your body. You need beta-carotene. You get it from orange stuff like pumpkins, carrots, papayas, and sweet potatoes. Cheez Whiz doesn't count.

Broccoli

The ultimate green. Buy it organic, steam it gently, and squeeze a lemon on top.

Spinach

Think Popeye, but with a beard. Buy the organic stuff and add it to everything—scrambled eggs, smoothies, sandwiches, soups and stews, burgers. When we're home, I make a greens pie about once a week.

Don't like veggies? You can also lift weights to boost testosterone. But you really should do what your mama told ya and eat your greens. Real men listen to their mamas.

CHAPTER 25

Saint Patrick

SLAVE TO SNAKE FIGHTER

BY AARON ALFORD

Meditation: I have given you authority to trample on snakes and scorpions and to overcome all the power of the enemy; nothing will harm you.

—LUKE 10:19

Quote of the Day: My name is Patrick. I am a sinner, a simple country person, and the least of all believers.

—SAINT PATRICK

The runaway slave fell to the ground, exhausted. The scent of salt water and the sound of crashing waves filled his senses, and the possibility of freedom filled his eyes with tears. Six years ago, he had landed on these same shores in chains, torn from his family and everything and everyone he loved. He was only a boy of sixteen. Now he was a young man of twenty-two, and his heart was nearly bursting with hope. If he could find passage on a sailing vessel, he would soon be home.

Patrick was born into Roman citizenship on the British Isles in 387. His father was a deacon of the church, and his family was wealthy and well respected. Patrick's life was comfortable, and his future seemed secure. He would probably obtain a position of service within the church, as his father and grandfather had. Nothing too grand or demanding great sacrifice, of course, but of service. Perhaps he would work in government or teaching, or another respectable and comfortable area. He would live a good, pleasant life, free from much hardship.

But there's just no accounting for pirates.

They came through his town like a storm, and when they reached Patrick's home, he found himself kicking and screaming, desperately trying to escape the hold of an Irish marauder, to no avail. Afraid and confused, the young man who had been given everything found himself on a slave ship, stripped of everything, and sailing west. When they landed on the shores of Ireland, land of the Celts, Patrick was sold to a cruel Druid named Milchu and taken to work in what is now Northern Ireland.

Although Patrick had been raised with the Christian faith as part of his family's lifestyle, he had no true knowledge of God, no interest in Jesus, and certainly no desire to live a holy Christian life. With iron manacles around his hands, this all changed. Suddenly God was no longer a nice idea, but the object of Patrick's desperate prayers. Young Patrick discovered a God he had never known before.

> The Lord opened the sense of my unbelief that I might at last remember my sins and be converted with all my heart to the Lord my God, who had regard for my abjection, and mercy on my youth and ignorance, and watched over me before I knew Him . . . and comforted me as would a father his son.[1]

Milchu put him to work in his fields as a shepherd, and as Patrick tended these sheep, he found his relationship with the Shepherd of his soul growing ever deeper. Patrick spent days in the fields with the sheep, often with meager provisions. Through snow, through frost, through rain, through hunger, the presence of God became warmth to his soul.

Patrick also learned a great deal of the language and culture of his captors. Beneath the barbaric practices of the religion common to Ireland, which may even have included human sacrifice, Patrick saw the beauty of people made in the image of God. Something of Himself remained in them, some piece of eternity in their hearts.

One night he had a dream that seemed to be sent from God, and Patrick received it as a sign to make an escape. Through darkness and cold and over the forbidding wilderness, Patrick ran. Two hundred miles later, he reached the shores of northeastern Ireland and begged for passage on a ship bound for Britain.

Months after setting sail, Patrick returned to his hometown a different person than the boy who had been stolen away years before. His faith was alive, even dangerous. He began studying for the priesthood and even went on dangerous missionary journeys throughout Britain. But Patrick never forgot the people of Ireland, and one night in a dream, he heard the voice of the Irish people calling out from their shores: "We ask you, boy, come and walk among us once more."[2]

Patrick obeyed. While Christianity was not unknown in Ireland, missionary efforts to bring the true faith to its people were limited both in scope and success. Many considered these isolated people simply too barbaric and violent to ever hear and understand the gospel. But Patrick knew the Irish people and their culture intimately. He knew their joys, and he knew the fears that drove their pagan practices. Because of this, he knew how to communicate the gospel effectively.

When he landed with his missionary companions on the shores

of Ireland, one of the first things he did was to seek out his former master and pay him the price of his own ransom. From there he traveled throughout Ireland. When he met a chieftain named Dichu, who intended to strike him down with a sword, the man found he could not lift his arm to do so. Patrick preached the gospel to the man in a way he could understand, and Dichu was converted. Dichu gave Patrick one of his barns, which became the first church dedicated to Christ by Patrick.

On Easter of 433, Patrick found himself engaging in a spiritual duel of sorts with the Druid priests and magicians. There was a great pagan gathering of chieftains, and the Druid priests tried once and for all to silence Patrick and drive him (and his religion) out of their midst. Patrick had lit an Easter fire, a bonfire traditionally lit on the evening before Easter morning that symbolizes the light of Christ and His resurrection. The Druids could not extinguish it. They called down a demonic darkness. Patrick dispelled it with a prayer. In a demonstration of their supposed power, "the Arch-Druid Lochru, like Simon Magus of old, was lifted up high in the air, but when Patrick knelt in prayer the druid from his flight was dashed to pieces upon a rock."[3]

The inferiority of Druidism to Patrick's Christian faith was dramatically demonstrated to chieftains gathered from all over the country, and there was an extraordinary breakthrough for the gospel. One of the legends surrounding the life of Saint Patrick says that he drove all the snakes off the island. Truth be told, there is no evidence that Ireland ever had any snakes (New Zealand, Iceland, and Greenland are also snake-free). It's likely, though, that this legend came about because of the way snakes often symbolize evil in Scripture. Patrick did not drive literal snakes from Ireland, but by his work and witness, the serpent-like stranglehold of Druid superstition was loosened and eventually driven out. In Patrick's enslavement, the snake of paganism had struck at Patrick's heel, but Christ in the end had crushed its head.

Patrick would spend the rest of his days as an itinerant pastor, a shepherd of the people he loved so dearly. Somehow, in the evil that had been done to him in his kidnapping and enslavement, Patrick found his calling. Evil had been turned to good. The runaway slave had returned a free man, a slave of Christ, and a servant of the Irish people.

Patrick is said to have prayed this famous prayer in preparation for his confrontation with the Druids. It's a prayer that beautifully summarizes the depth of his faith and the source of his courage:

I arise today
Through a mighty strength, the invocation of the Trinity,
Through a belief in the Threeness,
Through confession of the Oneness
Of the Creator of creation.
I arise today
Through the strength of Christ's birth and His baptism,
Through the strength of His crucifixion and His burial,
Through the strength of His resurrection and His ascension,
Through the strength of His descent for the judgment of doom.
I arise today
Through the strength of the love of cherubim,
In obedience of angels,
In service of archangels,
In the hope of resurrection to meet with reward,
In the prayers of patriarchs,
In preachings of the apostles,
In faiths of confessors,
In innocence of virgins,
In deeds of righteous men.
I arise today
Through the strength of heaven;

Light of the sun,
Splendor of fire,
Speed of lightning,
Swiftness of the wind,
Depth of the sea,
Stability of the earth,
Firmness of the rock.
I arise today
Through God's strength to pilot me;
God's might to uphold me,
God's wisdom to guide me,
God's eye to look before me,
God's ear to hear me,
God's word to speak for me,
God's hand to guard me,
God's way to lie before me,
God's shield to protect me,
God's hosts to save me
From snares of the devil,
From temptations of vices,
From every one who desires me ill,
Afar and anear,
Alone or in a multitude.
I summon today all these powers between me and evil,
Against every cruel merciless power that opposes my body and soul,
Against incantations of false prophets,
Against black laws of pagandom,
Against false laws of heretics,
Against craft of idolatry,
Against spells of women and smiths and wizards,
Against every knowledge that corrupts man's body and soul.
Christ shield me today

Against poison, against burning,
Against drowning, against wounding,
So that reward may come to me in abundance.
Christ with me, Christ before me, Christ behind me,
Christ in me, Christ beneath me, Christ above me,
Christ on my right, Christ on my left,
Christ when I lie down, Christ when I sit down,
Christ in the heart of every man who thinks of me,
Christ in the mouth of every man who speaks of me,
Christ in the eye that sees me,
Christ in the ear that hears me.
I arise today
Through a mighty strength, the invocation of the Trinity,
Through a belief in the Threeness,
Through a confession of the Oneness
Of the Creator of creation.[4]

CONTEMPLATION

1. Have you seen bad circumstances turn to good in your life? Did you discover some aspect of your own calling through them?
2. Are you in the midst of a difficult time now? What are you learning in the midst of it? Are you discovering anything about who God has made you to be?
3. What might God be speaking to you about your own calling?

PRAYER

Holy Spirit, speak to us in our worst circumstances, that in them we might find You.

Growing a beard
is too irritating?
ITCH, PLEASE!

THE LEGEND OF SAINT PATRICK AND THE FORMERLY DEAD GIANT

BY JONATHAN ROGERS*

Saint Patrick's beard was not an orange chinstrap. That's a leprechaun you're thinking about. According to the portraits and stained-glass windows, Patrick's beard was white and well groomed—not as well groomed as that of The Most Interesting Man in the World, but in that ballpark. Indeed, the legends that sprang up around Saint Patrick do have about them the aroma of The Most Interesting Man in the World, or perhaps Chuck Norris, that other bearded saint.

According to one legend, baby Patrick provided the holy water for his own baptism by causing water to spring out of the ground. The same holy water healed the blindness of the priest who was to baptize Patrick—and also gave the previously illiterate priest the ability to read the baptism!

In another legend, a young Patrick was out playing one cold day and came home with an armload of ice chunks. His nurse scolded him, saying he would have been better off to bring home an armload of firewood. So he piled up the ice chunks like fire logs, made the sign of the cross, blew on them, and they flared up into a nice little fire.

The Patrick legends demonstrate the connection between holiness and comedy—and by comedy I don't mean merely the humorous, but the divine comedy whereby every sad thing eventually becomes untrue, and life overwhelms death.

Perhaps this marriage of holiness and comedy—both high comedy and low comedy—is most apparent in a story recorded in *The Life and Acts of Saint Patrick* by Jocelin of Furness.

Patrick, according to the story, was traveling across Ireland on one of his preaching journeys, accompanied by the disciples who often accompanied him, when he came across an enormous tomb. The tomb was so enormous, in fact, that Patrick's followers wouldn't believe that it could contain the body of any man.

Patrick, however, was convinced that this was the tomb of a giant. To prove it, he prayed that God would raise the dead giant back to life. And it happened even as Patrick had prayed. A living, breathing giant, "horrible in stature and in aspect," awakened from the dust and stood before the saint and his followers. When he looked on Patrick, the terrible giant broke down weeping. For he had been suffering the punishments of hell since his death and was grateful to have been released if even for just an hour.

The giant begged Patrick to allow him to join his travel party. But Patrick refused on the grounds that the giant was just too big and ugly and scary to accompany him on his evangelistic travels: "No man for very terror could stand before his countenance." But Patrick did him one better: he preached the gospel to the giant. The giant believed, was baptized, then died again, this time freed from the torments of hell.[5]

The monstrous, the horrible, and the barbaric folded into the love of a God who laughs. Those great reversals are the divine comedy.

---

* *Jonathan Rogers is the author of* The Charlatan's Boy, The Wilderking Trilogy, *and* The Terrible Speed of Mercy. *Portions of this piece previously appeared in an excellent biography he wrote about Saint Patrick called . . .* Saint Patrick!

CHAPTER 26

Thomas Barnardo

MUTTON-CHOPPED CITY BUILDER

BY JARED BROCK

Meditation: Jesus said, "Let the little children come to me, and do not hinder them, for the kingdom of heaven belongs to such as these."

—MATTHEW 19:14

Quote of the Day: The work to me is everything, and I would throw every rule overboard and send them to the bottom of the sea tomorrow, if I felt there were a more excellent way.

—THOMAS BARNARDO

Thomas John Barnardo was born in Dublin, Ireland, in 1845. He converted to Christianity as a teenager, and just before his seventeenth birthday, he decided to become a medical missionary in China. He enrolled at the prestigious London Hospital in Whitechapel in 1866 and set sail for England.

Victorian London was in the throes of the Industrial Revolution, and the East End slums of London were overcrowded and rife with poverty and disease. Within months of Barnardo's arrival, a cholera outbreak swept through the neighborhood and killed more than three thousand people. Thousands of children were abandoned to the streets and forced to beg.

On March 2, 1868, Barnardo started an East End mission in two small cottages in Limehouse called Hope Place. He named it the Ragged School.

One evening after classes had finished at 9:30 p.m., a young boy named Jim Jarvis was slow to leave on a cold evening. Barnardo shooed him out the door, not wanting the boy's mother to get worried. Little Jarvis explained that he had no mother, and that he slept in a hay cart in Whitechapel. The young medical candidate needed to see for himself. The boy guided Barnardo through the East End and showed him children sleeping on rooftops and in gutters. This discovery had a profound impact on him. A member of Parliament and fellow Bearded Gospel Man, Anthony Ashley-Cooper, the Seventh Earl of Shaftesbury, encouraged him to do something about it. At age twenty-three, young Barnardo gave up his plan of going to China, dropped out of university, and devoted his life to serving destitute children.

At first Barnardo placed a limit on the number of boys who could stay overnight at his shelter. One evening, an eleven-year-old named John Somers—nicknamed Carrots because of his red hair—was turned away because the shelter was full. Two days later the boy was found dead from exposure in an old barrel. Barnardo vowed never to turn away another child, and hung a sign that read: No Destitute Child Ever Refused Admission.[1]

Within two years Barnardo purchased property and started training boys in metalwork, carpentry, and shoemaking, enabling them to gain apprenticeships and careers. In 1872—way ahead of his time—he converted an old gin joint into a coffeehouse and mission church.

The following year he married a fellow evangelist and philanthropist, Sara Louise Elmslie, and leased sixty acres to open a home for girls. Within three years he owned the land. The Girls' Village

Home—affectionately nicknamed Barnardoville—grew to include sixty-five cottages, a church, a hospital, and a school for fifteen hundred girls. The training provided was so thorough that the girls were hired by wealthy and aristocratic families.

The couple had seven children of their own, including Marjorie, who was born with Down Syndrome. Caring for his daughter taught Barnardo about the needs of disabled children, and he set up several specialist homes for kids with both physical and learning disabilities.

Barnardo took regular forays into the slums to find destitute boys and was attacked on many occasions, having two of his ribs broken in the process. He even visited the brothels and encouraged the prostituted women—one of whom was later murdered by Jack the Ripper—to let him care for their children.[2]

In the meantime, the Ragged School continued to grow. By his thirtieth birthday, Barnardo had purchased a dozen properties and a children's magazine, and had started an employment agency, a church, a coffeehouse, a village, and a school. He also managed to go back to school himself. Though he was known as Doctor Barnardo throughout his life, he didn't actually complete his studies until 1876.

According to the *Irish Post*, Barnardo also found time to write 192 books, which we can all agree seems preposterous. Barnado died of heart complications at age sixty, completely worn out from his exhausting service to humanity. At the time of his death, Barnardo's mission cared for eighty-five hundred children across ninety-six homes, had sent more than seventeen thousand children to start a new life in Canada, and had protected and raised more than sixty thousand children in all.

Shortly after his death, a fund was established to ensure the homes would be maintained in perpetuity. One hundred fifty years later, you can still visit the Ragged School Museum in London. And Barnardo's is now the biggest children's charity in the United Kingdom, raising around a half billion dollars per year to help kids in need.

CONTEMPLATION

1. When was the last time you encountered the poorest of the poor?
2. How can you help ensure no child goes destitute in our world?
3. In what ways can you help in raising the next generation of gospel children?

PRAYER

Father of the fatherless, thank You for adopting us. May we, as princes in Your kingdom, do our part to serve Your children.

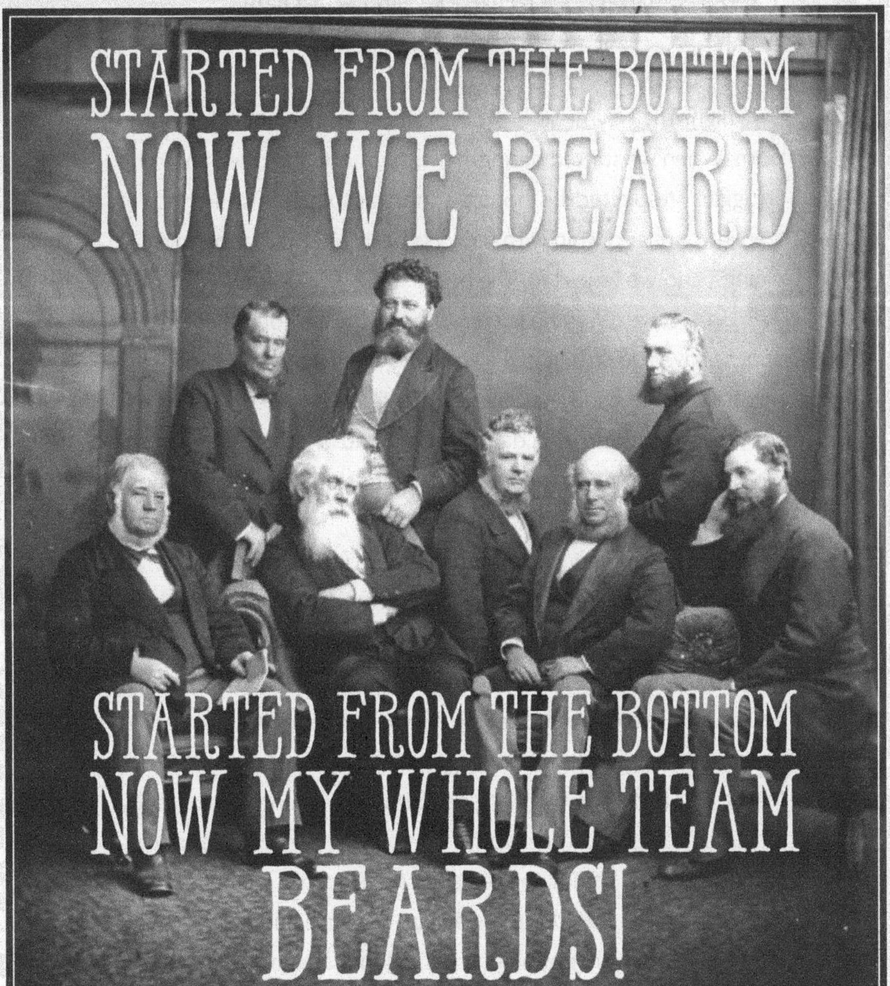
STARTED FROM THE BOTTOM
NOW WE BEARD
STARTED FROM THE BOTTOM
NOW MY WHOLE TEAM
BEARDS!

AN OPEN LETTER TO ALL MY BROTHERS WHO STRUGGLE WITH PORN

BY (NAME WITHHELD)

Last night my boyfriend and I broke up because he's addicted to porn. When we started dating, he was upfront and open about his struggle. I respected his honesty and transparency, so I chose to step into a relationship with him. We both believe that people can change, and we hoped for the best.

Unfortunately, the patterns of behavior we hoped would disappear have too strong of a grip on his life right now. He couldn't forget what he had been engaging in for over a decade. He was powerless to undo the damage that had shaped his views of women, sex, marriage, and faithfulness. For these reasons, we chose to step away from the relationship.

For all you men out there who wonder if porn is really a problem, you need to know this: engaging in pornography is unfaithfulness. Entertaining a sexual image of any woman other than your wife—whether present or future—is sinful. And by *sinful* I mean that it breaks relationship between you and God as well as other people. It bears far-reaching consequences that you may not realize, but I promise will bring deep regret. Viewing pornography changes the way you see women, it changes the way you understand sex, and it denies you the ability to step into true manhood.

Pornography shapes the way you perceive and interact with women. Women are not objects to be dominated or controlled for your own selfish pleasure. On the screen they may do your bidding, but this breeds an unrealistic expectation. When you dominate or control a woman, you oppress her. She is no longer free to choose love or to live out of a place of beauty and strength. When you meet a woman who will not be dominated or controlled, you will be confronted with your own insecurities and weaknesses. A good man never dominates or controls another person for his own pleasure. You forfeit your ability to grow into a godly man if you allow the lie of porn to invade the way you think about women and sex.

You attack the security and identity of women when you engage in porn. Most women do not look like the women on the screen. When your woman finds out that you've been choosing porn instead of her, she will think something is wrong with her, that she is not enough. She will compare herself to the thousands of women you have consumed. She will never be enough because she can't compete with the buffet you have gorged yourself on. She will question her value and her very identity. She will grow in insecurity, not because she isn't beautiful, but because you are not satisfied. This will destroy your intimacy. It will threaten to destroy her.

Pornography changes the way you understand sex. When you engage in porn, you are denying yourself the ability to experience true intimacy. Sex is meant to be the fullest expression of love and commitment in marriage. Sex is meant to be mutually enjoyed and celebrated. At the heart of marriage is the commitment to "forsake all others." This is because the commitment of marriage is built on trust. Engaging in pornography is inviting other women into your sexual experience. Trust is broken when another person enters that sacred union.

You were wired for intimacy. When you seek gratification through porn, that wiring is short-circuited and your brain bonds to those pornographic images rather than to your (present or future) wife. By bonding to porn, you experience an unnatural high that cannot be reached in marriage. Your body begins to crave porn more and more and your wife less and less. Take note: men who regularly view porn can have decreased attraction to their partner. They can be unable to be aroused by their partner.

Thousands have experienced porn-induced erectile dysfunction, and many more are increasingly dissatisfied with their partner's looks and their sexual experiences.

Godly manhood is defined by selfless responsibility. This kind of man is worthy of respect and submission. Porn denies you the opportunity to step into godly manhood because porn breeds selfishness. By seeking immediate gratification you strip yourself of the ability to act in love. True love is patient. Lust is demanding. Love waits for the other to be ready. Lust demands sex now. Love runs the other way when temptation is aroused. Lust consumes without consideration of others or the consequences. Love fights with every tactic for the intimacy it knows is worth it. Lust is too proud to do whatever it takes, especially if it exposes weakness. Porn ultimately denies you the ability to truly love.

Porn also breeds insecurity. The imbalance in your brain due to the unnatural highs you've experienced lead to problems such as anxiety, frequent masturbation with little satisfaction, an inability to concentrate, and a lack of motivation. Porn makes you unable to cope with the challenges of life. When the stress comes, you resort to childish reactions. It exposes your weak foundation. You need a stronger, more secure foundation.

Men, you need to know: not every guy does it. Yes, men are visual, but not every man watches porn. Godly men don't watch porn because they realize that the women on the screen are our sisters, our daughters, and our friends. They are real people. They have value and they are worth more than your momentary pleasure. The most joy-filled men I know are not mastered by porn. They are the ones who have embraced their responsibility of selfless love and are living out godly manhood.

While pornography may have a grip on your life, you can choose to move toward freedom. I hope that you will find help so you can enjoy the sexual fulfillment you were created for. Speak up and be honest about your struggle.

Most of all, repent fully before the Lord and begin to let love, rather than lust, be your standard. May we all have strength to live into the life-changing truth that love is patient and kind. Love does not envy or boast. It is not proud or rude. Love does not insist on its own way. Love is not irritable or resentful. It does not rejoice at wrongdoing, but rejoices in the truth.

My brother, you are loved. You have incredible worth. We need you to step up and overcome this. We need you to fight for purity. We're backing you 100 percent. Will you make a change today?

CHAPTER 27

Josiah Henson

A GREAT NORTH AMERICAN

BY AARON ALFORD AND JARED BROCK

Meditation: It is for freedom that Christ has set us free. Stand firm, then, and do not let yourselves be burdened again by a yoke of slavery.

—GALATIANS 5:1

Quote of the Day: I will use my freedom well.

—JOSIAH HENSON

Born into slavery in Maryland in 1789, Josiah Henson's first memory is brutal beyond words: His father, bleeding and weeping. His master's overseer had sexually assaulted the young boy's mother. Henson's father attacked the man in defense of his wife and was punished cruelly. For striking a white man, Henson's father was bound to a post and publicly whipped. He was given one hundred lashes to the whites of his spine. His ear was then nailed to a post and severed with a sharp knife. The man burst into the family cabin, howling in pain, back mangled, blood pouring down his face. Months later, he was sold south to Louisiana, never to be seen again.

Such a parting wasn't uncommon in Josiah's day. Husbands were routinely taken from their wives, mothers from their children. Two years later, Josiah's master died. The boy and his five older siblings were sold at the public auction. Mrs. Henson was sold to Isaac Riley, a blacksmith and drunkard. She begged the young man to purchase her baby, but he kicked her mercilessly until she crawled out of reach. Josiah was sold to Adam Robb, a tavern owner and stage-coach manager who also trafficked children for profit. Josiah was thrown in his slave quarters, surrounded by strangers. The shock of the separation took a toll on the tiny boy's body, and he soon lay gravely ill. Robb was convinced the boy was going to die, so he made Riley an offer: If the blacksmith took the kid and he died, Riley owed him nothing. If Josiah's mother managed to nurse him back to health, Riley would owe Robb some horseshoeing services. A deal was struck, and Josiah was reunited with his mother.

Josiah survived and grew into a strong young man. He became a profitable asset to Isaac Riley, and soon he ran the whole plantation. As horrific as the conditions of slavery were, Josiah refused to attempt an escape. It was all he'd ever known, and he was proud of his position and achievements. He was convinced he could purchase freedom for himself rather than become a fugitive slave.

One Sunday Josiah received a travel pass to go hear John McKenny, a baker, preach the gospel outside a local mill. McKenny was an "upright, benevolent Christian"[1] who despised slavery and refused to use slave labor in his business dealings. Josiah wasn't allowed inside the church building, but was so overwhelmed by the message that he gave his life to Jesus in the woods on the way home. He later wrote of this event:

> The divine character of Jesus Christ, his tender love for mankind, his forgiving spirit, his compassion for the outcast and despised, his cruel crucifixion and glorious ascension, were all depicted, and

> some of the points were dwelt on with great power; great, at least, to me, who then heard of these things for the first time in my life. Again and again did the preacher reiterate the words "for every man." These glad tidings, this salvation, were not for the benefit of a select few only. They were for the slave as well as the master, the poor as well as the rich, for the persecuted, the distressed, the heavy-laden, the captive; for me among the rest, a poor, despised, abused creature, deemed of others fit for nothing but unrequited toil—but mental and bodily degradation. O, the blessedness and sweetness of feeling that I was loved![2]

Josiah's inner life was transformed. "Swallowed up in the beauty of the divine love, I loved my enemies, and prayed for them that did despitefully use and entreat me," he later wrote in his autobiography.[3] Led by this divine love, Josiah, while still a slave, took every advantage for religious education his position as a superintendent on the plantation afforded him. He got married to a fellow slave and became an ordained Methodist minister in his early twenties.

Isaac Riley was an inveterate gambler and constant drunk who, despite Josiah's skillful management of the plantation, managed to get himself into so much debt that his slaves were to be confiscated. Josiah was terrified to be sold south, away from his wife and children, so he volunteered to smuggle all of Isaac's slaves to his brother's plantation in Kentucky. Amos Riley's plantation was far larger—thousands of acres and more than one hundred slaves—and soon Josiah managed multiple farms. He was given a travel pass and started to save money by preaching on Sundays at churches that favored abolitionist causes.

Still convinced that he could obtain his freedom through "legitimate" means, Josiah struck a bargain with his owner to purchase his freedom for $450. Josiah put a down payment of $350, and a contract was written that he would obtain his freedom when he had paid the last $100. But he soon discovered a treacherous trick. The Riley brothers had doctored the legal note: a zero added to the one hundred. It was a debt he could never repay.

Devastated by this deceit, Josiah realized he would not obtain his freedom by any legal means. It would be another two years, however, before he and his family had an opportunity for escape. The day came when Josiah's owner planned to sell him away from his wife and four children. Desperate, Josiah arranged an escape. The family journeyed hundreds of miles on foot, through wilderness and woods, traveling by night and resting by day, facing near starvation and capture at every turn. At last they came to the Niagara River near Buffalo, New York. Just across that river was Canada, and freedom.

On October 28, 1830, in his early forties—and with the help of a kind Scottish captain who paid the way—Josiah Henson's feet touched the Canadian shore. Overcome with joy, he wept and danced and kissed the soil. He and his family were free at last.

But Josiah's escape from slavery was only the beginning. He had promised the captain that he would use his freedom well, and Henson went straight to work. The newly freed man saw that many slaves who had escaped to Canada only knew how to live in subservience and found themselves in economically servile situations. Some worked on farms, some in tobacco fields, often doing the same kind of work they had done as slaves, with no thought toward improving their circumstances. So he began to create a self-sufficient school where former slaves had the opportunity to learn a variety of trade skills. He eventually began selling high-quality Canadian black walnut lumber, hiring and training many former slaves and finding great success in exporting his lumber to Great Britain.

Josiah often returned to the United States, sometimes at great personal risk, to assist other fugitive slaves in finding their freedom through the Underground Railroad. Both as a Methodist minister and as an abolitionist, Father Henson preached the gospel and spoke out against slavery from the pulpit and other public forums. He personally returned to rescue 118 slaves and welcomed another 500 to his free-man settlement, called Dawn. Father Henson wasn't content with enjoying his personal freedom. He traded the oppression of slavery for the freedom of servanthood.

CONTEMPLATION

1. What is the difference between physical freedom and freedom in Christ?
2. What freedoms do you enjoy that others don't have?
3. How can you use your freedom to free others?

PRAYER

Father of the free, help us to use our freedom on behalf of the poor and powerless.

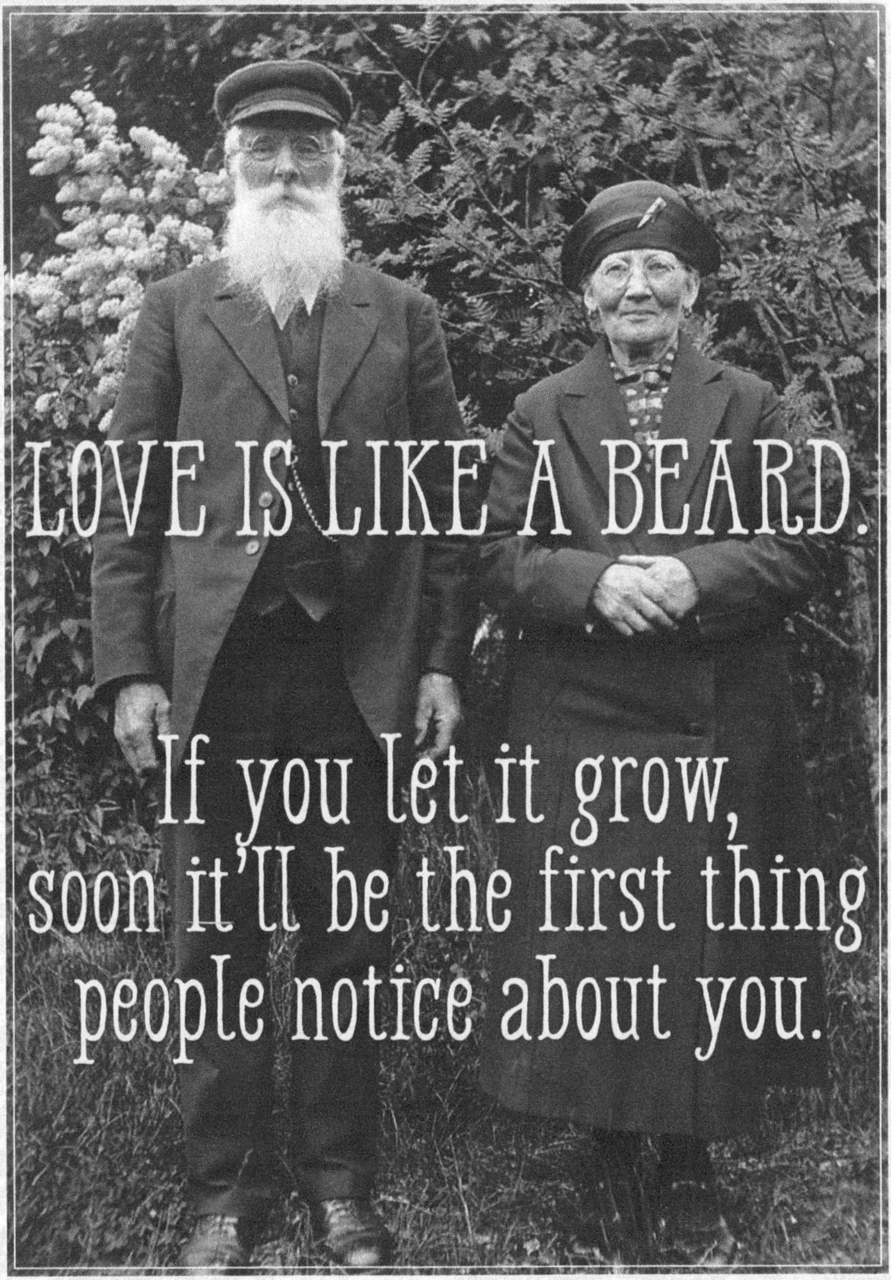
LOVE IS LIKE A BEARD.
If you let it grow,
soon it'll be the first thing
people notice about you.

GODLY GOSPEL WOMEN

BY AARON ALFORD

We have presented in this book an impressive list of remarkable Bearded Gospel Men, from the earliest church fathers to more recent saints. Each of these men holds a unique place in the shared history of the church, and God's grace was revealed in their lives in a unique way. But we would be remiss if we did not acknowledge that Jesus did not establish a church of only men, nor has He given a mandate that only men should inspire men and women inspire women! In a culture that experiences a lot of confusion over gender identity issues, sometimes Christian men overcompensate by defining our masculinity by what it is not. We are masculine by not being feminine. But this can lead to an empty, Christianized form of chauvinism and machismo. If you want to have a truly rich gospel life, you have to get in touch with your feminine side. God has blessed His church with amazing women who led astonishing lives of devotion, and we men need the gifts God wants to give through these women.

Here are just a few Godly Gospel Women whose lives have rich treasures to discover.

CLARE OF ASSISI (1194–1253)

Later in this book, you'll read the story of Saint Francis of Assisi. But one of the greatest influences on his life was his friendship with Clare. When she was eighteen years old, Clare heard Francis give a sermon about poverty and joy. Within a year, she would take religious vows of poverty and chastity and establish an order, which later became known as the Poor Clares. Her love for Jesus was profound and passionate, and she referred to Jesus as her "heavenly spouse."[14] When faced with a difficult decision, Francis often relied on the wisdom of Clare.

THÉRÈSE OF LISIEUX (1873–1897)

Thérèse died at the age of twenty-four, having lived her short adult life in obscurity as a nun at a small convent in northern France. But when her private letters and journals were published as the spiritual autobiography *The Story of a Soul*, they revealed a portrait of a young woman of both astonishing wisdom and childlike love. Thérèse could express deep theological truths with the quaintness of a little girl, and through everyday, often unnoticed acts of service and kindness, she found a way of loving Jesus with remarkable devotion.

CORRIE TEN BOOM (1892–1983)

Corrie and her family lived in Nazi-occupied Holland during World War II, as recorded in her classic book, *The Hiding Place*. After being arrested, Corrie spent ten months in Nazi concentration camps where her sister, who had been arrested with her, died. After the war, Corrie went on to become a kind of ambassador of forgiveness and reconciliation, preaching a message of love for enemies as she traveled Europe and the United States as an author and public speaker.

ELISABETH ELLIOT (1926–2015) AND RACHEL SAINT (1914–1994)

In 1956 Jim Elliot, along with his missionary companions Nate Saint, Ed McCully, Pete Fleming, and Roger Youderian, was speared to death by men of the Waodani tribe in the jungles of Ecuador. The five friends were making first contact in an attempt to bring the Waodani people, known as one of the most violent tribes in Ecuador, the message of the gospel. The story might have ended with their demise if not for the work of Elisabeth Elliot, widow of Jim, and Rachel Saint, sister of Nate, who took up the work of reaching the Waodani people. Nine years after the martyrdom of the five men, one of the children of those men, Steve Saint, was baptized by Mincaye Enquedi, his father's killer. Mincaye had given his life to Jesus as a result of the work of Elisabeth and Rachel, and a once violent people embraced the peace found in Christ. You can read more of their story in *Through Gates of Splendor* by Elisabeth Elliot and *End of the Spear* by Steve Saint.

DOROTHY DAY (1897–1980)

No, not Doris. Dorothy! Doris was a famous actress who sang "Que Sera, Sera." Dorothy was a woman who revolutionized what it meant to serve the urban poor in a modern context. She was an avid pacifist and worked as a peacemaker in both her local community and the world. Jesus Christ, the ultimate bringer of peace, was for her an endless source of love and compassion for the homeless, the addicted, and even her enemies. A prolific writer, she authored several books including her autobiography, *The Long Loneliness*.

These are just a few Godly Gospel Women who have changed and influenced the lives of more than a few Bearded Gospel Men (my own included!), and there are thousands more. So make your mama proud! Get that bearded face of yours into a book and learn about the lives and spirituality of these mothers in the faith.

CHAPTER 28

Charles Monroe Sheldon

MORE THAN BRACELETS

BY JARED BROCK

Meditation: Follow my example, as I follow the example of Christ.

–1 CORINTHIANS 11:1

Quote of the Day: Good resolutions are like babies crying in church. They should be carried out immediately.

–CHARLES SHELDON

Charles Monroe Sheldon was born on February 26, 1857, in Wellsville, New York, but like the epic Bearded Gospel Man that he was, Sheldon grew up in the Dakota Territory in a log cabin that he helped his parents build. His father was the territory's first missionary superintendent, and he didn't mess around: the man started one hundred churches in ten years.

Sheldon started writing at age twelve and managed to sell his work to a Boston newspaper. He was educated at Phillips Academy and took a job as a minister in Waterbury, Connecticut, after graduating from seminary. Sheldon was liberal, innovative, and unorthodox.

The young preacher believed deeply in the social gospel movement, which encouraged Christians to help solve real-world problems, and brought this message to his new flock. The conservative New Englanders weren't interested.

An elderly visitor from Kansas encouraged the struggling preacher to bring his ideas south and introduced his granddaughter in hopes of sweetening the inducement. It worked. Central Congregational Church in Topeka hired the passionate pastor in 1889, and Sheldon and Mary Merriam married three years later.

Sheldon announced he would preach "a Christ for the common people. A Christ who belongs to the rich and poor, the ignorant and learned, the old and young, the good and the bad . . . a Christ who bids us all recognize the Brotherhood of the race, who bids throw open this room to all."[1]

In the early years, Sheldon supported himself by selling articles to the local papers. By 1891 the church began to flourish and was running four Sunday services. Sheldon noticed that attendance at the Sunday night service was poor, so he wrote a series of stories to attract young people. The audience loved the tales, and Sheldon left each with a cliff-hanger to ensure they'd return the following Sunday. Soon the evening service was packed.

A weekly religious magazine from Chicago, *The Advance*, caught wind of the innovative sermons and bought the serial rights. Starting in November of 1896, they published the chapter-by-chapter stories in a weekly column.

Once the series ended the following year, *The Advance* published the entire story as a book titled *In His Steps*. Critics panned the novel as overly simplistic, but the book's core question, summed up in its now-famous subtitle, was revolutionary at the time—"What Would Jesus Do?"[2]

The book was a smash hit, but Sheldon received almost no reward for his effort. The publisher made a mistake while registering the copyright, and the book was thrown into the public domain. Since no one had legal ownership of the book, publishers around the world did the Christlike thing and pounced on the opportunity. Sixteen American publishers and over fifty international publishers printed their own copies. Since they didn't have to pay any author royalties, publishing houses slashed prices in a frantic race to the bottom. One publisher in London sold more than three million copies for one penny apiece. The sheer irony of the subtitle is palpable.

According to *Guideposts*, "*In His Steps* appeared in millions of copies of newspapers, comic books, magazines, and was translated into scores of different languages and produced in countless plays."[3]

Sheldon received almost no royalties, but what he did receive he donated to charity. When Sheldon was informed by *Publishers Weekly* that *In His Steps* had sold more copies than any other book besides the Bible, his response was perfectly BGM: "No one is more grateful than I am, as it confirms the faith I have always held that no subject is more interesting and vital to the human race than religion."[4]

The slighted author set aside any bitterness and wrote nearly fifty more books and hundreds of magazine articles, including several sequels to *In His Steps*. But the WWJD principle was more than just talk for Charles Monroe Sheldon.

Kansas at the time was in a deep recession and was full of jobless men. To understand their experience, Sheldon donned a set of old clothes and went job hunting for a week. He applied at mills, coal yards, and general stores but came up empty-handed. So he joined a chain of laborers and shoveled snow off the Santa Fe railroad tracks for free.

On Sunday he climbed back in the pulpit with a renewed love for the working man.

He spent the following week with laborers and professionals, "living as nearly as I could the life they lived, asking them questions about their work, and preaching the gospel to them in whatever way might seem most expedient."[5]

Soon, Topekans found him attending classes with college students, hopping freight trains, riding streetcars, joining lawyers in court, making rounds with doctors, chasing leads with reporters, trading with merchants, and shadowing businessmen.

Sheldon's empathy and understanding grew deeper and deeper, and he relayed the message to his upper-middle-class congregation in small meetings held after the usual services.

His social fervor increased. Seeing the damage that alcohol was doing to families, he campaigned against local saloons. He promoted solid housing and support for local businesses. He started Bible study groups, a town newspaper, and a local library. When typhoid killed more than twenty townspeople, Sheldon relocated the pigpens that were too close to the town's water supply and ended the outbreak.

The inquisitive pastor spent three weeks visiting Tennessee Town, a neighboring shanty village of "Exodusters"—freed former African-American slaves who'd moved to Kansas after the Civil War. He was shocked by the brutal reality of 1890s racism and helped many of them find work.

In 1892 the concept of kindergarten arrived in America from Germany. The very next year, Sheldon sponsored two kindergartens—one at his church and one in Tennessee Town. The latter was the first African-American kindergarten west of the Mississippi. Five years later, the church built one of the first kindergarten teacher training schools in America, and its graduates were hired across the nation.

But kindergarten was only the start. In later years Sheldon helped one of his Tennessee Town students, Elisha Scott, attend law school. Scott became a respected attorney, as did his son, Charles Sheldon Scott, who successfully argued for school desegregation at the Supreme Court in the 1954 landmark ruling, *Brown v. Board of Education of Topeka*.

Sheldon challenged the men of industry to question their morals and encouraged business leaders to conduct their affairs like Jesus. In March of 1900, the editor and owner of the *Topeka Daily Capital*,

Frederick O. Popenoe, offered Sheldon complete control over his paper for one week, to run it "as Jesus would do."[6]

Sheldon worked thirteen to sixteen hours per day and tried to publish the paper as he thought Jesus would. He refused to print ads for alcohol, tobacco, or pharmaceuticals. He listed every staff member in the editorial column, including the janitor. Daily circulation exploded from less than 11,000 copies locally to more than 387,000 copies internationally. The spike overwhelmed the local printing press, so an extra 120,000 copies were ordered from both Chicago and New York.

Sheldon retired from his pulpit in 1919 to become editor in chief of the *Christian Herald*. He used his new platform to fight against prejudice and later to oppose the Nazi persecution of Jews in 1939. He continued to serve the community and voluntarily spent a week in jail to push through local prison reforms.

As he grew older, Sheldon spoke with great anticipation of his new life to come: "It is not death but life I greet . . . when he who loves me calls me home."[7] On February 24, 1946, two days before his eighty-ninth birthday, Charles Monroe Sheldon died peacefully in bed.

In His Steps remains one of the top one hundred bestselling books of all time with more than thirty million copies in print.

CONTEMPLATION

1. What changes would Jesus make to your life if He took over today?
2. How are you spending your money and time differently from how Jesus would spend it?
3. What practical needs are going unaddressed by the church in your local community?

PRAYER

Father of our hearts, conform us to the image of Your Son, Jesus.

TELL ME AGAIN
ABOUT YOUR
"MANSCAPING."

TECHNOLOGY—A TOOL OR A WEAPON?

BY JAMES KELLY*

Have you ever played Grand Theft Auto?

In 2013, the year GTA 5 released, Guinness World Records declared it the fastest entertainment property to gross $1 billion.[8] It only took three days. For perspective, the New York Yankees' revenue for the same year was $461 million.[9]

Stealing, murder, and prostitution. That's the hallmark of GTA.

I recently asked an employee of a video game store: What genre sells best? Her answer: "Killing." In 2015 Shooter was the leading genre.

Why do these games compel and addict us? Is technology a toy, a weapon, or perhaps a tool?

I like to ask people, "Is Google the new God?" We are currently witnessing one of the most significant cultural shifts in history regarding how we ask questions. When smartphones entered our lives, we started using them to find restaurants or to ask for directions. Now people are asking Google for life advice before they ask their families and friends.

I run a conference for geeks called FaithTech Hackathon, where we build practical solutions for real-world problems in less than seventy-two hours. One team discovered that every month, tens of thousands of people Google "how to kill yourself." The top result: "7 Easy Painless Ways to Kill Yourself." The third result was a video showing you how. To find help on staying alive, you had to get all the way to the second page of results. When was the last time you went to page 2 in Google for anything?

So the FaithTech team decided to do something about

it. They purchased www.howtokillyourself.org and partnered with a counseling organization and a search engine optimization expert. When you go on their site, the first thing you read is, "You're Not Alone." Their goal is to be the number one search result when people type "how to kill yourself."

That is using technology to save lives, not harm them. That's viewing tech as a tool, not as a weapon or a toy.

Technology has incredible power both to harm and heal. Porn, via the Internet, harms. However, the Internet has the power to educate a remote village in South Sudan on creative uses of agriculture.

Technology doesn't addict us. We addict ourselves. We ignore God's prompts in our hearts, minds, and spirits to "stop and go to bed" or "talk to someone about that." Our posture becomes arrogant, resentful, and rebellious. We consume without thought or pause. Yet there is a world of opportunity to use technology as a tool to heal, save lives, and make a difference.

May we challenge ourselves to transform the way we view, use, and play with technology. And may we remember that our Savior transformed a tool of torture for our salvation, so perhaps it's time we take up our crosses and follow Him.

---

* *James Kelly is the founder of FaithTech.*

CHAPTER 29

Saint Nicholas

HE CAME HERE TO GIVE PRESENTS AND SLAP HERETICS. AND HE'S ALL OUT OF PRESENTS.

BY AARON ALFORD

Meditation: [Jesus] took a little child whom he placed among them. Taking the child in his arms, he said to them, "Whoever welcomes one of these little children in my name welcomes me; and whoever welcomes me does not welcome me but the one who sent me."

—MARK 9:36–37

Quote of the Day: The giver of every good and perfect gift has called upon us to mimic God's giving, by grace, through faith, and this is not of ourselves.

—SAINT NICHOLAS OF MYRA

If you ever find yourself facing execution for a crime you didn't commit, jolly old Saint Nicholas is a good man to have in your corner. But if you find yourself denying the divinity of Christ, get ready for a beatdown.

Arguably one of the most famous figures in Bearded Gospel

history, Saint Nicholas of Myra has had a long association with the Christmas season, one that predates his Santa Claus persona by about a millennia and a half.

Nicholas was the son of Theophanes and Nonna, a wealthy Christian couple, in the late third century in what is now Turkey. His parents were devout, and they dedicated their only child to the Lord. The stories of the miracles of Nicholas start early, for it's said that while the baby Nicholas was still in the baptismal font, he stood up by himself on his wobbly infant legs and remained standing there for three hours, in honor of the blessed Trinity. With an infancy story like that, it's not surprising to learn that Nicholas had a passion for good theology throughout his life.

While Nicholas was still very young, Theophanes and Nonna died, leaving him a healthy inheritance. But Nicholas, remembering Jesus' admonitions about wealth, held his inheritance lightly. As he grew up, instead of using that wealth for his own comfort, he dedicated himself to helping those in need, especially children. Perhaps it was his own experience of being orphaned that inspired such tenderness toward children in difficult circumstances.

The earliest story of his care for children involves a widower and his three girls. The father, having almost nothing, could not provide a sufficient dowry for his daughters as they came of age for marriage, which was essential in his culture at the time. The father faced a reality that still happens in many parts of the world today; he had nothing, no options for gaining money, work, or status for himself or his children, so the risk of his girls being sold into slavery or prostitution was great.

But jolly old Saint Nick was not about to let that happen.

The story goes that as each daughter reached the age for marriage, Nicholas secretly tossed a small bag of gold coins through their window. Some say these bags of gold fell in the girls' shoes or stockings. Others say Nicholas dropped them down the family's chimney.

However he did it, Nicholas's generosity forever changed the lives of these three young women and their father. And although the world's first Secret Santa operation was eventually discovered, Nicholas always tried to keep his good deeds and gift giving on the down-low.

Another story is told of an unjust governor who had taken a bribe and knowingly sentenced three innocent young men to death. Nicholas raced to the spot where the execution was to take place, and as the executioner raised his sword over the condemned boys, Nicholas snatched it from his hands. He then proceeded to publicly rebuke the corrupt governor until he admitted his horrible crime and begged forgiveness.

Nicholas tried to do justice for others, but he experienced injustice himself. When he was made a priest, and later a bishop, Nicholas learned what it meant to suffer for his faith. When the Roman emperor Diocletian came to power, he brought severe persecution on the church. He rounded up hundreds of Christian clergy, casting them into exile and imprisoning them. Nicholas and many other leaders were among them. He would face torture and remain in captivity for years, all the while encouraging and sustaining with a word his fellow prisoners for the Lord. It was not until the emperor Constantine came to power that Nicholas and the others were released.

After his release, Nicholas is said to have been present at the famous Council of Nicaea, in which the early church confronted many heresies and clarified essential elements of Christian teaching. One such heresy was put forth by a man named Arius, who vehemently denied the divinity of Christ. Arius stood before the bishops of the church, explaining the silliness of believing that Jesus was actually God in the flesh. Nicholas, the infant who had stood in his baptismal font in honor of the Trinity, listened, fuming. Finally, he could stand it no longer. He stormed right up to Arius, slapped him in the face, and gave him a verbal beat-down.

Although the council disciplined Nicholas for the outburst, it went on to proclaim what became known as the Nicene Creed, which says this about Jesus:

> We believe . . . in one Lord Jesus Christ,
> the only-begotten Son of God,
> begotten of the Father before all ages,
> Light of Light, very God of very God,
> begotten, not made, being of one substance with the Father;
> by whom all things were made;
> who for us men, and for our salvation,
> came down from heaven,
> and was incarnate by the Holy Ghost of the Virgin Mary,
> and was made man.[1]

Take that, Arius!

The Arian heresy was one that was especially present in Nicholas's city of Myra, and Nicholas worked and preached tirelessly against it. A later biographer, Methodius, wrote this about Nicholas: "Thanks to the teaching of St. Nicholas, the metropolis of Myra alone was untouched by the filth of the Arian heresy, which it firmly rejected as a death-dealing poison."[2]

Nicholas died at a healthy old age, with a long white beard, sometime between AD 345 and 352. His stories and legends took on a life of their own. In the years and centuries that followed, children throughout Europe began leaving stockings by the fireplace for Saint Nicholas to give a gift on his feast day, December 6. With the proximity of Saint Nicholas's day to Christmas (not to mention the gifts of the wise men), and the old bishop's association with being a protector of children and a giver of gifts, it's easy to see how gift giving became a Christmas tradition.

At the root of our Santa Claus mythology lies a real man named Nicholas. However incredible some of the stories about him may seem, they were born from the reputation he had for proclaiming the truth, caring for the poor, and protecting the innocent.

So when you see Santa on TV or on your coffee cup, don't get mad about him stealing the limelight from Jesus. Let him remind you of Nicholas of Myra, a kind and passionate follower of Christ, a Bearded Gospel Man who made his very life a gift to Jesus. Remember his desire to honor God through study and preaching. Remember, too, the spirit of generosity that marked his life, especially toward the helpless and children, for there are families today facing the same difficulties of poverty and injustice that the people of Myra faced seventeen hundred years ago. Let that sidewalk Santa remind you to give of yourself and your resources for the sake of the kingdom. Let the white-bearded man on his throne at the mall remind you to welcome the little ones, as Jesus did, and as Nicholas did. Whatever you may be faced with, ask yourself how Saint Nick might respond.

Just try not to slap any heretics.

CONTEMPLATION

1. Are there children in need in your city? Consider volunteering time with a community organization that helps families in need.
2. Is there a family facing difficulties or financial struggles in your church? How might you help?
3. Do you devote time to theological reading or study? If not, consider adding such time to your devotional life.

PRAYER

Heavenly Father, grant us generous hearts and giving hands.

MAN'S BEST FRIEND.
AND SOME DOG.

HOW TO SHAVE IN NINE EASY STEPS

BY AARON ALFORD

1. Be stupid.
2. Be dumb.
3. Buy stupid, dumb razor.
4. Put razor on stupid, dumb face.
5. Use stupid, dumb razor to slice precious, innocent whiskers, whose only wish is to make you better looking and to generally make you a better person, from your stupid, dumb face.
6. Go do whatever it is shaven men do, like talking about how great stupid things are while doing dumb things.
7. Weep bitterly for doing something so stupid and dumb as shaving.
8. Stop shaving.
9. Refer to steps one through five, "How to Grow a Great Beard in Five Easy Steps" on page 8.

CHAPTER 30

William Booth

PROPHET OF THE POOR

BY JARED BROCK

Meditation: I will build my church, and the gates of Hades will not overcome it.

—MATTHEW 16:18

Quote of the Day: Go for souls and go for the worst!

—WILLIAM BOOTH

And the award for longest beard in this book goes to . . . General William Booth.

Born in Nottingham in 1829, Booth was born into a wealthy family that quickly descended into poverty. Writing about his father, William said, "He had been born into poverty. He determined to grow rich; and he did. He grew very rich, because he lived without God and simply worked for money; and when he lost it all, his heart broke with it, and he died miserably."[1]

Booth went to work as a pawnbroker's apprentice in the poorest part of Nottingham when he was thirteen and his father couldn't afford to send him to school any longer. Booth's father died the following year, and the young pawnbroker's job helped provide for his family. The year after that, Booth attended a Wesleyan chapel and found faith. He wrote in his diary, "God shall have all there is of William Booth."[2]

Five years later, Booth moved to London and met Catherine Mumford. They eventually married and became a formidable team. Booth took a job as a local pastor, but within five years of marriage, he was tired of being tied down to one location. He and Catherine became itinerant evangelists. They traveled all over Britain to the struggling districts—places like Wales, Cornwall, and the Midlands—on a crusade to win souls. Catherine was asked to speak in London, and Booth agreed to go along as a temporary minister at a local church.

One writer in Booth's time described East London as "a squalid labyrinth, with half a million people, 290 to the acre."[3] The writer claimed that every fifth house was a gin shop, and that most had special steps so that even children could reach the counter. After witnessing East London, Booth said to Catherine, "I seemed to hear a voice sounding in my ears, 'Where can you go and find such heathen as these, and where is there so great a need for your labors?'"[4]

They decided to stay.

In 1865, in the area near George Holland's George Yard Ragged School, they started preaching from a tent in Whitechapel. They used secular songs as a way to attract crowds, and Booth scoffed at religious folks who gave him a hard time: "Secular music, do you say, belongs to the devil? Does it? Well, if it did I would plunder him for it, for he has no right to a single note."[5]

The Booths' East London Christian Mission opened in 1870, and eight years later was renamed the Salvation Army. Booth's vision for the ministry was simple: "We are a salvation people—this is our speciality—getting saved and keeping saved, and then getting somebody else saved."[6] His passion was infectious, and the highly organized ministry quickly expanded around the world. His motto was simple and bold:

While women weep, as they do now,
I'll fight;
While little children go hungry,
I'll fight;
While men go to prison, in and out, in and out, as they do now,
I'll fight—
While there is a drunkard left, while there is a poor lost girl upon the streets, where there remains one dark soul without the light of God—
I'll fight! I'll fight to the very end![7]

Catherine died of cancer in 1890, and then one of Booth's children died in a train crash a few years later. Booth turned over the executive leadership of the Salvation Army to his oldest son, a magnificently plumed fellow named Bramwell Booth, and went back to itinerant preaching. He became known as the bearer of "soup, soap and salvation."[8]

Despite losing his right eye along the way, Booth made seven tours of Britain in the newly popularized motorcar, went on preaching tours in Australia, New Zealand, and fifty-six other countries, and visited the Holy Land to poke around the historical sites of biblical events. On returning home, he received awards from the cities of London and Nottingham, as well as an honorary doctorate from Oxford.

On August 20, 1912, at 10:13 p.m., it was reported that "the old warrior finally laid down his sword."[9] At the time of his death, the Salvation Army had 15,875 officers and cadets serving in fifty-eight countries. Seven of his children had taken leadership positions in the organization.

During the week after his death, 150,000 people passed by his casket. The paper described him as "the world's best-loved man," and a local mayor called him "The Archbishop of the World."[10] Thirty-five thousand people attended his funeral service, including an undercover Queen Alexandra. It took seven thousand Salvationists, forty marching bands, and 2,950 police officers nearly four hours to travel the five-mile processional route.

Booth's son offered the final graveside eulogy: "If you were to ask me, I think I could say that the happiest man I ever knew was the General. He was a glad spirit. He rose up on the crest of the stormy billows, and praised God, and laughed at the Devil's rage, and went on with his work with joy."[11]

Today the Salvation Army boasts more than fifteen thousand congregations, twenty-six thousand ministers, and more than 1.1 million members across 127 nations. Many continue to heed the great general's words: "We must wake ourselves up! Or somebody else will take our place, and bear our cross, and thereby rob us of our crown."[12]

CONTEMPLATION

1. Have you ever fallen asleep on the battlefield?
2. Where is your time and talent needed most?
3. What would you need to do for Jesus in order to earn the title of "warrior"?

PRAYER

Father of the poor, make us rich in good deeds and service to Your people. Make us warriors in Your army of love and peace.

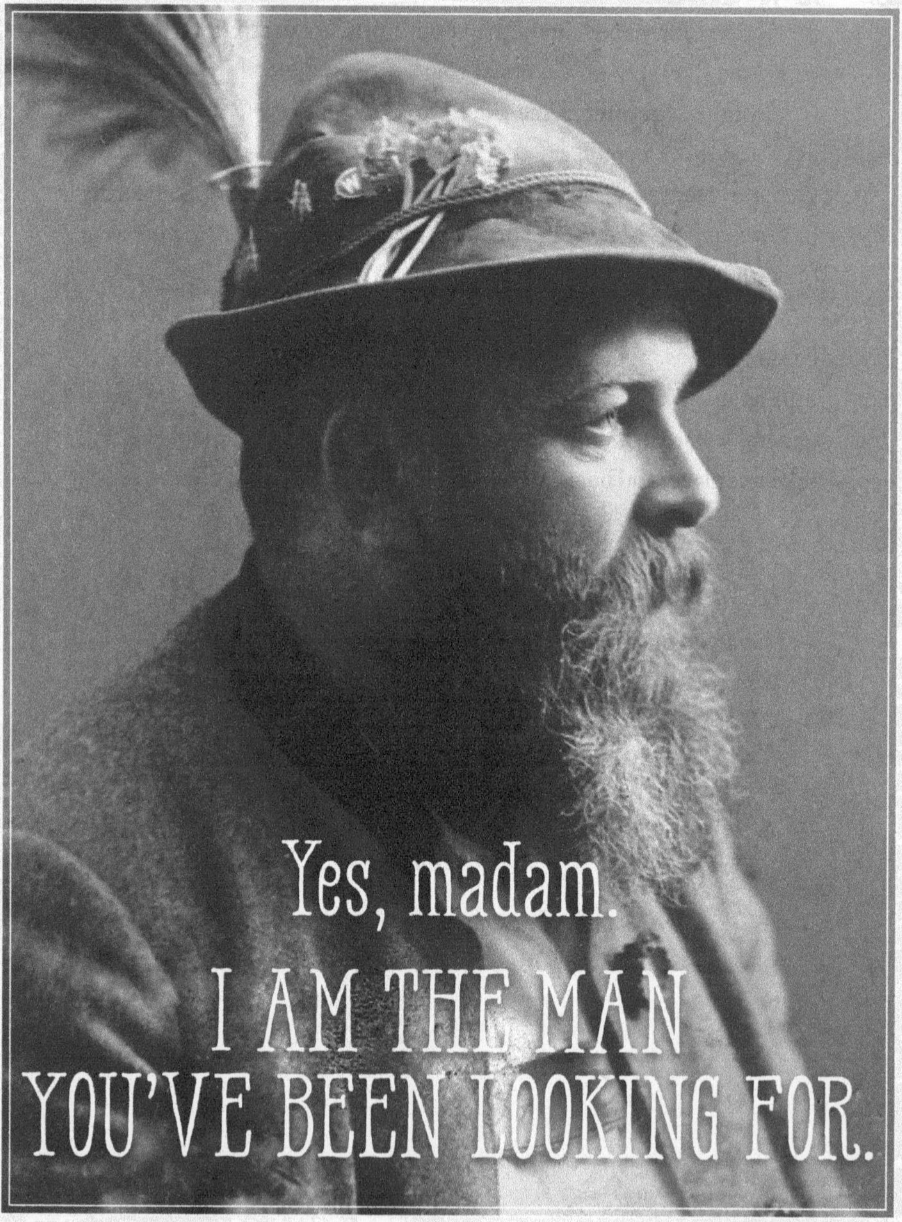
Yes, madam.
I AM THE MAN
YOU'VE BEEN LOOKING FOR.

LOVE AND MONEY AND THE LOVE OF MONEY

BY JARED BROCK

It seems like most Christians pretend that money doesn't exist. Like it's a necessary evil and a topic of conversation to be avoided at all costs. One thing I noticed while researching various Bearded Gospel Men is that most of them were total bosses when it came to money. Unlike the masses around them who lived in a cycle of "earn, spend, repeat," men like William Booth and Anthony Ashley Cooper seemed to employ a cycle of "learn, give, repeat." They saw a need, responded with generosity, and then relied on God to refill their coffers so they could do it again.

Let's not fool ourselves—our finances are a highly accurate indicator of where our faith is at. The Bible talks about money more than heaven and hell combined. Here are a few principles that many BGMs had in common when it came to Christ's cash:

1. Use Money as a Tool, Not a Weapon

> For the love of money is a root of all kinds of evil. Some people, eager for money, have wandered from the faith and pierced themselves with many griefs.
>
> —*1 Timothy 6:10*

Bearded Gospel Men combated evil by investing their money in their mission. Moses the Black stopped stealing from others and started giving, even going so far as to make the ultimate sacrifice. Josiah Henson knew how financial power could absolutely ruin lives, and instead used his considerable resources to build a community of hope for others.

2. Become Poor for the Sake of Others

> For you know the grace of our Lord Jesus Christ, that though he was rich, yet for your sake he became poor, so that you through his poverty might become rich.
>
> —*2 Corinthians 8:9*

That verse isn't the end of the story. Since we have been called to live like Jesus, we in turn choose to become poor so that others may become rich. Bearded Gospel Men virtually drained their accounts to enrich the lives of others. John Wesley died with little more than a few coins in his pockets, but tens of millions of people are part of our faith family because he invested his millions in God's economy. Mother Teresa could have taken a big paycheck from her charity, or at least could have kept her million-dollar Templeton Prize money, but was known instead for wearing the worst pair of donated shoes so her kids could have better ones.

3. Let Money Change Your Heart (In a Good Way)

> For where your treasure is, there your heart will be also.
>
> —*Luke 12:34*

When I was a younger, dumber man, I took out a huge loan and bought a gorgeous car with upgraded rims, heated leather seats, a sunroof, and volume control on the steering wheel. I loved that car. I cleaned it, cared for it, treated it like a fine stallion. I was invested. Now I've discovered that the more I give away my "treasure," the less I love money and the more I love the thing I give it to. I don't care about cars anymore. I care about the poor. I want human trafficking to end. I want fair wages for coffee farmers. I want clean water to be a human right. The more I give, the more I'm invested.

Bearded Gospel Men demolished their love of money by putting it to kingdom use. Duke Václav could have let the poor man freeze, but he showed him the true meaning of Christmas instead. Keith Green could have lived like a rock star with his music millions, but instead he bought up a row of houses and filled them with former prostitutes.

4. Don't Be Like Others

> Do not conform to the pattern of this world, but be transformed by the renewing of your mind.
>
> —*Romans 12:2*

While it's really tempting to take on a few car payments and a hefty mortgage on a sizable house, those with purposeful margin get to live on purpose. Bearded Gospel Men were consistently "in this world, but not of it." C. T. Studd could have stayed at Cambridge, then used his inherited millions to build an empire. Instead, he gave it away, and his kingdom investments continue to pay dividends to this very day.

5. Give, Give, and Give Some More

> Whoever is faithful with very little will also be faithful with much, and whoever is dishonest with very little will also be dishonest with much.
>
> —*Luke 16:10 BSB*

If you study this passage, it's not saying that if you're good with a little bit of money, God will magically give you more. It's simply a straight-up observation on human nature. People who aren't faithful with little won't be faithful with much. That's it. So what's the point?

We need to transform our character if we want to be faithful, regardless of the amount entrusted to us.

Then consider the next verse: "If you have not been trustworthy in handling worldly wealth, who will trust you with true riches? (BSB)" Bearded Gospel Men were trustworthy with their finances, and God entrusted human lives to their wise stewardship. Instead of buying himself a mansion, Thomas Barnardo bought up ninety-six homes to house his eight-five hundred kids. If George Müller hadn't been faithful with his finances, there's no way he could have cared for 10,024 orphans with integrity.

The bearded (and unbearded) gospel men (and women) throughout history had a deep understanding that if they chose to love money, it would ruin them. So they changed their minds, opened their wallets, and allowed their provision to fuel their vision. They gave away their treasure, and their hearts committed fully to the work to which God had called them. They gave away their money, and found their true love.

CHAPTER 31

Francis of Assisi

PREACH THE GOSPEL AT ALL TIMES; WHEN NECESSARY, USE BEARDS

BY AARON ALFORD

Meditation: Therefore I tell you, do not worry about your life, what you will eat or drink; or about your body, what you will wear. Is not life more than food, and the body more than clothes? Look at the birds of the air; they do not sow or reap or store away in barns, and yet your heavenly Father feeds them. Are you not much more valuable than they?

—MATTHEW 6:25–26

Quote of the Day: Preach the gospel at all times. When necessary, use words.

—SAINT FRANCIS (EXCEPT HE NEVER ACTUALLY SAID THAT!)

Saint Francis, arguably the church's most famous saint, may also be its most misunderstood. He is embraced by some as a vaguely pantheist animal lover and appreciated by others as a nonthreatening hippie Jesus-follower who liked to hang around birdbaths. But both of these miss who Francis really was by a wide margin.

Francis was born into a well-to-do cloth merchant's family in Assisi, Italy, in 1182. Dancing and drinking and carousing into the wee hours of the morning, Francis was famous in his younger days for being the city's most enthusiastic partygoer.

He was a respected citizen of Assisi, and when the city went to war against the neighboring city of Perugia (cities at war with each other being not uncommon at the time), Francis enthusiastically enlisted. But his first day of battle did not bode well for him. He was captured and taken as a prisoner of war. For over a year, Francis rotted away in a dank cell, breathing in sickness and disease.

Eventually his family ransomed him and brought him home, where he remained homebound for another year, convalescing from his illness. He would never again be completely whole and healthy; sickness would return to him from time to time for the rest of his days.

The fourth crusade to Jerusalem was about to begin, and Francis insisted that he was well enough to fight. He set out to join a company of men in southern Italy, but turned back one day after leaving Assisi. The people of Assisi whispered of rumored visions from God that had cut his journey short. Others labeled him a coward. Most concluded that his imprisonment and sickness had taken more than his health; it had also taken his mind.

But Francis wasn't just hearing voices. He was beginning to hear the whisperings of the Holy Spirit. To his father, Pietro's, consternation, Francis was no longer held in high esteem by the townsfolk and no longer attended the parties over which he had once been crowned king. Instead, he spent his days riding the plains beneath the town and was even known to visit the nearby leper hospice. He stopped wearing the decadent clothing he used to wear and began wearing a plain brown fieldworker's robe. The people's suspicions about his mental health seemed to be confirmed when he began to talk of hearing Jesus speak to him in the ruins of an old chapel. He said that Jesus had told him to rebuild His church.

Francis took this command quite literally and set out to rebuild the ruined walls of the church where he had heard Jesus speak, the chapel of San Damiano. As any good son on a mission from God would do, he began to raise funds for his construction project by selling his father's stuff.

Pietro became so enraged with his son that he locked him in a tiny stone closet under the stairs for several days. Then he dragged Francis before the bishop, publicly demanding justice. This he received in a form he never could have imagined. Of his own accord, his son returned to him every cent he had taken, and, along with the money, his sonship and the clothes off his back. Francis stood naked in front of his father, declaring that from that day forward, his Father in heaven would be enough.

From this place of profound confidence in the immense love of Father God, Francis began an accidental revolution in the town of Assisi, and eventually in all of Christendom.

Some of his closest friends left partygoing behind to join him in his life of poverty and service to the lowest and the forgotten. His small fraternity of friends became a movement that continued to grow, eventually inspiring thousands to embrace a life of poverty and simplicity. They spent their days communing with lepers and beggars, serving their needs, and creating friendship with those whom society deemed outcasts.

The effect Francis's life would have on the world, and the renewal his spirituality of simplicity and trust brought to the church, would be immense. By his witness, not only did many people come to faith, but those within the church found new meaning in being Christians. The Christian life was suddenly an adventure in following in the footsteps of Jesus, serving the "least of these" and living in joyful trust of the heavenly Father.

Francis never did join a crusade, but he did risk his life behind enemy lines for his faith. Francis saw the violence happening around him in the name of God and decided that the best way to bring peace would be not to kill Muslims, but to convert them. Francis traveled to Egypt and crossed enemy lines into the camp of Sultan Malik Al-Kamil. Francis preached the gospel of Christ to the sultan, boldly and with great humility (for the two qualities are not mutually exclusive). Al-Kamil did not convert, but he was so taken by the love that Francis showed him that he arranged for Francis to visit Muslim-controlled Jerusalem as the sultan's guest, a pilgrimage that would otherwise have been impossible at the time.

This quality of humility was perhaps the most integral part of who Francis was, and it may be surprising to find out that this is why he is so often depicted with sparrows on his shoulders. Sparrows are small and often go unnoticed when compared with lovely little hummingbirds or great, soaring eagles. They are clothed in brown feathers and receive their sustenance, quite literally, off the crumbs from our tables. They do not reap or sow, but their Father in heaven knows their needs and sends them our leftover doughnuts and Big Mac buns. For this reason they have come to represent the poor, especially in art, and whenever you see an image of Francis with a sparrow on his finger, it's saying less about his communion with animals than it is about his spirit of humility and his communion with the lowly.

And here, perhaps, is where that non-quote comes from about preaching the gospel at all times. You see, Francis actually spent quite a lot of time preaching. When he couldn't find people to preach to, he preached to the birds, exhorting them to praise their Father in heaven. What made Francis's preaching so unique, however, was the authority with which he spoke. It's one thing for a wealthy man to tell you to live simply and trust your Father, but quite another for a poor man to tell you that. Francis made his life a sermon about the love of Jesus.

Francis, in his poverty, experienced the love of his heavenly Father in such profundity that everything in his life, whether he was washing the feet of a leper or preaching the gospel to a sultan, flowed from that deep well of trust.

Saint Francis, the former partygoer and soldier, became a bearded beggar. He traded the wealth of his earthly father for the riches of his heavenly Father. The gospel was not a matter of words for him, but a matter of trust, of simplicity, and of the deep joy of walking in the footprints of Jesus.

CONTEMPLATION

1. Are there ways you could simplify your life? How might simplifying help you become closer to your heavenly Father?
2. Are there people near you living in poverty or on the margins of society? What can you do to reach out to them in friendship?
3. Where might you see the footprints of Jesus in your life, or in your city? What can you do to walk in His steps today?

PRAYER

Lord, make us instruments of Your peace and channels of Your love.

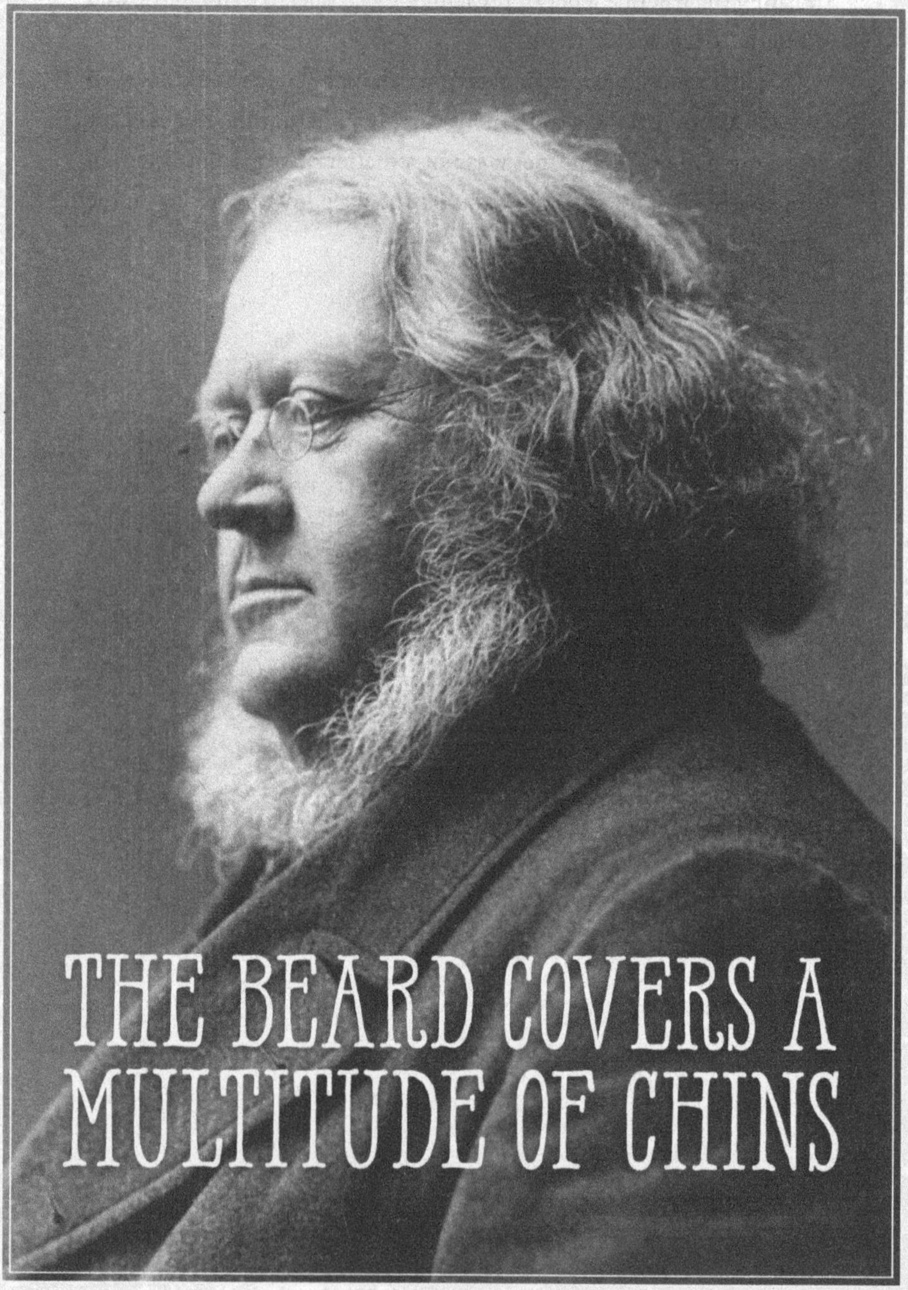
THE BEARD COVERS A
MULTITUDE OF CHINS

THE HOLY FAMILY

BY AARON ALFORD

"You are barren and childless, but you are going to become pregnant and give birth to a son" (Judg. 13:3).

This was the angel's proclamation to the mother of Samson. She dedicated her child to God even before his birth, and Samson was raised according to the strict vows of a Nazirite.

Hannah wept in the temple, begging God for the gift of a son. God heard her prayer, and the formerly barren woman gave birth to Samuel. In gratitude, Hannah gave her child to the Lord's service, and Samuel grew up in the temple.

Christ Himself had a miraculous birth, the most miraculous of all. He, too, was dedicated to God at the temple. But unlike Samuel, He wasn't raised there. Unlike Samson, He took no religious vows. Instead, Jesus' childhood was spent living with an average family in the unremarkable town of Nazareth.

For thirty years, He lived a quiet life among family and friends who knew Him simply as Jesus, son of Joseph and Mary. And in His infinite humility, the Son of God subjected Himself to everything that being part of a family entails. Joseph was not a priest, and Mary was not a prophetess, but Jesus' first earthly experience of love came in the embrace of His parents. He learned to walk by holding Joseph's pinky finger and wobbling toward His mother. He learned to talk by staring into Mary's eyes and listening to the sounds coming out of her smiling mouth.

He also learned the deeper things as He "grew in wisdom and stature" (Luke 2:52) in His experience of being in a family. He probably learned what patience looked like by watching His father work. Perhaps He learned grace by watching Mary bring a warm meal to the family in need down the street. And when Joseph fell short and had to ask his wife's forgiveness for an unkind word, little Jesus was watching, learning what humility and grace looked like. He learned to love, just as He learned to walk and talk, by watching the way Joseph and Mary gave of themselves to each other.

Samson and Samuel were made holy by separating themselves from their families. But Jesus did the opposite. He made all families holy by becoming part of one.

If you are a parent, you have been given the highest and holiest of callings: to teach another human being how to love. As Jesus watched His earthly parents, your children are watching you. And it's in watching this day-to-day vocation to love—the calling of every family—that your children will remember the delectable scent of holiness. They will remember it just as warmly as your homemade cookies. The first and best thing a child can learn is love, for love is the source of all that is holy.

Don't be intimidated by this task, and don't back down from it. Jesus has assured you not only of the sacredness of this vocation, but of His faithfulness to meet you there. He will give you the grace to live it. No family is perfect, but in Christ's incarnation, God has made every family holy.

Afterword

And so we have come to the last beard in our pantheon of hirsute greatness, and that beard belongs to none other than you. You, friend, are destined for nothing less than the bearded gospel greatness achieved by each of the men and women profiled in this book. Remember that. Just as every beard is unique, so, too, is every man's holiness. You may not write theological works of greatness like Augustine or Chesterton, and you may not preach to thousands like Festo Kivengere or become a great social leader like Frederick Douglass, but you are called to live the gospel as thoroughly as any martyr or theologian. You are called to the greatness of the gospel as it is meant to be expressed in your totally unique, never-to-be-duplicated life. Our prayer is that by meeting the men in this book, you are inspired to become like them.

The men in this book were not perfect, of course, and so varied are the places, eras, cultures, and Christian traditions they came from that we're pretty sure some of these men would have a hard time getting along with one another. (D. L. Moody and Keith Green would probably be great friends, but Thomas More and Francis Schaeffer would likely have had a tussle.) But imperfect as they were, with weak points to counter their spiritual strengths and blind spots in their vision of faith, these men passionately pursued the love that had taken possession of their hearts. They aimed to be wholly God's, and they did this by embracing humility and walking in the way of righteousness, peace, and joy.

A great beard must be cultivated with healthy eating, a good beard oil, and regular brushing. These things encourage growth. So, too, must a gospel-centered life be cultivated with Scripture, humility, prayer, grace, and community. These things encourage growth, and if you immerse yourself in them, you will soon find the flourishing of the gospel in your own heart.

When you let the gospel grow *in* you—like a big, healthy beard grows *on* you—it will soon be the first thing people notice about you.

Acknowledgments

The authors wish to thank:

Ann Spangler, literary agent par excellence, for faithfully representing two rowdy beardsmen in their stumbling pursuit of Christlikeness.

Our girl boss and personal editor, Beth Fisher-Adams a.k.a. "Ballin' Betty," for her watchful eye, careful prodding, and rightfully sensitive defense of femininity.

Joel Kneedler, Sam O'Neal, Megan Dobson, Jesse Wisnewski, Meaghan Porter, Lori Cloud, Laura Decorte, Kimberly Golladay, and the rest of the team at W Publishing, for being so passionate about beards . . . and all the stuff that actually matters.

Elisabeth Sullivan and Adria Haley, who kindly edited our 4,788 mistakes. Any leftovers are obviously ours.

Our contributors: Chris Wignall, Michelle Brock, Eric Fusilier, Catherine Greene, Richard Saunders, James Kelly, Jonathan Rogers, Bradford Loomis, Jimmy Sustar, and Malcolm Guite for sharing moving pieces that only they could write.

Aaron Alford wishes to personally thank:

My YWAM Modesto community, especially Chris Whitler and Jimmy Sustar, for giving me the space and encouragement to write, to create, and to become more and more the person God has made me to be. I am honored to have you as brothers and family.

Each of my friends and supporters who has made my life as a YWAM missionary possible. Your prayers, presence, friendship, and sacrificial giving continue to humble and inspire me.

Joe Thorn, thank you for starting that little Tumblr blog so long ago, and thank you for the faith and trust you gave when you handed me the keys.

And Jared, for helping to make this happen. You are a man of integrity, passion, and mission, and I'm so blessed to get to work with you.

Mary, Francis, and Arley: Thank you for your presence in my life and for your prayers. I'm closer to Jesus than I ever could have been without you.

Jared Brock wishes to personally thank:

The gospel men and women in my life, bearded or otherwise: Richard Saunders, Dave McSporran, Matt Naismith, James Kelly, Eric Fusilier, Gordon Daman, Dave Arnold, Jacob Miles, Bobby Clarke, plus Steph Vandenboomen, Ruthann Brock, Cat and Cody Greene, Rob and Andrea Filgate, Mark and Cheryl Buchanan, Christy and Trevor McClelland, Lewis and Ellie Jones, James and Cammy Lockwood, Ron and Helena Zacharias, Robin and Ingrid Kent, Ben and Joanne Brock, and Chandler and Maria Horne. I'm a better man for knowing each of you.

My fifty-plus prayer partners and supporters. Your generosity allows me to create books like this one. I'm so grateful for each of you.

The hundreds of Bearded Gospel Men throughout history—most of whom lived quiet lives of greatness and will never be profiled in a book—upon whose shoulders I stand.

Karen and Gord—Mama and Papa—for loving me more than any son such as I deserves.

Ari and Lea Uotila, for generously providing the space for me to write in solitude, keep warm in the sauna, and sleep in heavenly peace.

Aaron Alford, your character outweighs your magnificent beard, and I stand in awe of both. I've met few men as great as you.

Michelle, my love, life, and muse. You're the bestest beans in the mud.

You, dear reader, who I don't for a moment take for granted.

Jesus—I cling to Your feet.

Notes

Introduction

1. R. B. C. Huygens, ed., with a contribution by Giles Constable, "*Apologia de Barbis*," in *Apologiae Duae* (Turnhout, Belgium: Brepols Series, 1985).
2. Dilwyn Knox, *Ironia: Medieval and Renaissance Ideas on Irony* (Leiden, Netherlands: E. J. Brill, 1989), 81.
3. Thomas S. Gowing, *The Philosophy of Beards* (London: British Library, 2014).
4. Francis Bacon, *Essays and Apothegms of Francis Lord Bacon* (London: W. Scott, 1894), 235.
5. *Liberty University Student Teaching Handbook* (Lynchburg, VA: Liberty University, 2009), 18.

Chapter 1: Ignatius of Antioch–Lion Food (And Loving It!)

1. "Ignatius to the Romans," *Early Christian Writings*, from *Apostolic Fathers* (New York: Lightfoot and Harmer, 1891), www.earlychristianwritings.com/text/ignatius-romans-lightfoot.html.
2. Kevin Knight, ed., "The Martyrdom of Ignatius," New Advent, www.newadvent.org/fathers/0123.htm.
3. "Ignatius to the Philadelphians," *Early Christian Writings*, from *Apostolic Fathers* (New York: Lightfoot and Harmer, 1891), www.earlychristianwritings.com/text/ignatius-philadelphians-roberts.html.
4. Kevin Knight, ed., "The Epistle of Ignatius to the Ephesians," New Advent, www.newadvent.org/fathers/0104.htm.
5. Ignatius, *The Epistles of Ignatius* (London: Aeterna Press), chapter V.
6. Knight, "The Martyrdom of Ignatius."
7. Knight, "The Epistle of Ignatius to the Ephesians."

Chapter 2: Good King Wenceslas–The Merry Christmas Boxer

1. Mark Forsyth, *A Christmas Cornucopia: The Hidden Stories Behind Our Yuletide Traditions* (London: Penguin UK, 2016).

Chapter 3: Saint Boniface (Versus the Mighty Thor!)

1. Henry van Dyke, *The First Christmas Tree and the Story of the Other Wise Men* (North Chelmsford, MA: Courier, 2013), 27.
2. William J. Federer, *There Really Is a Santa Claus: The History of Saint Nicholas and Christmas Holiday Traditions* (St. Louis, MO: Amerisearch, 2002), 47.
3. Roberts Liardon, *God's Generals: The Martyrs* (New Kensington, PA: Whitaker House, 2016).

Chapter 4: Moses the Black–The Murderer Marauder Martyr

1. "History of St. Moses the Black Priory," St. Moses the Black Priory, 2009, www.stmosestheblackpriory.org/about_history.html.
2. Jared Brock, *A Year of Living Prayerfully* (Colorado Springs: NavPress, 2016), 280.
3. Ibid.

Chapter 5: D. L. Moody–Gospel, Music

1. William Revell Moody, *The Life of Dwight L. Moody* (Murfreesboro, TN: Sword of the Lord, 1980), 41.
2. Edgar Johnson Goodspeed, *A Full History of the Wonderful Career of Moody and Sankey in Great Britain and America* (New York: Henry S. Goodspeed and Co., 1876), 24.
3. Ibid.
4. Moody, *The Life of Dwight L. Moody*, 82.
5. Goodspeed, *A Full History of the Wonderful Career of Moody and Sankey in Great Britain and America*, 29.
6. Ibid., 38.
7. Ibid., 28.
8. Ira David Sankey, *Sacred Songs and Solos: Twelve Hundred Hymns* (London: FB & C, 2016).
9. Goodspeed, *A Full History of the Wonderful Career of Moody and Sankey in Great Britain and America*, 25.
10. Ibid., 15.

11. George Thompson Brown Davis, *Dwight L. Moody, the Man and His Mission* (Chicago: K. T. Boland, 1900), 168.
12. Moody, *The Life of Dwight L. Moody*, 55.
13. C. S. Lewis, *The Lion, the Witch, and the Wardrobe* (New York: Macmillan, 1983), 99.
14. C. S. Lewis, *That Hideous Strength* (New York: Simon and Schuster, 1996), 140.

Chapter 6: Daniel Nash—Spiritual Napalm

1. J. Paul Reno, *Daniel Nash: Prevailing Prince of Prayer* (Asheville, NC: Revival Literature, 1989).
2. "Daniel Nash: Prevailing Prince of Prayer," The Interceders, www.prayforrevival.org.uk/encourager35.html.
3. Bryan Cutshall, *Armorbearers: Strength and Support for Spiritual Leaders* (New Kensington, PA: Whitaker House, 2013).
4. J. Paul Reno, "Prevailing Prince of Prayer (Daniel Nash)—J Paul Reno," Hope Faith Prayer, 1989, www.hopefaithprayer.com/prayernew/prevailing-prince-prayer-daniel-nash/.
5. Christopher Oldstone-Moore, *Of Beards and Man: The Revealing History of Facial Hair* (Chicago: University of Chicago Press, 2015), 161.
6. C. S. Lewis, *The Screwtape Letters and Screwtape Proposes a Toast* (New York: Macmillan, 1961), 102.

Chapter 7: Saint Luka of Crimea—Doctor of the Church

1. "Saint Luke the Surgeon, Archbishop of Crimea (1877–1961)," Pemptousia.com, June 11, 2013, pemptousia.com/2013/06/saint-luke-the-surgeon-archbishop-of-the-crimea-1877–1961-june-11/.
2. "Life of Saint Luke of Simferopol and Crimea," Mystagogy Resource Center (blog), June 11, 2010, www.johnsanidopoulos.com/2010/06/life-of-saint-luke-of-simferopol-and.html.
3. Victor Potapov, "One Who Came to Love Suffering," Pravoslavie.ru, June 11, 2013, www.pravoslavie.ru/62097.html.
4. Stavros J. Baloyannis, "Saint Luke Metropolitan of Simferopol as Physician, Surgeon and Academic Professor," *Encephalos*, 52, no. 3 (July–September 2015).
5. Potapov, "One Who Came to Love Suffering."

6. G. K. Chesterton, *Tremendous Trifles* (CreateSpace Independent Publishing Platform, 2016), chapter 19.

Chapter 8: Frederick Douglass—Abolitionist Extraordinaire

1. Niral R. Burnett, *Voices of Hope: Timeless Expressions of Faith from African Americans* (Colorado Springs: Honor Books, 2005), 141–42.
2. "Frederick Douglass," Goodreads, accessed July 20, 2017, www.goodreads.com/quotes/335571-once-you-learn-to-read-you-will-be-forever-free.
3. Frederick Douglass, *Narrative of the Life of Frederick Douglass: An American Slave* (New York: Cosimo, 2008), 71.
4. "Frederick Douglass Biography," Biography.com, updated February 1, 2016, www.biography.com/people/frederick-douglass-9278324.
5. Frederick Douglass, *Frederick Douglass on Slavery and the Civil War* (North Chelmsford, MA: Courier, 2014), 41.

Chapter 9: John the Baptist—Less Is More

1. "San Juan Baptista," Solstice Chronicles, accessed July 20, 2017, solsticechronicles.org/#!/services-view/san-juan-bautistas.
2. Charles Souvay, "St. John the Baptist," New Advent, accessed March 19, 2017, www.newadvent.org/cathen/08486b.htm.
3. Edward Graham, "Essenes," New Advent, accessed March 19, 2017, www.newadvent.org/cathen/05546a.htm.

Chapter 10: Dirk Willems—Anabaptist Lifeguard Martyr

1. Neta Jackson, *The Complete Book of Christian Heroes: Over 200 Stories of Courageous People Who Suffered for Jesus* (Carol Stream, IL: Tyndale House, 2004), 379–80.
2. Ibid., 380.

Chapter 11: Sir Thomas More—The Beard Hath Committed No Treason!

1. Henry Smith Williams, *The Historians' History of the World: England, 1485–1642* (New York: Outlook Company, 1904), 154–55.
2. Gilbert Huddleston, "Sir Thomas More," New Advent, accessed March 19, 2017, www.newadvent.org/cathen/14689c.htm.
3. "Pilgrimage to the Home of Sir Thomas More," *Harper's New Monthly*

Magazine, 1, no. 3 (August 1850), www.gutenberg.org/files/29655/29655-h/29655-h.htm.

4. "Christian History: 1534 The Act of Supremacy," *Christianity Today*, accessed March 19, 2017, www.christianitytoday.com/history/issues/issue-28/1534-act-of-supremacy.html.
5. Sir Thomas More, *Utopia: With the "Dialogue of Comfort"* (London: J. M. Dent & Sons, 1957), 394.
6. William Cobbett, Thomas Bayly Howell, and David Jardine, *Cobbett's Complete Collection of State Trials and Proceedings for High Treason* (Charleston, SC: BiblioLife, 2015), 396.
7. Gerard Wegemer and Stephen W. Smith, *A Thomas More Source Book* (Washington, D.C.: Catholic University of America Press, 2004), 357.
8. Thomas More, *The Last Letters of Thomas More* (Grand Rapids: Eerdmans, 2001), 114.
9. Frederick Buechner, *Beyond Words: Daily Readings in the ABC's of Faith* (Grand Rapids: Zondervan, 2009), 61.

Chapter 12: Charles Spurgeon—Cigar-Chomping Prince of Preachers

1. "Charles Spurgeon: England's 'Prince of Preachers,'" Christian History Institute, issue 29 (1991), www.christianhistoryinstitute.org/magazine/issue/charles-spurgeon-englands-prince-of-preachers/.
2. G. Holden Pike, *The Life and Work of Charles Haddon Spurgeon*, 5 vols. (London: Cassel, n.d.), 5:138-40.
3. Andrew Steinmetz, *The Smoker's Guide, Philosopher and Friend* (London: Hardwicke & Bogue, 1876), 78.
4. "Spurgeon's Love of Fine Cigars," The Spurgeon Archive, www.romans45.org/spurgeon/misc/cigars.htm.
5. Trevin Wax, "Spurgeon the Drinker: The Rest of the Story," The Aquila Report, www.theaquilareport.com/spurgeon-the-drinker-the-rest-of-the-story/.
6. "Philip Yancey Quotes," Goodreads, accessed July 31, 2017, www.goodreads.com/author/quotes/9204.Philip_Yancey.
7. C. H. Spurgeon, "Salvation of the Lord," The Spurgeon Archive, sermon 131, http://archive.spurgeon.org/sermons/0131.php.
8. Christian George, "Spurgeon Almost Quit," Desiring God, www.desiringgod.org/articles/spurgeon-almost-quit.

Chapter 13: G. K. Chesterton—Frenemy

1. Maisie Ward, *Gilbert Keith Chesterton* (Lanham, MD: Rowman & Littlefield, 2006), 323.
2. Gilbert Keith Chesterton, *The Paradoxes of Mr. Pond* (North Chelmsford, MA: Courier, 1937), 35.
3. G. K. Chesterton, *Orthodoxy* (North Chelmsford, MA: Courier, 2012), 94.
4. G. K. Chesterton, *What's Wrong with the World* (London: Aeterna Press, 1910), 13.
5. Paul Asay, "G. K. Chesterton: The Sinner Who Might Be a Saint," Six Seeds (blog), March 20, 2015, sixseeds.patheos.com/watchinggod/2015/03/g-k-chesterton-the-sinner-who-might-be-a-saint/.
6. Ward, *Gilbert Keith Chesterton*, 496.
7. G. K. Chesterton, *G. K. Chesterton: The Autobiography*, ed. Randall Paine, (San Francisco: Ignatius, 2014), 221.
8. Ward, *Gilbert Keith Chesterton*, 371.
9. Hugh Latimer, *Sermons* (New York: E. P. Dutton, 1906), accessed by Project Canterbury, March 20, 2017, anglicanhistory.org/reformation/latimer/sermons/.
10. James E. Kiefer, "Hugh Latimer, Bishop and Martyr," Biographical Sketches of Memorable Christians of the Past, accessed March 20, 2017, www.justus.anglican.org/resources/bio/269.html.

Chapter 14: C. T. Studd—Mustachioed Gospel Cricketer

1. Eric Gilmour, "The Little Foxes and 'the D.C.D. Soldiers,'" Voice of Revolution, May 9, 2011, accessed July 20, 2017, www.voiceofrevolution.com/2011/05/09/the-little-foxes-and-the-d-c-d-soldiers/.
2. "History of Mission: C. T. Studd," Traveling Team, accessed March 20, 2017, www.thetravelingteam.org/articles/ct-studd.
3. "Charles Thomas (C. T.) Studd," European American Evangelistic Crusades, accessed March 20, 2017, www.eaec.org/faithhallfame/ctstudd.htm.
4. Ibid.
5. "History of Mission: C. T. Studd."
6. Dan Graves, "C. T. Studd Gave Huge Inheritance Away," Christianity.com, May 2007, www.christianity.com/church/church-history

/timeline/1801–1900/c-t-studd-gave-huge-inheritance-away-11630616.html.
7. Norman Grubb, *C. T. Studd: Cricketer & Pioneer* (Cambridge: Lutterworth, 2014).
8. Graves, "C. T. Studd Gave Huge Inheritance Away."
9. Stephen Ross, "Charles Thomas (C. T.) Studd," Wholesome Words: Missionary Biographies, accessed March 20, 2017, www.wholesomewords.org/missions/biostudd.html.
10. Zacharias Tanee Fomum, *Church Planting Strategies* (CreateSpace, 2017).
11. "History of Mission: C. T. Studd."
12. "Objectives," WEC International, accessed March 20, 2017, www.wecinternational.org/who-is-wec/objectives.php.
13. Ross, "Charles Thomas (C. T.) Studd."
14. Grubb, *C. T. Studd: Cricketer and Pioneer*, 203–4.
15. Ibid, 129-130.

Chapter 15: Zacchaeus—Of Camels and Trees

1. *The Sacred Writings of Apostolic Teachings and Constitutions* (Lochsberg, Germany: Jazzybee Verlag, 2012), sec. 4.

Chapter 16: Saint Valentine—Patron Saint of Lovers (and Beekeepers)

1. Brendan Nolan, *Dublin Folk Tales* (Stroud, UK: The History Press, 2011).
2. Ted Olsen, "Then Again Maybe Don't Be My Valentine," *Christianity Today*, February 1, 2000, www.christianitytoday.com/ct/2000/februaryweb-only/11.0a.html.
3. "Valentine's Day," Religion Facts, accessed March 20, 2017, www.religionfacts.com/valentines-day.
4. Ibid.

Chapter 17: Joseph of Cupertino—The Beard Who Could Fly

1. Angelo Pastrovicchi, *St. Joseph of Cupertino* (St. Louis, MO: B. Herder Book Co., 1918), 118.
2. Ibid., 30, 61.
3. Ibid., 92.
4. Ibid., 22.
5. Ibid., 25.

6. Frank Sheed, *Saints Are Not Sad: Short Biographies of Joyful Saints* (San Francisco: Ignatius, 2012), 387.
7. Pastrovicchi, *St. Joseph of Cupertino*, 119.

Chapter 18: Festo Kivengere–The Billy Graham of Africa

1. "Festo Kivengere," Dictionary of African Christian Biography, accessed March 21, 2017, www.dacb.org/stories/uganda/kivengere_festo.html.
2. Bridgette Kasuka, *Prominent African Leaders Since Independence* (Dar es Salaam, Tanzania: New Africa Press, 2013), 92
3. "7 Popular Quotes of Idi Amin of Uganda," Nigerian Bulletin, accessed July 31, 2017, www.nigerianbulletin.com/threads/list-7-popular-quotes-of-idi-amin-of-uganda.144875/.
4. "Festo Kivengere," Dictionary of African Christian Biography.
5. Michael Newton, *Famous Assassinations in World History: An Encyclopedia* (Santa Barbara, CA: ABC-CLIO, 2014), 305.
6. Richard H. Schmidt, *Glorious Companions: Five Centuries of Anglican Spirituality* (Grand Rapids: Eerdman's, 2002), 314.
7. "Festo Kivengere," Dictionary of African Christian Biography.

Chapter 19: Keith Green–You Put This Love in My Heart

1. Melody Green, *No Compromise: The Life Story of Keith Green* (Nashville: Thomas Nelson, 2008), 37.
2. Ibid., 148.
3. Keith Green, "The Man Behind the Message," *Last Days Ministries*, January 13, 2012, www.lastdaysministries.org/Groups/1000086203/Last_Days_Ministries/Articles/By_Keith_Green/Keith_Green_The/Keith_Green_The.aspx.

Chapter 20: Agnes Bojaxhiu–Is That Even a Dude's Name?

1. Mother Teresa, *Mother Teresa: Come Be My Light*, ed. Brian Kolodiejchuk (New York: DoubleDay, 2007), 192–93.
2. Ibid., 210.
3. Ibid., 187.
4. Ibid., 288.
5. Mother Teresa, *Blessed Mother Teresa* (London: St. Paul's, 2003), 1.

Chapter 21: Saint Augustine—Earnest, Active, Vigorous, Bearded

1. Augustine, *Confessions of St. Augustine*, bk. 2 (London: Watkins Media Limited, 2002), chap. 9.
2. Augustine, *Confessions of St. Augustine* (London: Burns and Oates, 1954), xvi.
3. Augustine, *Confessions of St. Augustine*, bk. 7 (London: Watkins Media Limited, 2002), chap. 20.
4. Ibid., chap. 5.
5. Ibid., chap. 12.
6. Kevin Knight, ed., "Exposition on Psalm 133," New Advent, accessed March 21, 2017, www.newadvent.org/fathers/1801133.htm.
7. I am indebted to Dr. Anthony L. Lillies for introducing me to this concept in his book *Fire from Above: Christian Contemplation and Mystical Wisdom* (Bedford, NH: Sophia Institute Press, 2016).

Chapter 22: Johannes Kepler—Bearded Space Man

1. "Johannes Kepler," *NASA: Ames Research Center*, accessed March 21, 2017, https://kepler.nasa.gov/Mission/JohannesKepler/.
2. Christine Dao, "Man of Science, Man of God: Johann Kepler," Institute for Creation Research, accessed July 21, 2017, www.icr.org/article /science-man-god-johann-kepler/.
3. Ibid.
4. Ibid.
5. Ibid.
6. Ibid.
7. Ann Lamont, "Johannes Kepler: Outstanding Scientist and Committed Christian," December 1, 1992, Answers in Genesis, www .answersingenesis.org/creation-scientists/profiles/johannes-kepler/.
8. Ibid.
9. Dao, "Man of Science, Man of God."
10. "History," Samaritan's Purse, accessed March 20, 2017, www.samaritanspurse.org/our-ministry/history/.
11. Maltbie D. Babcock, "This Is My Father's World," 1901, www.hymnary .org/text/this_is_my_fathers_world_and_to_my.
12. "Maya Angelou Quotes," Goodreads, www.goodreads.com /quotes/7273813-do-the-best-you-can-until-you-know-better-then.

Chapter 23: Saint Denis–Heads Above the Rest

1. Kevin Knight, ed., "Chapter 39: The Persecution Under Decius, and the Sufferings of the Origen," New Advent, March 21, 2017, www.newadvent.org/fathers/250106.htm.

Chapter 24: Francis Schaeffer–Fundamentalist for Jesus

1. Francis Schaeffer, *True Spirituality* (Carol Stream, IL: Tyndale House, 2012), 155–56.
2. Ibid., xxx.
3. "Francis Schaeffer on Hospitality," Church of the Resurrection, January 2009, rezchurch.org/2009/01/francis-schaeffer-on-hospitality/.
4. Edith Schaeffer, "L'Abri Fellowship," L'Abri Fellowship International, accessed March 21, 2017, www.labri.org/history.html.
5. Michael S. Hamilton, "The Dissatisfaction of Francis Schaeffer," *Christianity Today*, March 3, 1997, www.christianitytoday.com/ct/1997/march3/7t322a.html.
6. Ibid.
7. Francis A. Schaeffer, *A Christian View of the Church* (Wheaton, IL: Crossway, 1994), 71.
8. Owen Strachan, "Everything but the Knickers: The Enduring Significance of Francis Schaeffer," The Gospel Coalition, September 14, 2011, www.thegospelcoalition.org/article/everything-but-the-knickers-the-enduring-significance-of-francis-schaeffer.
9. Schaeffer, *A Christian View of the Church*, 93.

Chapter 25: Saint Patrick–Slave to Snake Fighter

1. William Federer, *Saint Patrick* (St. Louis, MO: Amerisearch, 2002), 15.
2. "The Confession of St. Patrick," EWTN, 1996, www.ewtn.com/library/MARY/PATCONF.htm.
3. Patrick Moran, "St. Patrick," New Advent, accessed March 20, 2017, www.newadvent.org/cathen/11554a.htm.
4. "Lorica of Saint Patrick," EWTN, accessed March 20, 2017, www.ewtn.com/devotionals/prayers/patrick.htm.
5. Jocelin of Furness, *The Life and Acts of Saint Patrick* (Dublin: Hibernia Press Company, 1809), 96–97.

Chapter 26: Thomas Barnardo—Mutton-Chopped City Builder

1. "The History of Barnado's," Believe in Children: Barnardo's, accessed March 20, 2017, www.barnardos.org.uk/barnardo_s_history.pdf.
2. "Dr. Thomas Barnardo," Casebook: Jack the Ripper, accessed March 20, 2017, www.casebook.org/ripper_media/book_reviews/non-fiction/cjmorley/12.html.

Chapter 27: Josiah Henson—A Great North American

1. Josiah Henson, *Uncle Tom's Story of His Life* (London: Christian Age Office, 1876), 29.
2. Ibid., 31.
3. Ibid., 32.
4. Joan Mueller, *Clare of Assisi: The Letters to Agnes* (Collegeville, MN: Liturgical Press, 2003), 98.

Chapter 28: Charles Monroe Sheldon—More Than Bracelets

1. "The Story of 'In His Steps,'" Master's Image Productions (blog), August 2, 1996, www.mastersimage.com/the-story-of-in-his-steps/.
2. "Charles Monroe Sheldon/Central Congregational Church Collection," Kansas Historical Society, collection 222, accessed March 20, 2017, www.kshs.org/p/charles-monroe-sheldon-central-congregational-church-collection/14115.
3. "The Story of 'In His Steps.'"
4. Ibid.
5. Ibid.
6. Ibid.
7. Ibid.
8. "Confirmed: Grand Theft Auto 5 Breaks 6 Sales World Records," Guiness World Records, 2014, www.guinnessworldrecords.com/news/2013/10/confirmed-grand-theft-auto-breaks-six-sales-world-records-51900.
9. "Revenue of the New York Yankees (MLB) from 2001 to 2015 (in Million U.S. Dollars)," Statista: The Statistics Portal, 2015, https://www.statista.com/statistics/196673/revenue-of-the-new-york-yankees-since-2006/.

Chapter 29: Saint Nicholas—He Came Here to Give Presents and Slap Heretics. And He's All Out of Presents.

1. "Nicene Creed," Association of Free Lutheran Congregations, accessed March 21, 2017, https://www.aflc.org/wp-content/uploads/2014/05/Creeds.pdf.
2. "Saint Nicholas of Myra Bishop, Confessor c. 342," EWTN, accessed March 21, 2017, www.ewtn.com/library/mary/nicholas.htm.

Chapter 30: William Booth—Prophet of the Poor

1. "William Booth: The Founder of the Salvation Army," The Salvation Army, accessed March 21, 2017, https://www.salvationarmy.org.uk/history-william-booth.
2. "William Booth: First General of the Salvation Army," *Christianity Today*, accessed March 21, 2017, www.christianitytoday.com/history/people/activists/william-booth.html.
3. Ibid.
4. Ibid.
5. Eliakum Littell and Robert S. Littell, *Littell's Living Age*, vol. 179 (New York: T. H. Carter & Company, 1888), 313.
6. "William Booth: The Founder of the Salvation Army."
7. "William Booth: First General of the Salvation Army."
8. "Soup, Soap and Salvation," The Salvation Army, accessed March 21, 2017, www.salvationarmy.org.nz/our-community/bcm/archives-heritage/did-you-know/soup-soap-and-salvation.
9. "William Booth: The Founder of the Salvation Army."
10. Ibid.
11. Ibid.
12. Dr. Purushothaman, *Words of Wisdom*, vol. 5 (Kollam, India: Centre for Human Perfection, 1987), 83.

About the Authors

Jared Brock is cofounder of Hope for the Sold, a nonprofit organization dedicated to combating exploitation, and author of *A Year of Living Prayerfully*. He's happily married to his best friend, Michelle, and his writing has appeared in *Esquire*, Catalyst, *Relevant*, *Huffington Post*, *Elite Daily*, and *Writer's Digest*. Brock runs a documentary production company, is the director of *Over 18* and *Red Light Green Light*, and has been interviewed on TODAY.com, *100 Huntley Street*, and *The 700 Club*.

Aaron Alford is originally from Ontario, Canada. He has studied improv at The Second City, hitchhiked across Ireland and Italy, and, as a missionary with Youth With A Mission in Modesto, California, helps run a street café for the homeless with his friends. He is currently studying for the priesthood and enjoys beautifying the world with whimsy, compassion, pipe smoke, and an admirable beard.

CPSIA information can be obtained
at www.ICGtesting.com
Printed in the USA
LVHW040220231021
701078LV00001B/12

9 780718 099305